"If Life's Worth Doing, It's Worth Doing Well"

Finding Sane Fulfillment in an Insane World

GOWOR
INTERNATIONAL PUBLISHING

Tony Inman

The Elephant in the Room

When there is something going on that is clearly a source of controversy, confusion or tension, that issue is known metaphorically as 'the elephant in the room'. In other words, it's something that you can't really miss, so it's best to clear the air and talk about it.

During the writing of this book, someone glanced at my cover design, saw pictures of me at the Pyramids, and asked me, "Is this a travel book?" So, in reference to that particular elephant, here is my answer: *"No, it isn't, but in a way, yes, it is."*

I'm glad we got that cleared up! So now seriously, what I mean is that it's not a travel book in the sense of suggesting the best places to eat in downtown Cairo! Nor is it about riding camels along a beach in Broome at sunset. However, the lessons within, if applied, could well lead to more of those things in your life. If I can do them, so can you if you want to.

This book is written specifically for you if:

- You can see your life as a journey of self-discovery.
- You want to feel inspired to help you uncover some of your own secret talents.
- You like to hear a good story from which you can extract some deeper meaning.
- You can sense and be moved by the distilled wisdom of some of the world's leading transformational speakers.
- You are ready to use your attributes to touch the hearts of humanity.

On the other hand, this book is not for everyone. Before you buy it you need to ask yourself:

- Am I willing to take responsibility for committing to learn something new from this book?
- Am I curious and willing to consider some potentially new (to me at least) concepts or ideas?
- Am I willing to take action in some area (or many areas) of my business or my life?

I encourage you to take some notes, not just about what you read, but about what you think as a result of what you read. Things happen for a reason; there is a reason you chose this book. It has found you, just as surely as you have found it. So, here is my suggestion…

If a book is worth reading, it's worth reading well.

If you find this book useful to you on your journey through life, please recommend it to others. Help me spread the message that we *can* change the world – one human being at a time. We can *be* more, *do* more and *have* more inspirational experiences and uplifting relationships in our lives. If you help my words travel around the world, then yes, this is a travel book. I hope you enjoy your journey with me!

Thank you.

Tony Inman

"If Life's Worth Doing, It's Worth Doing Well" – Finding Sane Fulfillment in an Insane World © Tony Inman 2014

www.tonyinman.net

www.clubred.com.au

The moral rights of Tony Inman to be identified as the author of this work have been asserted in accordance with the Copyright Act 1968.

First published in Australia 2014 by Gowor International Publishing

www.goworinternationalpublishing.com

ISBN 978-0-9923493-1-8

Any opinions expressed in this work are exclusively those of the author and are not necessarily the views held or endorsed by Gowor International Publishing.

All rights reserved. No part of this publication may be reproduced or transmitted by any means, electronic, photocopying or otherwise, without prior written permission of the author.

Disclaimer

All the information, techniques, skills and concepts contained within this publication are of the nature of general comment only, and are not in any way recommended as individual advice. The intent is to offer a variety of information to provide a wider range of choices now and in the future, recognising that we all have widely diverse circumstances and viewpoints. Should any reader choose to make use of the information herein, this is their decision, and the author and publisher/s do not assume any responsibilities whatsoever under any conditions or circumstances. The author does not take responsibility for the business, financial, personal or other success, results or fulfillment upon the readers' decision to use this information. It is recommended that the reader obtain their own independent advice.

This book is dedicated to my father, Bill Inman 1922 – 2012
and to my mother, Vera Inman (94 – not out!)

A Personal Note from the Publisher

To the reader,

As the Founder of Gowor International Publishing, my publishing company, I make it part of my practice to offer a personal review for all authors about their book – which they can either use in promotion or in the book itself. The reason why I do this is so that YOU, the reader, can glean a further understanding into why this book is so valuable to you in your life.

Let me tell you about Tony…

Tony is one of those authors who has no fear about bearing himself on page. In fact, this book is very much like a journey inside Tony's mind. At first, Tony comes across as a professional (despite the collage of photos on the front cover), and it was only in working with him more closely that I realized just how rich the life and heart of this man is. Tony has an incredible gift for building relationships, nurturing connections and doing business – which I believe stems from his deep care for people. His crazy, dreamer streak is uplifting, and despite my being several years younger than him, he inspires ME to get out there and live even more fully.

For Tony, this is not *just* another self-help book or a simple motivational piece. It is an opportunity to go after what is most important to you: your goals, aspirations, dreams and ambitions. I know that Tony's dream has been to travel – it has been with him ever since he was a child – and that, in his adult life, he has been living it… something that many of us aspire to do.

This book is a powerful concoction of his life stories, wisdom and experience – both personal and professional. Read it, and it will move you. It has been written with intelligence and purpose. Every piece of this book fits together with every other piece, and reading it will be quite the adventure.

It has been an honour to welcome Tony as one of the Founding Authors of GIP. May you feel as blessed by his book and who he is, as I have.

With inspiration,

Emily Gowor

Founder of Gowor International Publishing

What People Are Saying About Tony

"I came across Tony when my business had fallen apart and my private life was in tatters. Fortunately, another friend put me in touch with Tony, and it proved to be a Godsend. The inspiration and foresight that the guy gave me enabled me to push through what I was doing. The fact that I had somebody there that had been through it all, that had walked the same path, made a big difference and actually gave me the confidence to be able to push on… which I've done! So thank you, Tony. Thanks for all your help, and I'll be dealing with you again one day in the future."

– **Kel Shipton, Retail Business Owner, Perth WA**

"I suffered a major illness and had to have a new shiny machine planted in my chest. Tony kept me inspired, and what I learned from him took me further than I could have imagined. When I went for a Bar Manager job in Broome, the life skills that Tony employed and his coaching under the most difficult of circumstances put me in the right time and place. In the last three months, I have surfed more beaches than I could name, driven in excess of twenty thousand kilometres, and have travelled across the Nullarbor twice in as many months. Some call it 'Living the dream!' Take the hint and get with Tony. His skills are solid, and the life coaching…? Well, the facts of my story say it all. If you're at a breaking point, look for your point break. Go surf life and have Tony assist!"

– **George Barr, No Fixed Address or Job!**

"Tony Inman is a guy who has no limits. I'm amazed at some of the things he does – like running in the City to Surf, still playing soccer at 50+, diving, travelling to exotic places, and now business and personal coaching. He is prepared to travel all over the country for training and to improve his knowledge, and most importantly his willingness to share is quite rare in the modern world. Above all else, Tony is a great guy with a genuine love of life and humanity. Having initially met in a business relationship, I now count him as a genuine friend. He is also a Man U supporter, so that says something about his impeccable taste for fine things. I've done business in the past with Tony Inman, and I can honestly say he is a man of the highest integrity. He firmly believes in what he teaches, and more importantly, he lives what he teaches. Last, but not least, Tony has invested enormous personal energy and capital in self-development, which makes him well qualified to be a business and personal coach."

– **Bernie Kroczek, Real Estate Principal, Perth WA**

"You can have an open communication with Tony easily. He really cares about people, and he is committed to making a contribution to other people's lives and happiness. He is a great life coach."

– **Halle Yilmaz, Financial Advisor, Melbourne VIC**

"Tony Inman was my life coach for ten months while I was redesigning my career, lifestyle and personal life. During that time, he successfully kept me focused on achieving the goals that I established – both at the outset of the coaching and also as additional goals were identified. His support and ability to cut to the core issues and highlight areas that I had yet to recognise and address were invaluable during this time. I am delighted with my continuing development."

– **Kym Chomley, Accountant, Sunshine Coast QLD**

"Tony helped me with an entrepreneurship unit at university. He was an excellent mentor, and his vast knowledge of business assisted us greatly in achieving success with our project. I have maintained contact with Tony in the following years, and he has been a terrific coach assisting me with achieving my goals in work and life."

– **Cuong Tran, I.T. Advisor, Perth WA**

"Although I have a successful business, I felt overwhelmed when my partnership broke up. Tony has been a fantastic sounding board and has helped me rebuild my focus, enthusiasm, vision and profitability."

– **Juan Rando, Dance Academy Owner, Perth WA**

"I met Tony (Inman) when we were both receiving our Certification as NLP Trainers in Sydney. During the course, we often had to work together in teams to help refine our ability to present on the topic in front of groups. Tony is a conscientious and charismatic leader and speaker with great compassion for and interest in, his fellow teammates. I have kept in touch with Tony since the course and I would highly recommend him as a trustworthy and committed professional, whom I am certain would go above and beyond to help his clients."

– **Kim Jewell, Specialist Consultant in Stress, Anxiety & Depression, Brisbane QLD**

"I have worked with Tony on several occasions and have found him to be a man of his words. He is honest, straight down the line, and I can recommend him highly to improve any business. I've known Tony for eight years now, and he is a man of inspiration – a great, all-round genuine guy who cares!"

– **Prak Sangthon, Real Estate Principal, Perth WA**

"Tony is not only an astute coach and mentor, but he possesses an exceptional ability to uncover the hidden issues underlying real problems. His charisma and charm are tantamount to being a true leader. Anyone who has a chance to experience working with Tony should grab it!"

– **Lune Lim, Business Owner, Sydney NSW**

"I've never met a more genuine individual who has such a devotion to providing authentic results. Since my time knowing Tony, he has mentored and coached me, allowing me to experience more and more about myself and empowering me to aid others. Through his support and guidance, I have been able to achieve a level of myself that was once a myth to me."

– **George Bastoli, Careers Advisor, Sydney NSW**

"I had the pleasure of working with Tony over a 6-month period at an advanced coaching training course. Tony is incredibly gentle with his clients and gently leads them to insights that he has picked up on almost immediately. He is very insightful, providing plenty of opportunities for seeing yourself and things in your life in ways you almost certainly would not have found by yourself. He clearly has excellent business acumen – not surprising given his many years of experience running various businesses, some simultaneously. I cannot recommend Tony highly enough as a coach for those venturing into business for themselves for the first time or for more experienced business owners who are looking to step up to the next level."

— **Dr. Haley Jones, Author and Life Coach, Canberra ACT**

"Tony has helped me define our company's purpose, values, vision and mission. We are now growing our business to the next level with even greater clarity and cohesion. I think that where he adds the most value is when he comes in and helps owners define what it is that they find hard to, or do not have the time to, articulate. I am definitely happy. "

— **David Payne, Management Accountant Principal, Perth WA**

"I felt like my business had become routine and was too dependent on me grinding away day after day. Tony recently helped me to re-evaluate my goals and direction, and together, we developed a plan whereby I could build the business, hire and develop new, competent staff, and review our systems. I am hoping this will free me up to have more time with my family – both here in Australia and overseas. I guess only time will tell. Tony helped me interview prospective candidates and gave me advice on our business proposition. We are now re-branding our business, and I am re-enthused. Tony genuinely believes in the people he helps. His business nous is invaluable. I am happy to recommend Tony's services to small business owners who seek the benefit of an experienced consultant to give them a fresh perspective."

— **David Price, Advertising Agency Owner, Perth WA**

"I still don't know exactly what it was that Tony did or said, but something's really clicked inside my head. I feel completely different. I've got so much more confidence. That started even after the first session! Since then, we've transformed my business. I've now got a unique brand and some systems that have made things much more professional. I'm getting more calls and making more money on a consistent basis, and our goals are much clearer. Working with Tony has really made a huge difference to our business and our lives."

— **Leroy Brown, Carpentry Business Owner, Perth WA**

"Tony got across good ideas to improve our present situation, both in our daily life and our business. We are now really busy, but we have taken our new caravan away three times so far, and we are about to go on holiday again."

– **Ivan and Ann De Souza, Odour Control Business Owners, Perth WA**

"Tony combines his being and his business to include those around him, which I think is the reason he has achieved and realised his goals in life. Tony is an inspirational person, who has encouraged me to start a successful business of my own. Tony knows how to have a laugh and develop those ideas around a life choice. Thank you, Tony, for your amazing input to my life! Tony has the qualities that you learn from."

– **Nicole Pitts, Children's Art Tuition Business Owner, Launceston TAS**

"I have known Tony for many years, so when he told me he had set up a coaching and consulting business, I wasn't at all surprised. I have seen Tony help hundreds of people during that time to improve their lives, in all kinds of areas – from relationships to career counselling to starting up or developing businesses. He is a natural coach in that people feel at ease with him, so they ask his advice on all sorts of issues. I have also seen his entrepreneurial skills first hand, where he has set up small businesses with ease and developed the people and the systems so that they could grow and flourish. Tony has boundless energy and drive, with a huge will to win, not just for himself, but also for those around him to win as well. Just like his brand message says, if you want to reinvent yourself or your business so that you win the game, look no further than Tony Inman."

– **Alan Wilkins, Tax Officer, Perth WA**

Contents

Preface xxi

Introduction xxv

PART ONE – BEING 3

  1 A Matter of Life or Death 5

  2 Be a Dreamer – It's the Starting Point to Fulfillment 9

  3 Take Advanced Dreaming: Freedom 201 19

  4 Bad Dreams and Nightmares 33

  5 Twenty-Twenty Vision 45

  6 Be Responsible– It's Your Life! 55

  7 Get Your Head Straight 65

  8 Sticks and Stones 71

  9 Behavioural Science and Mind Power 83

  10 That Matter of Life or Death, Plus Using Self-Talk 99

PART TWO – 'DOING' 105

  11 "Hello, Death, We Meet Again!" 107

  12 Kick Your Own Butt 109

  13 Life Is About Movement 117

  14 Managing Change and Habits 119

  15 *Carpe Diem* – Seize the Day 127

  16 Be Alert to Opportunity 131

  17 What if This Was Your Last Breath? 137

  18 Harness the Power of Universal Laws 141

19 With Each New Breath 145

20 Marriage Is Not Necessarily a Life Sentence 149

21 Every Step Is Like a Swig of a Sports Drink 157

22 Getting on the Bus.. 163

23 Don't Let the Bxxxxxxs Grind You Down!.................................. 169

24 Fears and Failures – The Dream Destroyers 173

25 It Ain't So Bad, So Don't Get Mad! 181

26 Touching Hearts and Serving Others.. 187

27 The Jigsaw Pieces of Character 195

28 Still Believing You Can Win When Life Deals You a Bad Hand 209

29 The Brighter Side of Life 221

30 Be the Change You Want to See 229

31 The Twists and Turns of Life.. 233

32 Empower Yourself or Be Overpowered 237

33 Twist or Stick 243

34 The Power of Leverage.. 245

PART THREE – 'HAVING' 253

35 So Have You Found Your Why Yet?... 257

36 Keeping the Wind Beneath Your Wings 263

37 Operating on Instinct and Being Congruent 267

38 Defying Logic 271

39 Inspiration and Joy – It's All Around You 275

40 What Next? – Winning the Games of Business and Life.............. 281

41 The Last Word	293
42 The Alternative Ending	297
Bibliography	299
Influential Training	307
Acknowledgments	311
About the Author	315

Preface

The following is one of my favourite quotes of all time. It's from a speech given by President Theodore Roosevelt entitled 'Citizenship in a Republic', which was delivered at the Sorbonne, in Paris, France on April 23, 1910. From the moment I read it, the words have influenced me profoundly, because they are an endorsement of my life's philosophy: Life is too short not to give it your best shot. When you are about to take your last breath in this world, you and your higher consciousness, whatever that means to you, are the only ones who can truly judge whether you did or did not do all that you could have in your life.

> *"It is not the critic who counts; not the man who points out how the strong man stumbles, or where the doer of deeds could have done them better. The credit belongs to the man who is actually in the arena, whose face is marred by dust and sweat and blood; who strives valiantly; who errs, who comes short again and again, because there is no effort without error and shortcoming; but who does actually strive to do the deeds; who knows the great enthusiasms, the great devotions; who spends himself in a worthy cause; who at the best knows in the end the triumph of high achievement, and who at the worst, if he fails, at least fails while daring greatly, so that his place shall never be with those cold and timid souls who neither know victory nor defeat."*

Theodore Roosevelt
26th President of the United States

In the occupation of being a business and lifestyle consultant, coach and mentor, as I am, we say to people, "Start with the end in mind." In business, that means think about your endgame or your exit plan. In life, it means think about the legacy you will leave behind you for your family, your friends, and perhaps even for mankind.

Greatness is a subjective perception.

You can greatly influence mankind by becoming a billionaire and making space flight available to the masses like Sir Richard Branson, or you can be relatively anonymous, yet still deeply influence another life or even several lives. You can be a great adventurer, a great sportsman perhaps, or you might simply be a great lollypop lady who helps children cross roads safely. In truth, the very fact that you exist means you are already great. To simply be a blend of the sperm that won the race among millions of contestants, with the egg that awaited its arrival, already makes you part of the miracle of existence.

Whatever your situation, whatever your circumstances, you have the power to evolve and become something greater still. What that greater being is, however, is for you to figure out. If you do figure out what 'it' is, then you probably also need to figure out why 'it' is worth going after. If you can't figure out, 'Why?' then maybe the question should be, 'Why not?'

Here's the ultimate twist in the game of life, in my opinion, and you don't have to agree with me – that's okay either way…

Whether you succeed or whether you succeed differently, either is fine.
There are always lessons to be learned from both.
It's not the destination that counts; it's the journey.

Maybe that's the ultimate answer to the question of the meaning of life! In the satirical TV programme, *The Hitchhiker's Guide to the Galaxy*, one of the characters asked, "What is the answer to the Ultimate question of Life, the Universe and Everything?" After painstaking and exhaustive research, many years later, the answer was given as "42." I think the point of the satire was that the answer is, "Whatever you want it to be." There is no right or wrong answer. There are only perceptions that we form, based on our understanding of the world and how it should be, which are based on our values and our beliefs. It is when other humans act in accordance with their values and beliefs, which may suit them, but may be diametrically opposed to our own, that we see no rhyme or reason to their behaviour. In such cases, we often label them as criminal, evil, stupid or worse. Another great man whose teachings have influenced me tremendously is Dr. Wayne Dyer. He said, "We are not human beings having a spiritual experience. Rather, we are spiritual beings having a human experience."

That is why, in your dreams, you can be anyone you want to be. You can do anything you can possibly imagine, because there are no limits. If you want to leap over a building with one jump, you can become Superman! You can dive with sharks, wrestle crocodiles, bed a famous movie star… (Watch out though. They might be similar experiences!). It also might explain that connection that we feel with other humans. You know how you can think of an old friend, and the next day, they call you out of the blue or you meet them unexpectedly? Thoughts are energy. In fact, human bodies are really a mass of energy. If you've ever seen a dead person, you'll know that the body seems totally different when that life force has gone somewhere else.

Another of my teachers, Carl Buchheit from the NLP Institute in Marin, California, explained the concept of duality in that spiritual connection with the example that you can't have a victim without a murderer or a murderer without a victim. The two spirits are inexorably linked. Furthermore, when he explained his research into family systems, he revealed that the families and descendants of both the murderer and the victim become linked spiritually, until forgiveness is achieved and peace takes the place of the unease. It's very powerful work and perhaps best left for another book.

A point I do wish to make to help explain my statement of 'no rights or wrongs', is that there is a duality to everything. Yes, there is a duality in 'good and evil', 'black and white' or 'yin and yang', because that's part of the balance that has to be there – right down to the fundamental building blocks of life itself: 'protons and neutrons'. Here's what another of my teachers, the incredibly inspirational Dr. John Demartini said:

> *"Most people think that when they get something else, life will be better, but all it does is transform the positives and negatives into new forms. I'm not saying you shouldn't seek, but if you seek something you think will give you more positives than negatives, you are living with an illusion. When you get what you imagine you want, you will find out that it has a new catch or twist to it that you didn't anticipate. If you live in the illusion that it's going to give you a lot of happiness, you may be let down, for it won't, at least for long. It only gives you a new set of pains and pleasures. Because like everything else, pain and pleasure are conserved through time and space."*
>
> **Dr. John Demartini**

You might now be asking, "What's the point of setting goals or trying to live your dreams if it doesn't matter whether you achieve them or not, or if, even when you do, you just end up with a different set of problems?" Well, I'm not saying that there's no point! I'm saying that life is about motion; it's about moving steadily forwards or, occasionally, firstly sideways or backwards, then forwards in the direction of your dreams and goals. It's about living your life congruently, in harmony with your values and your beliefs, but it's also about what I jokingly call 'rigid flexibility' – being willing to accept that if life doesn't go to plan, you need to 'improvise, adapt and overcome' in dealing with the curve balls that life throws at you. Ultimately, it's about finding your purpose, creating your vision and developing your mission – developing it in such a way that you achieve happiness and joy and that you leave a legacy of which you can be proud, of which your children can be proud, that you positively influenced others around you and that your time spent here in this realm, enabled your spirit, the essence of your being, to evolve.

I sincerely intend that you, the reader, get something valuable from this book – even if it's just 'one little thing'. In life, as it is in business, it's a collection of those 'little things' that make big differences. The best part about all of this is that the path is actually one of self-discovery. I wish you great enjoyment, peace and good health on your own unique journey.

Tony Inman

Introduction

"All men dream, but not equally. Those who dream by night in the dusty recesses of their minds, wake in the day to find that it was vanity: but the dreamers of the day are dangerous men, for they may act on their dreams with open eyes, to make them possible."

**T.E. Lawrence
Soldier, better known as 'Lawrence of Arabia'**

Hi!

I'm Tony Inman, and I'd like to congratulate you for following your instincts, taking action and finding this book, *If Life's Worth Doing, It's Worth Doing Well – Finding Sane Fulfillment in an Insane World*.

The reason I chose the book title was that I wanted to pay tribute to my late father, Bill Inman, who passed away in May 2012 at the commendable age of ninety. One of Dad's favourite sayings, one of the many that he drummed into me as a child, was, *"If a job's worth doing, it's worth doing well."* It was one of the values that I think his father, a self-employed mattress-maker (in the days when they were made by hand), had instilled in him. I heard it so often that it became one of my core values. I remember reading somewhere that the sayings of our parents are the little voices that pop into our heads as adults. Thus, I chose to paraphrase my father, extending it to the broader reflection on existence.

The sub-title, *Finding Sane Fulfillment in an Insane World*, is an explanation of some of the lessons I have learned in life about how to find your own inner peace, happiness and sense of satisfaction with your progress on your life's journey in a world that is often beset by what I call 'madness'. By that, I mean that our rapid advances in digital technology and accelerated communications have created a world where we are bombarded with 'noise'. We are deluged daily with mass consumerism, with more news than we can possibly keep up with and with more emails, text messages and social media updates than we could ever possibly read properly in a month. I don't know about you, but if I leave home and accidentally forget to take my smart phone with me, I feel naked! Technological and communications advances were supposed to make our lives easier, but in many cases, they have left people feeling inadequate, unworthy or redundant.

I've been a student of human behaviour and success ever since I began reading books as a child, and in managing people for around thirty-five years and setting up over 20 of my own businesses so far, I've consulted to, coached and mentored hundreds of business owners and managers and thousands of staff. This managerial career has enabled me to apply the lessons I have learned from studying success principles in a practical way with staff and customers alike. One of the commonly recurring themes among the behaviour of people who have achieved so-called high levels of success is that they solve other peoples' problems and they help other people get what they want. In fact, one of the well-known motivational speakers Zig Ziglar said, "You can have everything in life you want, if you will just help other people get what they want."

In my role as a business consultant and presenter, I often refer to both business and life as 'games'. Why do I call them that? Maybe it's because my father always used to ask me, "Are you winning, old son?" At first, that seemed to be an unusual, abstract question, but now it makes perfect sense. Or, maybe I refer to business and life as games because it helps me keep a sense of perspective. To me, if you lose one game, there is always a new game to play. If you win a game, there is always a bigger game to play. Games are played with rules, just as life and business have rules. Some people follow them, while others bend them. Some just break the rules, but there may well be consequences. Maybe the notion of playing games keeps us young at heart. When we no longer wish to play, it's time to leave the game and let someone else play. In the games of business and life, there doesn't necessarily have to be a loser to correspond with every winner. It's possible to negotiate and achieve 'win-win' outcomes.

If you've ever looked at my website, tonyinman.net, you may have noticed my catch cry of "Living the Dream!" So, what have games got to do with dreams, or with living the dream? Well, another thing that I have observed in my studies of human behaviour is that the person who firstly sees or imagines themselves winning the game has a far greater chance of doing so than the one who can only see a failure or a loss.

You may have heard of a book that was made into a movie, both by the name of *The Secret* by Rhonda Byrne. This achieved something of a cult following because it espoused the principle that the secret to success was to vividly imagine and focus on the things that you wanted in your life, and that by doing so, you would unleash the 'Law of Attraction' to bring you these results. It has been universally agreed that the power of creative visualisation of your dreams and goals is indeed one of the major steps towards their achievement. There is, however, another major ingredient in the recipe for success, which we will explore in this book. There are also a number of other traits that you may need to work on if you are to truly achieve the results that you want.

Many years ago, my life was changed when I came across a recording of a speech by a man named Earl Nightingale. It was called 'The Strangest Secret'. Earl's definition of success struck a chord with me…

> *"Success is the progressive realisation of a worthy goal or ideal."*
> **Earl Nightingale (From 'The Strangest Secret')**

In other words, he went on to say that you already are a success if you are doing the thing that you want to do. To express it another way, the person who is living the life that they had imagined for themselves, the life that brings them joy and fulfillment, is 'living the dream'. So, it's fair to say that 'the dream' is different for us all. That's a very good reason to not judge people, because their dream is different from your dream. Therefore, the things they value and hold dear may well not be the same as yours. Thus, their interpretation of what the world means is different than yours.

While some dreamers dream though, the world could be seen as having become an insane place, where people's ability to misbehave in astounding ways proliferates in nightmarish ways.

In fairness, however, there have always been conflicts and barbaric acts throughout the history of man, and armed conflict has never really been a rational solution. There have always been countries with economies in ascendance that rise to assume the mantle of power, while other empires crumble to make way. Meanwhile, our world has seen rampant technological advances during my lifetime that seem to accelerate on a daily basis, with communications so advanced that we are not only aware of our old friend's birthday on the other side of the world in a different time zone, but we can actually look at photos of him celebrating it within a second of them being taken. We can video call him and sing "Happy Birthday" to him live. In my lifetime, we've gone from black and white TV that you had to get off the couch to go and adjust, to digital downloads onto pocket-sized devices that contain more knowledge than an entire collection of the old encyclopaedias ever did.

We see suicide bombers sacrifice themselves in the middle of crowds of people they have never met, and we've gone from the Holocaust to Weapons of Mass Destruction in a way that shows little has really been learned in the last half century. Little by little, mankind is killing the planet on which we reside. We are making species extinct through hunting and fishing insanity and the quest for material gains over sustainability. In a world bursting with technology and inventions like super crops, there are still millions of people left starving to death. In a world of incredible medical advances, there are still millions dying each year of preventable diseases. In the struggle for global positioning and politicking, we gradually see the visions of Huxley's *Brave New World* and Orwell's *1984* coming into being, with perceived 'terrorist threats' broadcast incessantly so that extreme measures of power and control may be exercised with impunity and justification in the interests of national security. 'Big Brother' is alive and well.

Of course, while this is all happening, so too is the good stuff – the sane stuff. The heart-warming stuff where medical advances mean that people can donate a kidney to save a life; the inspirational stuff where people protest in the streets to save the sharks from finning; the humane stuff where televised appeals raise awareness of peoples' plights and millions of dollars can be raised within hours to help the needy, the victims of floods, fires and famines –all thanks to the lightning responses initiated by the stellar impact of social networking.

Perhaps it seems insane to me because it's all happening so fast – because we are drowning in a sea of over-communication with waves of noise extolling the virtues of foaming oceans of products and services, special offers, mega deals and rampant consumerism. However, it's all down to the way you choose. You alone choose what you will focus on – which news you will listen to, which politician you will believe in, which newspaper or TV channel you select, etc.

You can choose whether to see and hear the bad news, or see and hear the good news.

Perhaps the famous speaker, Jim Rohn expressed it best:

> "Things in the next six years will be the same as they were in the last six years – opportunity mixed with difficulty."
>
> **Jim Rohn**

We are spiritual beings on a journey of discovery where the concept of fulfillment is our theoretical destination.

So that's a little bit of an opening explanation about the title and about a few of the concepts we will explore in this book. I hope that by the time you have finished reading it, some new thoughts, ideas and sources of inspiration may have found their way into your mind and your heart and that they empower you to grab life by the horns and ride off into a lifetime of spectacular sunsets.

I just have a few words on how the book was written, so you know what to expect. I have blended some of my own personal journey with the lessons I extracted from my various ups and downs with ideologies and principles gleaned from some of the world's leading transformational thought leaders. I have sprinkled snippets from courses I've attended with books and stories I have read, and I've glued these together with quotations from some of humanity's most revered sources of inspiration. As a writer, my intention is keep you entertained, perhaps even a little in suspense, while I scatter a few pearls of wisdom in your path and you can choose which ones you like. It's also written so that you can read it as I wrote it. I had to fit my writing in between all of life's business, as and when I had the time. If that's the way you have to read it, then you should be able to flick it open randomly and still find something of value – something that you can use and plug in to your life in a way that brings you a result. Thus, a couple of my personal stories have been split apart like two pieces of bread in a sandwich, allowing you to savour the full taste of the ingredients that constitute the filling.

The book has an introduction, three main parts (the BE, DO and HAVE sections) and a conclusion. It also comes with an alternative ending, but you may read about this in the conclusion.

Although I like to keep busy and the entrepreneur in me keeps finding me new projects, my main roles today are those of coach, consultant, mentor, author and presenter of information and ideas. (My roles have changed many times over the years as I have constantly evolved and adapted, leading some people to see me as 'The Reinvention Specialist'.) Of course, I balance those with being a partner, father, grandfather, friend, confidante, scuba diver, soccer player, volleyball player, musician, occasional private pilot, movie buff, actor in training, avid reader, world traveller… well, the list is actually unlimited and subject to constant updates!

I hope that you will find enough of interest here to tap into my work as a resource for you, either as a coach, or via my blogs or newsletters, or even via one of my presentations, to help you 'do life well', 'follow your dreams' and find 'sane fulfillment'. Thanks for reading. If you enjoy it, please tell your friends to do the same.

Tony Inman

PART ONE:

BEING

Realising Who You Are

Tony the traveller and student of life, fulfilling a lifelong dream to visit the Pyramids of Giza

PART ONE – BEING

Realising Who You Are

"I think, therefore I am."

René Descartes

Part One of this book is about realising 'who you are'. The one thing that really holds the key to our life and the one thing that we will fight tooth and nail to protect and keep safe is our own identity, meaning, 'who we think we are'. That is why we feel so hurt or threatened when someone challenges that view that we hold of ourselves, such as when a lover jilts us or a boss or a parent berates us for some perceived flaw.

One of the things that I hope you will gain from this book is a little more clarity about who you are, what your beliefs and values are, and what your purpose is for being on this planet. The second key message that I hope you may discover is by changing some of your thoughts and introducing a few ideas or concepts that may be new to you, you truly can be the master or mistress of your own destiny.

Whatever things you wish to achieve during your time on this Earth may well be achievable by you, if you are willing to think differently, to perhaps take some different actions, and thus to succeed in obtaining results that previously may have seemed a little crazy. I sometimes wear a tee-shirt that has a slogan which reflects my (possibly) quirky way of looking at life, "I don't suffer from insanity – I enjoy every minute of it!" This world and the actions of the human race can certainly cause you to wonder sometimes if we are all insane. I hope that amidst what I call insanity, you can find your own key to sane fulfillment.

1

A Matter of Life or Death

"The greatest revolution in our generation is the discovery that human beings, by changing the inner attitudes of their minds, can change the outer aspects of their lives."

Professor William James

From Death to New Life

It was a fairly dull, overcast day on the South Pacific Island of Espiritu Santo – then known as New Hebrides, now the proud country called Vanuatu. The jungles on these islands were to witness some of the most ferocious combat to take place in the Second World War, between the Japanese, who had invaded them, and the Americans, who were trying to liberate them. The South Pacific Ocean that surrounds them is now the watery grave of many rusting ships and aircraft that were shot down and sunk in this unforgiving arena.

On one particularly fateful day, October 26, 1942, a US navy ship named the *SS President Coolidge* was steaming towards the natural harbour off the coastal capital town of Luganville on the northern island of Espiritu Santo. This island had been reclaimed by the Americans. The ship was bringing reinforcements and much needed medical supplies – quinine in particular, to combat the effects of malaria caused by mosquito bites – a condition that ironically did more damage than the warring factions.

The ship was a beautiful and graceful, gigantic vessel that, prior to commencement of hostilities, had been a luxury cruise liner. Having been converted to a new role of troop carrier, it was the transitory home to five thousand souls. The cargo holds were filled with trucks, jeeps and munitions ready to reinforce the garrison. Despite the practicalities of its conversion, such as rows of toilets on the deck, the inner chambers, such as the dining room and smoking lounge, bore the hallmarks of its splendid past.

The military high command had not entrusted the ship's captain – who was a commercial skipper, rather than a naval officer – with the location of their own minefield. Fearing a Japanese submarine attack, the captain was concerned when no friendly ship arrived to greet them, so he made the decision to quickly seek safety in the harbour. Before the troops on land could signal him a warning, however, the ship struck the first mine, and the explosion in the engine room killed one sailor immediately. The *Coolidge* was a very fast ship for its size, but with all of that weight on board, it was never going to turn around quickly enough.

Just as the word, 'Stop' was signalled, the stern of the ship caught a second mine, thus spelling its death knell. Fortuitously, the captain steered hard to shore so that his passengers could flee the doomed vessel. Over the next ninety minutes, 4,998 men disembarked safely, scaling down the sides of the ship on ropes in a mass exodus. Only one other man lost his life that day as he tried to help his men off the stricken cruise liner. They thought they could return and salvage the vehicles and supplies later, but the ocean was too greedy. The ship listed, sank and slid back down the slope into the channel. She now rests on her side with the bow at a depth of around twenty metres and her stern at around seventy metres.

Today, the *Coolidge* is protected by Vanuatuan law and provides a spectacular opportunity for scuba divers to test their ability at deep diving. The dual persona of the ship means that divers can see both a pre-war cruise liner and a naval vessel of war, simultaneously. The ship is a breeding ground for coral and all manner of marine life, including turtles and eels. The unexpected rapidity of her demise means that there are artefacts galore to discover, from typewriters and binoculars to guns and helmets, though by law they must not be removed. So it seems that *as one thing dies, another thing lives in its place.*

Is It Time to Die?

In August 2010, my partner, Joanne, and I were progressing on our umpteenth dive of the *SS President Coolidge*. This massive ship really reminded me of the footage I have seen of the *Titanic* in terms of both its opulence and its eeriness. We were in the safe hands of a local dive master, Dave, who had been guiding tourists around this mesmerising vessel for over eighteen years. As well-travelled scuba enthusiasts who were both qualified as advanced rescue divers, our holiday had really been planned around this opportunity to complete some of the best wreck penetration diving in the world. We actually went inside the dark cargo holds full of rusting vehicles, identifiable as such only by the tyres, and we explored the intact gauges of the engine room at a depth of fifty-five metres! (Normal, open-water level diving is to a maximum of eighteen metres.) For those who don't know much about diving, one single breath at that depth is equivalent to about nine on the surface, so you maintain slow motion to conserve air, and you stay focused.

We were doing the 'swimming pool' dive. As the ship had been a luxury cruiser, the first class passengers had the delight of a swimming pool on the rear deck. With the ship now on its side and covered in coral and silt, it was a very strange notion. We completed a vertical lap of the pool, which was most bizarre, and just so we could be sure of what we had done, Dave swished away the silt with his hand to reveal the ceramic tiles on the pool's side.

Sometimes, when you inhale the dry air from a dive tank, you can lose the moisture in your throat, which is exactly what happened to me. In trying to swallow some saliva, I felt the urge to cough, in an effort to clear my throat. This was neither the time nor the place to start coughing. I desperately felt the urge to rip the regulator out of my mouth. After all, it is not normal to breathe through a tube with only your mouth (your nose is inside your mask). Another effect of the pressure on your body from being so deep is that you think much slower than you do on the surface. Some people don't handle it very well, and as your body absorbs more nitrogen, you can start to experience a condition called nitrogen narcosis. This can take the form of euphoria – a feeling like you've had a few alcoholic beverages – or you can experience anxiety. My coughing triggered a sense of anxiety, which was probably exacerbated by slight narcosis. I immediately grabbed my regulator and held it firmly in my mouth, lest I should accidentally cough it out.

I looked up, and I couldn't even see the surface. Not that it would have made a difference if I could, because I would not have been able to shoot up there without seriously endangering myself. When you go that deep, you have to take a long time to return to the surface, and you do it in stages, with multiple 'safety stops' to allow for decompression, which means giving the nitrogen time to dissipate from your bloodstream. Failure to do so could result in a condition called 'the bends', where nitrogen bubbles could find their way to your brain, which could be fatal.

Despite the depth and reduced speed of reaction, my mind was racing. It was like a Hollywood movie, where you see the actor with a devil on one shoulder and an angel on the other. Have you ever experienced that kind of crazy conflicting conversation inside your head? I'm sure I'm not the only one!

The angel tried to reassure me that I was an experienced diver and I could handle this. The devil was telling me I had no right to be down here. I didn't belong in this dark, eerie world. He told me that I should spit out my regulator and breathe deeply, but I knew that to do so would most likely lead to my premature death by drowning.

Had you told me a few years earlier that I would find myself fifty-five metres below the surface, exploring a World War II shipwreck, I would have definitely laughed at you. I had a fear of opening my eyes under water, so there was no way I would *ever* learn to scuba dive. Yet, there I was, facing a life or death situation. *Is this going to be my final moment?* I wondered. *We all have to go some day. Is this to be the time and place where my adventure ends?* Then, something surreal happened. Remind me to tell you later just what that was…

2

Be A Dreamer – It's The Starting Point to Fulfillment

"Happy talk, keep talkin' happy talk,
Talk about things you'd like to do.
You got to have a dream,
If you don't have a dream,
How you gonna have a dream come true?"

Rodgers and Hammerstein
From the musical South Pacific

How many times have you heard of someone being called 'a dreamer' as if it's an insult?

Now, if we're talking about a highly paid staff member, whose wages you are paying while they dream only of what they will do on the weekend instead of serving your customers, I completely understand! However, what I'm talking about is the big dreams we have about what we want to achieve on this planet. Those are the kind of dreams that can lead to new discoveries, to decisions that might affect humanity, and to changes in direction that could put you personally on the path to fulfillment.

The Questions Some People Avoid Asking Themselves

I could have given this particular section the title, 'Are You Happy?' However, you would have probably cringed, said to yourself, "Of course I am!" and zoomed away to a more interesting question. Now, don't panic. I'm not going all religious here either! (That's definitely not my style, though I will mention spirituality later on!) Let's expand on the question at hand. Here are three sub-questions for you to consider. (I call them the 'BE', 'DO' and 'HAVE' questions.)

1. Are you the person you wanted to be when you were younger? (If not, then who or what kind of person do you want to be now?)

   _____

   _____

2. Are you doing the things you really wanted to do? (If not, then what are they and when *will* you do them?)

   _____

   _____

3. Do you have the result you wanted? (If no, then what will let you know when you have?)

   _____

   _____

Let's strip away some of the dirt that may be preventing the diamond that you know that you are from sparkling to the full extent that you could be!

1. What if you had unlimited time? (Then what?)

   _____

   _____

2. What if you had 'enough' money? (Let's say that money was no object – indulge me here for a moment!)

_____

_____

Were those easy questions to answer? Did the answers immediately leap out of your brain onto the page or are you stuck? If you really did just go blank, then it may mean that you haven't given yourself permission to dream yet, or you have given up on your dream. Well, you're not doing that on my watch! I would really recommend that you create a few minutes of thinking time today in a quiet place where you won't be disturbed. Grab a pen and paper, throw caution to the wind, and write down whatever comes out of your head. Think back to when you were just a child. If someone had asked what you would like to 'be' when you grew up, you could have said whatever you wanted and no-one, except the most cynical souls, would have laughed. They would more likely have said, "Of course, you can be whatever you want to be when you grow up!"

I, on the other hand, have now come to terms with the fact that my childhood fantasy career as a professional football player is highly unlikely to come to fruition – although my team did have a spell a few years back when I considered making a phone call to a certain Premier League Manager! Even had I been of a suitable age and fitness level, however, if I had said in my 20s that I was quitting my job and flying to England to pursue my childhood dream of becoming the next George Best, people would have said I was nuts. Furthermore, had I also said anything out of the norm, like, "I'm quitting my job to go travelling around Australia!" which I actually did do in 1994, then I'm sure people probably *did* say I was nuts!

In fact, they definitely did. In truth, I actually was nuts(ish), but I did it anyway – except that half way around, I changed plans and flew from a forty-degree day in the Australian Outback to a minus five-degree night in London to chase after a girl with whom I had fallen in love (That particular story could be a whole other book in itself!). So what's even more amazing about that decision is that I had virtually no money. I created the time of course by quitting the job. The funny thing is that when you 'go with the flow' and trust in your own ability to handle whatever comes along, you'll find that you just figure out the small details as you go. Other people just shook their heads in disbelief. The trouble is though that it's a bit addictive. Once you've broken the shackles and escaped the rat race, you know that, if you can do it once, you can do it again.

I'll expand on that more in a moment, but first I'd like to make the point that life is really made up of a series of dreams – some of which you are able to make come true. Others may fall by the wayside, and we'll talk about why that happens later on in the book. I'd like to share just a few of the bigger dreams that came true for me so far in my journey, because maybe you'll identify with some of the ups or downs and perhaps you may find something of use to you in your own situation. Hopefully, you'll be able to see that it was through me being willing to dream increasingly bigger dreams and take action toward achieving them, that I learned the lessons I have.

My First Big Dream – The Freedom of the Road

Most teenagers, or people who have been teenagers or are about to become teenagers, would relate to this one. Wheels on the road meant freedom from my parents, so at the age of sixteen, I used my savings and some Christmas money to buy a 50cc motorbike. With an engine that small it was really a moped, but it looked and felt like a proper big bike – except for the whiney sound it made as I revved it full tilt. By cunningly leaning forward to cut down wind resistance, I could reach speeds of fifty-four miles per hour on an island with an all-island speed limit of forty miles per hour! All of my mates had these bikes, and we raced around the town believing ourselves to be the 'Kings of Cool'. I'm not sure that spectators to our coolness as we zoomed past would have agreed, but we didn't care what lesser mortals thought.

Lesson learned: The ability and means to travel where I wanted represented freedom to me.

I expanded further on this dream a year later, when I bought my first car. My parents were cunning here because Mum sold me her old Hillman Imp for the princely sum of seventy-five pounds. She could have given it to me, but she knew that it was better I paid something. The vehicle eventually featured six different body colours as it fell apart bit by bit! It's fair to say that I spent as much time pushing that rascal of a car as I did driving it, but it was mine. When it needed a new clutch, Dad fixed it, with me as his 'go-fer'. Being a car with a rear engine, we had to take the whole thing out to even get at the clutch. It was a big job, and I learnt a lot about cursing at bolts that you can't reach and nuts that won't undo – along with a bit about how cars work and the importance of tea as a calming influence.

Lessons learned: Spending time with people and showing an interest in them is important, and you value things more if you have invested in them in some way.

At the age of seventeen, I decided I needed to upgrade my bike and my level of coolness. I researched intently and found the bike of my dreams: a Yamaha RD 250cc machine. I went to the dealer, brought home a leaflet, and stuck it on my bedroom wall. I saved and saved until I was able to buy myself a brand new, shiny white motorbike. I now owned a 'chick magnet'. The only problem was that I was too shy to meet any 'chicks'.

Lessons learned: Focusing on your vision of what you want is very powerful. Backing this up by following a plan is more so. Being willing to delay gratification to achieve that plan adds value and is even more empowering. I was so proud of that motorbike.

My Second Big Dream – As Free as a Bird

Learning to fly may not seem so special these days, but to me it was a big goal and a big accomplishment at the age of nineteen. I will always be thankful to an old school friend, Steve Hill, who took me up for a spin one glorious sunny afternoon in a Cessna 150 light aircraft. With about sixty-kilometres visibility, we could see across the sparkling blue ocean, the whole island of Jersey, and all the way up the French Coast towards the Cherbourg Peninsular. As soon as he let me take the controls, I knew immediately that I just had to get my private pilot's licence.

I asked my mum for a loan, and although my parents agreed, they also said, "But we'll charge you the same interest that the bank would." That was actually really empowering of them because it made me use my own initiative and self-reliance Take note of that if you are a parent or prospective parent!). Thus, I think it was only about a week later that I secured a bank loan, and only a few weeks or nine flying hours later, I made my first solo flight at a grass airfield in France. Flying then became a huge part of my life, with many jaunts to France and England. I also became a significant organiser of social events at the Aero Club. I spent a great deal of my time cooking barbecues for visiting pilots, being captain of the pool team, and being the captain and match-organiser of the football team.

> *When you know instinctively that you have found something that you want desperately to do, something so special that you know it is non-negotiable, listen to your intuition and do everything within your power to make it happen.*
>
> **Tony Inman**

What is there in your life that you know you desperately want to do more than anything else?

My Third Big Dream – The Girl of My Dreams

Women were a mystery to me because I went to an all-boys school. I dated some lovely girls, but I found my first wife, a Glaswegian lass, named Joyce McIlwaine – a vivacious and pretty blonde, with whom I quickly fell madly in love. We met in the bar of my second home in Jersey, the Channel Islands Aero Club, at one of the regular disco parties. Unfortunately, not long after we started going out together, we broke up for a spell. Actually, she dumped me to go back out with an ex-boyfriend, but I knew she was the one. I remember telling my mother, "I'm going to get her back again." I never gave up on my belief that she would in fact return to me, and sure enough, she subsequently gave in to my charms and persistence. I won her back at my twenty-first birthday party.

> *When you love someone and you know it's right, a 'no' is a 'maybe'. I'm not suggesting you stalk people, but don't give up til you know it's a no'. Nevertheless, be true to yourself. If it's meant to be, it will be.*
>
> **Tony Inman**

Have you found the partner of your dreams? If not, I recommend you do this exercise: Write down as detailed a description of what that person would be like physically, mentally and spiritually. What would their personality traits be? The more detailed and specific you can be, the more likely you are to finally come across that person!

The most important part about finding someone is to know who you are looking for.

Lesson learned: Love conquers all.

My Fourth Big Dream – Rising Up through the Managerial Ranks

I really had no idea what to do when I left school, so I found myself attending job interviews, largely to get my mother off my back! Luckily I had learned a strong work ethic from my hotelier parents. Their greatest gifts to me were to give me a fantastic education at Victoria College, founded by Queen Victoria, and the opportunity to work in the family hotel businesses from a young age – including running their bar, checking in guests, taking bookings… the works!

My first full-time job though was to wash hire cars for Hertz and to pick up the gorgeous female sales reps from the various hotels, but my parents thought I was wasting my education. They were right of course (No disrespect intended to anyone doing that job; I had a lot of fun)! I then applied for a job as a trainee journalist, but didn't get it. Even then, I loved writing and travel. I also applied for a job with British Airways as a flight attendant. My dad was an aircraft engineer; my sister was a stewardess; and one brother was a pilot – so aviation was in my blood. Plus, I wanted the cheap travel benefits!

Having been rejected for my chosen fields, I wanted to do a tourism degree and take over my parents' hotel. They said it wasn't big enough to afford me and pay them, and the Jersey Government gave grants for every degree you might wish to study, except… you guessed it: tourism (It was only their major economic resource at the time. Go figure)! I think I partly wanted to go to a university in England because (a) we didn't have one in Jersey, and (b) all my mates, including best mate, Tony Pitcher, were heading off to what seemed like an adventure. They never talked about the studying, just the parties!

I had no idea what else I wanted to do, so to appease my nagging (concerned) mother, I went for an interview at the local supermarket chain (the 'Co-op') with seventy other applicants for a trainee manager position. I was shortlisted before becoming one of the five who were successful, along with an older and more experienced man who later became my great friend and mentor, David Palmer.

Lesson learned: If you don't know what to do, find someone who does. Always seek out mentors – people who are willing to pass on their pearls of wisdom to help point you in the right direction.

I think my social life and my flying took priority at first, but one day I got serious – and here is an important lesson. At the age of eighteen, I had started working full time as a trainee manager. I set two goals: to be a deputy manager by twenty-five and a store manager by thirty. They were pretty realistic targets if I worked hard. I also studied the art and skills of management – much of which I learned from my mentor – and I became a good manager. How powerful it can be to set some goals! Only a year later, at nineteen, I became the youngest deputy manager in the company, overseeing twenty-three staff members. By age twenty-three, I was deputy manager at the second biggest store in the company. I won a major industry award, presented at the London Hilton, and I had been told I was in line to get the next manager's job.

I was young and ambitious. However, by the time I was twenty-three, Joyce and I wanted our own house. It still wasn't happening fast enough for me. I remember thinking that I wanted to have my own company 'someday'.

> *"A goal is a dream with a deadline."*
>
> **Napoleon Hill (Author of Think and Grow Rich)**

Here's another important question for you: Have you put deadlines on your dreams and goals? If not, please grab that piece of paper, or better still a book or a spreadsheet so that you don't lose it, and add some dates to those goals. You can always start by separating them as goals to achieve by: this month, this quarter, this year, the next 3 years… this lifetime. With the longer term goals, put some stepping stones of things to do as milestones towards their accomplishment. This exercise is really great fun to do because you suddenly realise that you actually can make things happen!

Building Blocks

- Questions are the answer.
- Define what 'freedom' means to you.
- Invest in the right people – the ones who inspire you, not the ones who drag you down.
- Giving people your attention is your greatest gift.
- Find time to reflect and focus on what it is that you want.
- Take action, but be willing to be patient. What you seek will appear when you are ready for it.
- Take responsibility for your life and the outcomes you achieve.
- Love is the greatest force on Earth.
- Seek out mentors and coaches if you are serious about the results you want.
- Put dates on your dreams and goals. It will take them from 'I could' to 'I will'.
- You will 'do life well' if you think about what you want and you go for it.

3

Take Advanced Dreaming: Freedom 201

"Just when I thought I was out...They pull me back in."

Michael Corleone
(From *The Godfather* by Mario Puzzo)

My experience has been that the more you set goals and achieve them, the bigger and more daring your dreams will become. Success on the little things gives you the self-confidence and self-belief to move on to bigger things, just as when you go from basic studies to advanced studies.

My Fifth Big Dream – A Home, a Family and a Career in 'The Lucky Country'

In 1984, I persuaded Joyce to leave the delightful but frustrating Channel Island of Jersey to honeymoon in Perth, Western Australia, which of course impressed her sufficiently so that she agreed to emigrate here. My brother Geoff had already emigrated years before and ever since visiting him several times during my teens, it had been my dream to move here as well when I was grown up. We wanted a land of opportunity where we could raise a family and buy our own home – a luxury that was looking like an increasingly problematic task with escalating property prices on the island. All I had to do was to take my wife to see some builders' display homes, and she was hooked on the 'Great Australian Dream' of home ownership. Despite doing well in my career, I felt frustrated and as if I was waiting for 'dead men's' shoes' for promotion opportunities. Everything seemed so much more optimistic in Australia.

The challenge of securing permission to emigrate is another lengthy story. The quick version is that, whilst on my honeymoon, I approached retail department store giants, Target, secured an interview the day before our flight home (talk about pressure!), and convinced the state personnel manager, Ross Backshall, to break company policy to offer me a job, which I then upsold him to making it an official sponsorship offer. I just happened to have the necessary forms in my briefcase with me!

Lessons learned: Always set your intention up front, imagine yourself getting the result you want and be prepared!

The bureaucracy of emigration, or immigration as we who now live here call it, was, and still is, a drawn-out pain in the butt. I had to keep writing to Ross to reassure him I was still intent on moving, but that the wheels of government were spinning ever so slowly. When we finally did receive the go-ahead, some eighteen months later, I'll never forget one friend saying to me, "What do you want to go to Australia for? It's full of spiders and snakes isn't it?"

> *What you may see as an opportunity and a challenge to relish, others will see as a ridiculous idea, fraught with problems. Do your research and make an informed decision, but develop your trust in your intuition or gut feeling. The more you do this, the more you will operate at a higher level and play a bigger game, both in business and in life.*
>
> **Tony Inman**

At Target, I achieved good results and was promoted three times in two years from management trainee in the smallest store in the state to area sales manager at the biggest store in Australia. Then, I found myself with one of those bosses who just makes life miserable. I was promoted to a store that required me to spend three hours per day driving to and from work, under constant pressure, and for less money because of the additional fuel costs. It was one of the most challenging strains on our relationship as a young couple – that of being poor. I was paid a monthly salary, but the month lasted longer than the money. I learned to add up the grocery bill when we went shopping and put items back on the shelf so that I wouldn't be embarrassed at the checkout. I was working and travelling too many hours to get a second job, so I left and ran a Wonderland of Toys supermarket as a licensee for two years, recruiting and training my own staff team. We had a lot more fun than the Target people, yet my team and I still worked hard and increased the sales and the profits significantly. I'll always be grateful to Target and to Ross in particular for helping me gain residency, but I vowed to never again work in a job that made me feel miserable at the thought of going to work.

Nevertheless, with the toys retailer, I wasn't getting the rewards for effort that my family deserved, so I joined the world of selling insurance for about two years. Direct sales is a fantastic experience for learning more about people and their behaviour. Joyce and I achieved our dream of building a house within a year of our arrival, which became a home to our two fantastic children, Craig and Kim, who will always represent our greatest achievements in this world.

Sadly, we struggled financially through the Labour Government's period in power and almost went back to Jersey under Prime Minister Keating's reign – our mortgage rate went up to eighteen percent during what Keating called, "The recession we had to have." I had just started a new career in management coaching, but it was a commission position that took time to develop contacts. I took an evening telemarketing job and even a paper round to top up my earnings through the early stages as I was determined to make it work. I loved the intellectual stimulation of working with business owners and executives. The career was short-lived though as we needed a steady income, and that was going to take time to develop. You may have heard the saying, 'Happy wife, happy life'? The opposite is also true! When times are tough, and your wife refuses to have sex with you until you do what she wants and get yourself a 'proper job' with consistent pay checks, you go back to what you know best!

Economic Slavery

So I went back to retail management. I scored a great job at Big W and was a deputy store manager, overseeing up to 120 staff. There, I helped manage the transformation of a store undergoing a pioneering conversion to be based on the Walmart model (the most profitable retailers in the world). I was quite well paid in theory, but working anything from twelve hours up to sixteen hours per day made my hourly rate look somewhat pathetic.

One day as I recall, our whole management team worked back every evening for a week, and on the last day from about six a.m. to about eleven p.m. to get the store as perfect as possible for the visit of one of the big bosses from Melbourne or Sydney – we called them the 'Wise Men from the East'. It reminded me of the Scottish comedian, Billy Connolly, saying that the Queen must think everything smells of paint, because everywhere she visits, there is a team of painters about fifty metres ahead of her, painting everything to make it look perfect!

In our store, we always had problems with damaged goods. Managers never had enough time to go through these items, mark them down in price, and get rid of them to bargain hunters, so there was a backlog of trolleys full of this stock. If the big boss were to see this mess, it would reflect badly on our store and make us look disorganised. The store manager, Peter Bramble, who was a dry humoured but cynical pommy, thought quickly about how to solve the predicament. "Hide all those trolleys of crap in the ladies toilets!" he said. "The bugger'll never go in there!"

When the big boss' car arrived, he was running late and had a plane to catch. Our store management team was ordered to stand in a line at the front door of the store. When his car pulled up, he ran in, shook all our hands and promised to spend more time in our store next time. As he left, we all looked at each other in stunned silence. The ridiculousness of that situation in the world of retail management and of being used up and burnt out by corporations just trying to please shareholders altered my perspective *forever*.

Our whole team worked our socks off that year, completely refitting a massive store, whilst turning it around by ninety degrees and linking it up with the main shopping centre and trading through an increase in trade of about forty percent. The project was supposed to take six months, but it blew out to over a year because of the unions. Every time it rained, even if ninety-nine percent of the workers were working inside, they all stopped work. The same happened when it was too hot outside, even though most of them were working in air-conditioning. On Fridays, someone usually phoned in with a bomb hoax, so they all had to down tools and head for the pub instead!

I'll never forget the company flying in one of the Walmart board members as a consultant. He walked around the store making incisive comments in an American drawl, like, "I'd hang that sign about thirty centimetres lower." When someone told us they were paying him thousands of dollars per day for these pearls of wisdom, I thought, *How do I get a job like his – where people actually pay you for your knowledge and expertise?!* I tried to fix the 'managerial burn out' problem, so on my own initiative, I sent a lengthy report to the CEO of Big W, Roger Corbett, on the subject of management morale and how and why to build it – a brave move for a lowly deputy manager (Now, as I look back, it was the beginnings of what would later on lead me to the role of management consultant!).

The company had made a loss for the twelve years prior, and this was the first year we turned a profit. It wasn't because of my report, of course; it was because of Roger's leadership. Nevertheless, he was so impressed with my effort that he thanked me personally and told me he had made the whole board of directors read it. He said he had even passed it on to the board of the parent company, Woolworths Australia. They were all impressed apparently, but nothing appeared to change – except that Roger later moved up to command Woolworths, and I do remember getting a bonus that year. I think that the state manager was irked with me though, even though I cc'd him in on the report. Two years later, I got sick of long hours and never seeing my children, so I quit. It was great to hold true to my commitment not to do a job that was affecting my happiness and work/life balance, but realistically, I had a family to support and a mortgage to pay. I also needed an income… and quickly!

Around that time, while in search of the opportunity to earn more for my family, I came across the concept of multi-level marketing businesses. Before I knew it, I was building a business to a leadership level, driving hundreds of kilometres out to the wheat belt on weekends to give business lectures to farmers. We called it 'drawing circles', as we outlined the chance to make money by expanding your circle of influence and first helping other people to make money. I soon became disenchanted however, with people declaring their desire to have more in life but being unwilling to do more to get it. Nevertheless, the personal development programme that came with that business consolidated my belief that if you want to succeed at something, you have to study and observe those who are making it happen and duplicate what they are doing.

I joined a new retail company called Red Dot Stores, for way less money, but more autonomy and the chance to be creative, as it was a completely new venture, still at the concept stage. My team achieved nearly two and a half times the expected turnover on opening day, and within three weeks, I was managing two stores at once. As a senior store manager, I helped set up their first twelve stores and trained most of the managers. I also wrote a training manual that they said they didn't need, but they later used almost *ad verbatim* after I had left. I had made the mistake of telling the boss that I wanted to do what he was doing! I realised as a result though, that I had obviously been on the right track, that I knew my stuff, and that I wasn't getting the proper recognition or rewards for the conscientious effort that I consistently put in. I realised that I needed to be my own boss again and I set my sub-conscious mind to work on looking for the right opportunity.

Realising When You Have Changed

I'm not blaming anyone but ourselves, but through work pressures and financial strains, Joyce and I had drifted apart. I persuaded her to go to marriage guidance counselling, but after a few visits, she refused to continue. A few months later, I made a huge mistake of which I am not proud, but I allowed myself to be seduced one very drunken night at a party by a female friend of ours. Both of our marriages were in dire straits, but when it all came out, that was the final nail in the coffin for our marriage.

I really believe that things happen for a reason; however, even when we may not know til much later what that reason was.

Joyce and I began new separate lives in 1994. I will always love her for being a huge influence on my life and a fantastic mother to our children. I think that we just got together too early, and I didn't really know who I was or who I aspired to be. Joyce was older and had already done her partying, whereas I felt like I had missed out. She wanted security, and I was a risk-taker, but through all of those challenges, I learned the art of resilience and how to bounce back from adversity.

> *"Resilience is the ability to return to the original form after being bent, stretched, or compressed. That's the dictionary's definition of resilience. It's the ability to readily recover from illness, or depression, or adversity."*
>
> **Jim Rohn**

Are you happy with your home? Are you happy in your relationship? Are you happy in your work life? If the answer to any of those is 'no', then write down why you're not happy and ask yourself in what way have you brought this about, plus what could you do about it to fix it? When you have written down what you *could* do, organise those tasks into an action plan with dates for their achievement and start TODAY!

Whenever you set a goal, always take some action towards achieving it straight away so that your sub-conscious mind knows that you are serious about it.

My Sixth Big Dream – Freedom to Design a Life of Spontaneity and Adventure

Just before Joyce and I separated, an old friend from my Co-op days in Jersey came to visit us. The short story is that Ian Cassin and I got very drunk one night on a beautiful Scottish drink called Glayva and decided we should start our own business (No, I'm not a drunk by the way – it was just a phase!). I made notes which still, surprisingly, made sense the next day when we sobered up, and I had a solution for the problem of my frustrations with the corporate world. The full story is one that could easily consume a whole other book, but the outcome was that about a year later, we managed to get Australian Immigration to allow Ian to emigrate on the strength of the business plan it had taken us a year to research and write.

Perilously soon after the end of a thirteen-year stint with Joyce, and having lost any remote comprehension of how to chat up a girl or re-join the dating scene, I fell head over heels for a free-spirited and lovely Cornish girl, named Lesley Ough, who had been one of Ian's holiday conquests. A warm, brown-eyed brunette, she happened to be helping out the owner of the backpacker hostel we wanted to buy. We went out for a drink as friends and got on amazingly well. When I then asked her for a proper date, to my astonishment she said, "Yes!" I had already moved out of the family home and was sharing a house with young Aussie mates, Brett Kibblewhite and Glen Riggs, but I thought it was only fair to tell my ex that I had started seeing someone else. That wasn't as good an idea as I had thought.

Lesley and I began a whirlwind romance. I knew we couldn't marry because I still was married! Despite that technicality, I knew that this was serious and I also knew that she would be returning to England soon, so I bought her an engagement ring and proposed at King's Park, overlooking the lights of the city, that we be 'engaged to be engaged'. She was so shocked she didn't speak for the rest of the night! She kept the ring on, but she didn't answer the question. I thought I'd blown it! The following morning, Lesley joyfully said yes to the idea, and we were both very excited.

That joy was cut short in a very abrupt and somewhat terrifying way when Immigration Officers suddenly arrived at the hostel where Lesley was staying. They decided that she had been working illegally, so they confiscated her passport on the spot and told her to appear at their office that afternoon. They actually read Lesley her rights, so it was pretty daunting. She argued she had just been helping out a friend. But her visa was cancelled, and she had to leave Australia. Why Immigration acted that day is a matter for conjecture, but I did find hidden the number for the Immigration Department, torn out of a phone book, while baby-sitting for my ex-wife, who was going out on a date – I think just to try to make me jealous! Who tears pages out of their own phonebook… and why that particular page? Needless to say, I was not allowed back in the house for many years.

We pleaded with Immigration, but their only concession was to let us have a brief holiday down south before she had to leave Australia. She would not be allowed to return for another three years. That's when I suggested that if we got married, she could return sooner, as my wife. I had nothing to lose because my fairy tale dream of marriage for life had already been shattered. I knew that Lesley and I loved each other and wanted to be together, so why worry about what it would take for us to achieve that? The worst case if it didn't work was that she could visit whenever.

Saying goodbye to her was simply awful, and that's when I consoled myself by going on the first trip to the Australian Outback with my two good mates, Brett and Glen. We embarked on a drunken tour to circumference Australia, in a 5.8Ltr V8 Ford LTD, towing a caravan. We called it the 'Blind Tour of '94' because we planned to get drunk in a variety of adventurous locations (Don't worry. We took it in turns for one of us to stay sober and drive while the other two drank bourbon in the back of the limo)! I got as far as Kununurra, when I decided that I was not giving up on Lesley. I rang her in London from a country phone box and asked what she wanted for her birthday the following week. "Nothing," she replied. "I just wish I could have you."

I suppose I inherited an impulsive streak from my parents, but as soon as I put down the phone, I asked the guys if they would mind if I didn't finish the trip with them. I explained why, and they understood and wished me the best of luck.

I was penniless and had just been working on an Outback farm, sorting good green beans from bad ones to earn a few dollars. Nevertheless, a few days later, I left the guys and jumped on a plane from Darwin to London to go after her. I wanted it to be a surprise, so I didn't tell her I was coming. She wasn't answering her phone, and I was too broke to pay a big hotel bill for just a few hours. So, I spent the first night in a London phone box, having come from forty-degree heat to minus five degrees, freezing my 'you know what's' off!

The following morning was Lesley's birthday, and it was so cold I could see my breath as it steamed out of my mouth. I regaled the elderly American tourists with my story of rushing from the Australian Outback to chase after my Cornish damsel. When I jumped out from behind a pillar of the hotel reception in London sporting a newly grown big red beard, wearing an Aussie akubra hat and clasping a big bunch of roses, Lesley nearly fainted!

I then took Lesley with me to my old home town of Jersey and visited old friends and places of interest, including my old school. Then, we did the romantic trip to Paris, ticking off the Eiffel Tower, the Arc de Triomphe, and Napoleon's tomb from my 'bucket list'. This was a huge thing for me, because I had wanted to go to Paris for a long time. It wasn't far from England, but I had waited til I lived in Australia to go there. It was a fantastic example of creative visualisation, as one of my other important dreams had been one of sitting at a café on the Champs Elysees, sipping on hot chocolate and eating a croissant. I knew that I would make it there one day, and I had stuck photos of both the Eiffel Tower and the Arc de Triomphe on my bedroom mirror to keep that dream alive. As I actually sat at that café, enjoying doing exactly what I had repeatedly dreamt of, it gave me goose bumps – it was so surreal.

Lesley and I agreed that we would get married the following year. After all, I had to arrange a divorce first. In the meantime, I would be near my kids back in Perth. So once again we parted tearfully at an airport, and I came home to Perth. I returned to retail management full time, whilst researching and writing the business plan that would satisfy Immigration in my spare time. Ian and I couldn't raise the million dollars we wanted to build our own hostel, so we negotiated to buy the very backpacker hostel that Lesley had managed. I also sorted out my divorce. The cancellation of Lesley's visa meant that she could not return to Australia for three years, so we then had fourteen months apart, writing over one hundred letters each to the other.

Still, she was a bundle of nerves and uncertainty, and I was on the verge of losing her. So I jumped on a plane again to fly across the world and win back her heart, which I did, within a few days of being together again. Where in the world can you go when you just want to get married quickly? The answer was either Gretna Green or Las Vegas.

About two weeks later, we were married in Las Vegas at a drive-through chapel (No – not by Elvis – Everyone asks!). We were going to have married on a hot air balloon and would have been filmed for a Valentine's Day American TV special, but after three days of cancellations because of high winds, Lesley was so nervous that she almost couldn't go through with it! Ironically, we only realised later that we had married on Australia Day!

After flying back to London, I returned to Perth, went straight from the plane into a business meeting, and we tied up the vendor finance deal to buy the backpackers business. Lesley joined Ian and me at the backpackers a few months later. By 1998, Ian's heart was no longer in the business. We had very different goals. He wanted to be a tour guide instead, so we bought him out his share. Thus, my second wife was also now my business partner. We worked incredibly hard, insanely hard in fact, but we made up for it with trips to England, Ireland, Malta, and Tasmania. Our adventures together over the next few years were nothing short of amazing.

It had always been my dream to run my own company, and our little business empire had begun with a backpacker hostel in West Perth. We were 'Living the Dream' and within seven years of what I can only call absolute madness, working harder than either of us had ever worked before, we had achieved the following:

- We had gained the first 'special facility liquor licence' in a backpackers in Perth, and we extended the premises – increasing the capacity from forty-five to around sixty guests.

- We had purchased four apartments and were sub-leasing another two so that around eighteen extra people/long-term couples could stay in greater comfort nearby, but still join in with the social events.

- We had cooked Christmas Day and seasonal event barbecues for about one hundred people.

- We had gained an Open Tours and Charters licence, bought a bus, and were running our own wineries and adventure tours.

- We had set up the first, dedicated, backpackers' car dealership in Perth, along with a servicing workshop.
- We had established a car rental business that I later grew to a fleet of twenty vehicles.
- We had set up a cleaning business to create work for our backpackers.
- We had set up an office furniture relocation business to create work for our backpackers.
- In our spare time, we managed the twenty-eight unit residential strata complex where we lived. I was chairman, secretary, treasurer and caretaker of the strata company.

At one point, around 2001, a business broker named Robbie Robinson approached Lesley and I with an expression of interest in buying businesses. That led to serious negotiations whereby a South African migrant family was willing to buy our little business empire for over two million dollars. The deal was on, but just before it could all happen, sadly, one of their family members died. I don't think that Lesley ever really got over the disappointment of having that dream of retiring young and free with travel money in the bank snatched away from her.

There were other businesses that I undertook on my own later, but even as I write these words for you, it became glaringly obvious why my Cornish country girl finally cracked under the pressure when Perth's tourism market suffered the knock on effects of global downturns caused by terrorism (Bali bombs twice and 9/11, plus of course Asian Bird Flu). She returned to England on the verge of a nervous breakdown and said, "You deal with it all." The irony was that I had pushed really hard because I wanted to provide Lesley with the things she said she wanted – namely a big house in the country, but near the ocean, with lots of pet animals and staff to look after them, while we went travelling around the world. A dream like that requires a lot of money, so I was driving myself to work the plan to deliver it all. Such a huge commitment to such a big dream came at a price.

Sadly, my second marriage then ended badly when she cheated on me (Some would see that as my karmic payback). Still, we went to counselling and tried to fix it. I forgave her, but she did it again. It was as if she wanted me to kick her out so that she could leave and not feel guilty because she had abandoned her duty. She felt trapped, under pressure, and now just wanted to be free to travel with no responsibilities at all. She even talked me into seeing some other girls to 'even things up', but that just made the situation more bizarre as I was still in love with her. I even briefly had a Polish mistress, just as one of my heroes, Napoleon had done, but I discovered that I only really wanted my relationship with Lesley to work out. I know that my staff was completely bemused by proceedings, and the whole circus caused me to take my eye off the ball with the business at a very difficult and critical time.

I could not just throw the towel in though. I had staff that depended on me for their livelihood, and I had children who needed a father close by. Lesley left in April 2004, giving the impression she would return once she 'found herself', but in fact, she had no such intention. Somehow, we managed to overcome those disappointments and remain friends. Lesley was a huge influence on my life. We achieved heaps together, and I will always be fond of her. It is often said, "Be careful what you wish for." Our mini empire became a gilded prison for my wife, Lesley.

> "Life is either a daring adventure or nothing. To keep our faces toward change and behave like free spirits in the presence of fate is strength undefeatable."
>
> **Helen Keller**

Are you striving towards your goals or towards somebody else's? Are you working hard for the right reasons? Do you regularly review your goals and check that you and your partner (if you have one) are on the same track? If the answer to any of those is 'no', then I urge you to review and change that situation before it's too late.

Rich Realisations

- Achieving small goals creates momentum and belief towards achieving bigger goals.
- Start with what you know best, but work towards what you love doing most.
- Trust that everything you are learning now may have some greater unseen purpose later.
- Even when you seem stuck, and especially when you seem stuck, work on personal development. The more you know, the more you will think and, ultimately, the more you will achieve.
- Remember to regularly review your progress – in all areas of your life.
- The more you invest spiritually in your self-development, the more you will 'do life well'.

4

Bad Dreams and Nightmares

"Reality is never as bad as a nightmare, as the mental tortures we inflict on ourselves."
                                         Sammy Davis Junior

We've all experienced bad dreams. Some of them are so bad, we call them nightmares. In fact the imagery of that experience is so powerful that the concepts have found their way into our everyday language to describe poor performance or horrible events.

The Healing Powers of Nature

After my second marriage breakup, I hit a really low point in my life. I felt like everything I had worked for had been meaningless. It was as if the rug of life had been pulled out from under me, and it felt like my dreams had turned to a nightmare. I had even contemplated taking another man's life and my own, and that was a dark side of me I never want to revisit.

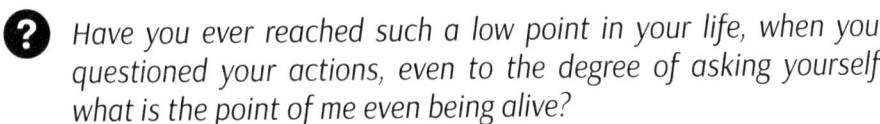 *Have you ever reached such a low point in your life, when you questioned your actions, even to the degree of asking yourself what is the point of me even being alive?*

That's when I took the brave and unusual step of rebranding the backpacker business, which allowed me to feel like I was starting again, 'brand new', with a new name, new colours, and a new logo, but with the existing infrastructure of an old business. It gave me the lift I needed to pick myself back up. I had not had holidays for two years while I slogged away in this 24/7 business that I rebuilt from the ashes of a failed relationship. The business had run down badly while my eye was off the ball, and I was busy trying to save a lost cause of a marriage. I literally 'buried myself' in my work to help me heal from the sadness and turn things back around. I also still had Club Red Cars, so there was no chance of being bored! Then age forty-four, I followed my staff's advice to take a long-overdue break.

I am incredibly proud of that period in my life. When you have run multiple businesses with an equal partner, with whom you make all of the decisions together, it is so unbelievably difficult and, in fact, downright lonely having to suddenly decide everything on your own. I hired a marketing girl, Hayley Barber, to bounce ideas with, and I will always be grateful to her and the fantastic staff I had working with me. Ironically, our new slogan for the rebranded business was, "You won't be lonely at Planet Inn!" I only just realised the irony that, for a while there, I was probably the loneliest person in the inn. That process of picking myself back up was tougher than I allowed anyone to see. My accountant, Diane Wilson, was later to remark, "You can see what happened even just by looking at the figures. I don't know how you didn't have a nervous breakdown!" I think in truth that I did have one, but nobody noticed (or so I thought)! The place itself was such an insane institution that you could easily disguise a nervous breakdown there. Those stories will have to wait for another book for another day!

I had started dating a lovely twenty nine-year-old Swedish girl, named Vicky, who was backpacking around the world with her friend, Malin. So I volunteered to drive them to Monkey Mia, about 800 kilometres north of my home in Perth, Western Australia. Having finally escaped, I was able to process some of the traumas I had gone through. Nature has fantastic healing properties, so climbing into the Karijini gorges, hand feeding a dolphin at Monkey Mia, and watching dugongs swim past (sort of grass-eating cows of the sea) from a catamaran – all had a big impact on me. The weight of perceived failure lifted off my shoulders. My staff was doing really well without me. My systems were really good, and I had built a solid and reliable team of good people.

I decided to continue on my adventure, and continue I certainly did! I found myself snorkelling with manta rays; enjoying a life-changing connection with a whale shark as I swam alongside, cathartically looking right into the creature's eye for an uninterrupted thirteen minutes; riding a camel on a beach at sunset; taking a helicopter ride over the Bungle Bungles; swimming under waterfalls and in thermal springs in the Outback; watching crocodiles jump out of the water to bite chunks of meat off the tour guide's fishing lines; driving through the spectacular Kimberley region. It was all breathtaking and incredible.

I managed to visit an old friend in Darwin, Glenn Treagus, where he recorded me in his studio, playing guitar and singing a song I had written (therapeutically about my marriage breakup). I drove down the centre and across Australia as we continued on to Townsville and up to Cairns. I certainly wasn't being a total slacker though. Firstly, I was healing my broken spirit with the power of nature. Secondly, I was learning a lot about how other people in my chosen tourism industry did things. I was networking, interviewing business owners and getting ideas I could adapt for my own enterprise. I could then talk with authority to my customers because I had done the things they wanted to do. Anyway, the reason I'm telling you that is that it was one of the best things I could ever have done for my own soul, which in turn, benefited my business and many other people in a sort of 'butterfly effect' kind of way.

> *"In chaos theory, the butterfly effect is the sensitive dependence on initial conditions, where a small change at one place in a deterministic nonlinear system can result in large differences to a later state. The name of the effect, coined by Edward Lorenz, is derived from the theoretical example of a hurricane's formation being contingent on whether or not a distant butterfly had flapped its wings several weeks before.*
>
> *"The butterfly effect is a common trope in fiction when presenting scenarios involving time travel and with hypotheses where one storyline diverges at the moment of a seemingly minor event resulting in two significantly different outcomes."*
>
> **Wikipedia Definition**

There will rarely be a 'perfect' time to do the stuff you have always wanted to do.

However, sometimes you just have to go for it because it feels right and that seemingly minor decision could result in a significantly different change of life direction, which would then in turn, impact on many other people. If you keep putting it off until 'someday', that could suddenly turn into 'shoulda, woulda, coulda…' (i.e., the stuff you wished you had done but never did).

My one week escape to a destination 800 kilometres away mutated into a nine week adventure, spanning 12,000 kilometres that I would not trade for the world – the memories are priceless. Vicky and I always knew that our holiday romance would end, that she would return to her family in Sweden, and that I would stay near my children in Perth, but the parting in Cairns was very sad. We will remain friends for life (thanks to modern technology like social media). One of the main reasons why I didn't complete the whole perimeter of Australia was that my daughter, who was a precocious fifteen-year-old at the time, found my ex-wife's old mobile phone in a drawer. It was still active on the business phone plan. She thought, "Wicked! Free phone!"

Within a month of chatting to her mates, she ran up a phone bill of over $2,200.00. I had little choice, but to sell my car in Cairns, say farewell to Vicky, and return home to work. Was I irresponsible to run away and take time out like Forrest did in the movie *Forrest Gump*? Was I unrealistic? Some might say so. As it happened, however, my staff achieved a record trading month in that time; I picked up loads of ideas and knowledge; and I returned, refreshed, re-energised and buzzing with excitement.

> "We owe it to ourselves to bring out the best of who we are, to use our talents for something beautiful and worthy. That requires a staying power that comes only with vision and determination."
>
> R. Henry Migliore

So, I challenge you to answer those questions I have posed for you today. Write them down. Think about how you would feel and what it would mean to you if you achieved those things (or even just one of them). Then ask yourself, when you are lying on your death bed one day (hopefully a long way into the future)…

Which things will I regret – the things I did, or the things I will wish I had done?

My grandfather was always going to take me fishing when I was a kid. Alas, the closest he came to it was to leave me his fishing rod. He really did intend to take me, but sadly his health gave way. Well, actually the hospital staff killed him when they gave him penicillin and failed to notice his medic alert bracelet that told them he was allergic to it (Showing the importance of attention to detail in your job!). Going fishing with his fishing rod wasn't quite the same without Grandpa there to show me what to do.

I'm not saying you have to quit your job, unless it's making you unhappy. Here are some ideas for you: think of places you'd like to visit; new skills or hobbies you'd like to learn; people you'd like to meet; another language you'd like to learn; a business you'd like to start; a car you'd like to buy, or a yacht, a house, etc. Just to be clear though, I'm not saying simplistically that making a list of material goals will suddenly make you happy if you are currently unhappy. These things should actually be treated as rewards for endeavour and progress. Your list could, and should, include things that you would like to do for other people, whether it's a gift for your family or doing something for a worthy cause or charity. The point is to create meaning and purpose.

> *If you don't set some kind of course to sail, you're going to drift awhile.*
>
> **Tony Inman**

So, the starting point really is to establish…

 Is your life going the way you would like?

Today's hi-tech world can be so crazy that we often forget about the things we really wanted to do in life, the people with whom we wanted to spend our time, the places we wanted to see and the adventures we would have liked to have had. In particular, it is far too easy to get so caught up in the rat race, stressing about all of life's details, that you can forget just how incredible this planet is that we inhabit and how when we actually take some time to stop a moment and appreciate the simple joys of nature, it actually regenerates our soul and re-enables us to return to the daily grind feeling truly invigorated.

 When was the last time you just stopped and quietly appreciated nature?

If you can't even remember, then stop what you're doing, right now, go outside to a garden or a park, and look around you. Then, close your eyes and listen.

Hear the sounds of nature, feel the wind on your cheek, and remember just how wonderful this planet is and how lucky we are to live on it. Enjoy the peace and stillness that nature brings you and take a moment each day for quiet reflection and contemplation. I promise you that you will be astounded by the results. New ideas will spring forth and you will find answers to many unanswered questions.

Bigger Dreamers Survive Nightmares

I mentioned earlier how at the pinnacle of our business empire, we could have sold everything and retired early, but a premature death scuppered the deal. From those dreamy heights, I later plummeted to despair over a marriage breakup, before reinventing myself and my business and surging again to greater heights. What I didn't yet mention was what happened after the Global Financial Crisis (GFC) struck.

Prior to the GFC my business was still looking strong enough to grow and prosper, despite numerous setbacks. One of the major challenges occurred when I had a run in with the local council. I had a property next door to my business – a large redevelopment block in a terrific location with a small but functional building that could house six paying guests. Long story short, the council closed it down in the middle of a peak summer season, simultaneously cutting my income and insisting on mandatory improvements to comply with technical clauses in legislation. Where you could normally negotiate to undertake work orders while you traded your way through paying for them, in this case, there was no such co-operation. This left me having to fund a substantial mortgage with no revenue from the property, plus a huge bill to upgrade it at a time when good tradesmen were in short supply, owing to Western Australia's mining boom. It took around seven months before we were finally given approval to use that property again and the loss of profits was significant.

There were plenty of other setbacks, but I won't dwell on all of those here. The net result was that subsequently the GFC caught us over-exposed financially. Whereas in the past we could and would have traded our way out of trouble, this time the hurdle was just too high.

In the summer of 2009-2010, our occupancy rate dropped from one hundred percent to around fifty percent, and the tourists who did arrive, turned up penniless and looking for jobs. Therefore, they were not doing tours or spending money on extras and were smuggling in alcohol rather than drinking in our bar.

I was down to owning three properties at that time, when I received the dreaded letter from the bank. In a week's time, unless I caught up my mortgage arrears, they would collect the keys of all three properties, including the apartment I lived in. They would put me out on the street unless I urgently contacted G.E. (the bank) to 'make arrangements'.

So imagine this… Everything you have created and worked your butt off to build over nearly fourteen years is about to be taken from you. I rang and rang the bank, but all I could get was a message bank and nobody would return the calls. The day before I was supposed to hand over my keys to persons unspecified, I resorted to a frantic search of any possible alternative G.E. phone number on the planet. When I finally got through to a real person, firstly, they told me I didn't exist in their system. I persisted. Finally, they found my records and replied that the department concerned was in the middle of moving offices from Sydney to Parramatta. They could see I had left messages, and they apologised for any 'inconvenience', but said 'someone' would get back to me in due course.

I thought the marriage breakup had been stressful, but this was way worse. Not knowing whether we even had a future to fight for was like having the 'Sword of Damocles' hanging over my head. When a banker finally called me, I undertook the greatest rear-guard action of my life, juggling bills, negotiating terms, trying everything that my supportive team and I could possibly come up with to stay afloat. We began organising music gigs to bring in bar drinkers; we did ad hoc tours again; we organised theme nights; and worked tirelessly on keeping up the atmosphere for which we had been so famous. I thought surely in the New Year, things would pick back up. Good times and bad times always follow one another in a cycle, but not this time. It just got worse. Tourists were not just leaving their homes in the UK and Ireland, and the phone was not ringing. So, it was time to salvage what I could and reinvent myself once more. I put my properties on the market and negotiated an extension with the bank.

In the March of 2010, even the 'Almighty' sent me a message that it was time to move on. Perth suffered a freak weather event with a hail stone storm that literally punctured holes in the roof of our backpackers' hostel. Our bar lounge was engulfed in a river of rainwater from the back yard that ran through the dining room and into the kitchen. The storm knocked out the power, which saved us getting electrocuted – though it was kind of ironic that we had just had a forty percent increase in the utilities and my electricity bills amounted to around $8,000. With help from our paying guests, we were scooping buckets of water off the carpets and into green council bins so that we could tip the water back outside. The hail stones were the size of golf balls, and people's cars were so dented they were written off. That was the day that I said to myself, "I hear You! It's time for Tony Inman to do something different – something bigger and better!"

I sold the business and two properties and managed to come out with a roof still over my head, even though the GFC knocked around half a million dollars off my property sale prices. Luckily, I had previously set up a cleaning business, specialising in strata complexes, and this gave me cash flow and time to reflect on what would come next.

I'm no different than anyone else in a lot of ways, but one thing I have found is that in order to make a dream come true, you must have a dream in the first place. There is, however, another crucial element to this equation for success – you must take action. Remember this though: If you keep doing the same stuff you've always done, guess what? You'll get the same results you always have!

> *"Definition of Insanity: Doing the same thing over and over again and expecting different results."*
>
> **Albert Einstein**

In the case of my tourism business, we constantly tried new things and kept evolving. We conquered several downturns, but sometimes you just have to recognise when a wave is too big to swim over, the storms are too wild, and you must be willing to change direction.

Since what seemed like a calamity to me at the time, I have reinvented myself and redesigned my life in wonderful ways. I have travelled to more places and done more exciting things than ever before. To me, life is an adventure, and I love it.

 As far as I know, we all get a limited time on this Earth, so if you want to realise some of those dreams and goals that you've been too busy to do, or too unfit, or too old, or too young... whatever the story and whatever the excuses are, it's time to stop and think. Ask yourself this question and be honest with yourself: Am I living my dream or have I settled for less? Worse still, has it become a nightmare? If so, what can I, and will I, do about it, and when?

TONY INMAN

A Dream of a Better World - The Story of Ruby Bridges

We all think we face big problems, but then we hear of someone facing a different kind of problem. It doesn't make our challenge disappear, but it can give a sense of perspective. Only fifty years ago, in New Orleans, USA, a six-year-old coloured girl walked into her local school for her first day's attendance. That is a big moment in anyone's life, though for most of us that first day would disappear as just another day in the haze of our distant childhood memories. For an innocent little Ruby Bridges though, it became an unforgettable day. For American citizens everywhere, it was an unforgettable day. For the human race, it became a significant day.

Ruby was one of only six African-American children who passed a test for selection to be admitted to an integrated school. ('Integrated' referred to the integration of Caucasian students with coloured students.) Of the six, two opted to remain in their existing schools, three were assigned to *another school* and only Ruby was assigned to nearby William Frantz Elementary School. Ruby's father was understandably concerned for his daughter's safety and was reluctant, but her mother insisted that she should go and set an example for all African-American students, who deserved an equal opportunity for education. On that particular day though, a seething and vociferous crowd gathered to protest this historic decision.

Ruby said later as an adult that she could remember the crowd chanting, "Two, four, six, eight. We don't want to integrate!" It did not really upset her, because she just recognised that it rhymed, but didn't know what 'integrate' meant. What does still give her nightmares is that one white mother protested with a black baby doll in a wooden coffin outside the school. She still relives that childhood trauma today. Another white mother threatened to poison her, such was the tide of feeling against African-Americans.

The child had to be escorted to her first day at school by US Marshals, who feared for her life. They insisted that she only eat food brought from her own home to be on the safe side. One of the Marshals, Charles Burk said of Ruby, "She showed a lot of courage. She never cried. She didn't whimper. She just marched along like a little soldier, and we're all very proud of her." As soon as Ruby started that first day, the white mothers came in and removed their children from the school. All but one of the teachers, refused to teach a class in which a 'black girl' was enrolled. Teacher Barbara Henry taught her as if she was teaching a whole class, alone for a year. This brave stance against appalling discrimination came at a price though – Ruby's father lost his job, and her grandparents were turned off their land in Mississippi.

Happily, both black and white people rallied to help however, and a neighbour employed her dad. A white lady babysat, others formed a neighbourhood watch to keep vigil over the family home, some formed a guard of honour behind the Marshals walking Ruby to school, and other white parents began to send their kids back to continue their education. A psychiatrist, Robert Coles, volunteered to provide counselling for little Ruby during her first year at school, so she survived the awful bigotry, though it would be impossible not to be affected by it through her whole life.

Ruby went on to work as a travel agent, married, and had four children of her own. In 1999, Ruby, now Ruby Bridges Hall, set up the Ruby Bridges Foundation: "To promote the values of toleration, respect and appreciation of all differences." Ruby summarises her mission, "Racism is a grown-up disease, and we must stop using our children to spread it."

One happy snippet was that recently Ruby had a 50th Anniversary reunion at William Franz Elementary School, where she met up with Pam Foreman Testroet, who was the first white child, then aged only five, to break the boycott and return to school. Ruby now travels as an inspirational speaker, promoting her message of respect and tolerance for all people of all races. How amazing to think that all of this was only fifty years ago!

It all starts with a dream. Martin Luther King had a dream. Ruby Bridges' parents had a dream. They faced huge adversity, yet their courage prevailed.

Be bold. Life is shorter than it should be, so make it count!

Write a list of places you want to visit, things you want to do, people you want to meet.

Then take action towards making your dreams come true!

Tony Inman

Dynamic Dreaming

- Having a dream of what it is that you most desire is an essential part of achieving one. If you don't know what you want, how will you know if you have it?

- To achieve turning your dream into a reality pre-supposes that you have not yet achieved it. Therefore, you must be willing to do something different than what you have already done.

- To do things differently requires that you think differently. Your philosophy of life, which has got you to where you are now, must require some changes.

- To 'Live the Dream' then, requires that you must BE different. You must become the kind of person who is capable and deserving of the result you seek.

- It is not enough to BE different; you must then DO whatever it takes. Without action, there will be no achievement. A goal is a dream with a deadline.

- The road to fulfillment is about enjoying the journey, no matter what detours you take from the path to your definition of success.

- In your dreams, anything is possible. If it can be conceived, it can be achieved, somehow, some day, by someone. Why not you?

- Learn to trust your gut feelings. Your intuition and instincts are usually right, so learn to trust and develop them.

- Be dynamic – massive action leads to massive results.

- If you are living in congruence with your dreams, then you will be 'doing life well'.

5

Twenty-Twenty Vision

"On a clear day, you can see forever"

Alan Jay Lerner

Our eyes have been described as 'The gateways to our souls', meaning that when you look deeply into someone's eyes, you can truly gain an understanding of who they really are, as if you can see inside them. We can tell if they are lying or speaking the truth; we know if they are fired up, dazed, passionate, angry or scared. A lot of the reason for that is revealed in the study of body language and sensory acuity, which we will touch on later.

If we accept that this is all true, then what do you make of what you can see when you look out at the world through your own eyes? And what about the legendary third-eye – the one through which you can sense all that is unseen?

Cutting through the Fog

Some people, when you ask them what they want out of life, respond with a blank expression or a kind of dazed look, even sometimes a look of despair. It's as if they're in a fog and can't find their way out. That's why it's one of the first things I address when I start coaching a new client. I always ask, "What do you want to achieve?"

Some of them respond with a line that really used to irk me, "I dunno, I just take life as it comes." Now as a student of behavioural science (we'll cover that in a later chapter), I know that I had a previous tendency to measure people against my own values, whereas I now understand that they have different values. I'm a very goal-oriented person, so the concept of just existing and waiting for life to 'happen to me' doesn't sit well with me. That's why I have designed a better life for myself and my family in a different country, why I have started my own businesses, and why I have done things like learning to scuba dive and to fly an aircraft. Had I just waited for something to happen to me, I doubt that any of those things would have happened. In my view, life is active, not passive. So what might those dreams be? Which things might make up your personal definition of success in life?

Here are just a few of the myriad of possibilities: crossing the finish line first; just reaching the finish line; just qualifying to be in the event; simply being there, actually in the arena; watching your hero or heroes achieve it from the comfort of your lounge chair; watching and encouraging your loved one; training or coaching someone to do it; a done deal; a new job; an exam passed; a baby born; a moment captured; a warm embrace; a glass of red wine; a beautiful smile; another breath taken; feeling at peace; hearing the birds tweet; seeing the sun rise; feeling the breeze on your cheek; knowing that you did it… and the list could go on. Any and every one of these and thousands more could be your dream or, to put it another way, your personal and unique definition of 'success'.

I was sitting here thinking, *What hot tips for success can I give people today?* So I did what all of us bright people do today – I Googled it!

Dictionary.com defines 'success' in logical terms:

1. The accomplishment of an aim or purpose.
2. The attainment of popularity or profit.
3. A person or thing that achieves desired aims or attains prosperity.
4. The outcome of an undertaking, specified as achieving or failing to achieve its aims.

As I continued searching, it soon became obvious that were you to ask a thousand human beings, you could potentially get a thousand different answers.

I was at a networking meeting a while ago and had a wonderful chat with a new friend I met by the name of Peter Hunt, who runs his own marketing business. I had talked about my coaching mission to help other people achieve their dreams and cross things off their personal bucket lists – like seeing the pyramids, climbing the Inca trail to Machu Picchu and so on. He congratulated me on my intentions and said that some of the things I had mentioned in my brief presentation to the group had struck some chords with him. Peter went on to remind me though, not to forget that not everybody wants to go on adventures, dive with sharks, travel the world, and so on. Not everyone would share my vision of what success means.

I said, "Peter, you're absolutely right." We agreed that for some people, success might be something as simple as having more time with their family, looking up at a blue sky, having a relaxing afternoon and so on. Success can take many forms, from the most simple to the most complicated. So this leads me to the question, "What is success?"

Defining Success

 What does the word 'success' mean to you?

It's a question I often like to ask the audience when I'm presenting my seminars because it fascinates me. At every seminar, I hear different answers, because everyone's perspective on life is unique to them. I've heard many formulae for success over the years and here are a few:

Source	Definition
Traditional interpretation from mining areas…	'Get a job' down the pit like your father and his father before him.
Suggestion from industrial areas…	Get an 'above ground job' at the local factory.
Get a better job…	Do an apprenticeship – get a trade.
Get an education…	Finish high school – work in a shop.
Get a better education at T.A.F.E. (polytechnic)…	Get a job in an office.
Get a diploma or degree…	Become a professional.
Win a load of money…	Buy Lotto tickets.

Source	Definition
Inherit it…	**Wait for a rich aunt to die and leave you a fortune.**
Marry it…	**Find a rich schmuck with a heart condition!**
Steal it…	**Rob a bank.**
Trade it…	**Become a drug dealer**
Or a definition from an old 'bludger' friend…	**Go on the 'dole' (social welfare).**
For those with bigger aspirations…	**Start your own business.**
For those who want to make their money work for them…	**Become an investor.**
Then, from the multi-level marketing companies, I heard…	**S = O + V + W** or **Success = The Right Opportunity + The Right Vehicle + Hard Work**

In seminars, I've heard answers like the following…

SUCCESS =	Good health
	Surfing
	Travel
	Fun
	Living in paradise
	Not having to work
	Time
	Money
	Self-satisfaction
	Power (Power over other people or in your own life)
	Happiness
	Being able to help other people
	Freedom

Upon reflection on all of the above and many more, I developed the following:

Tony's Ingredients for Success

To define and achieve your success recipe, mix the following ingredients in an unscrambled brain:

- **Imagination**
  Conceive what it is that you are looking for.

- **Vision**
  See yourself achieving what you have imagined.

- **Opportunity**
  Maybe you need to create one or look for it where others see only problems and disaster.

- **Resources**
  You can't do it all alone, so build a support team, funding, skills, knowledge, etc., and use other people's skills and experience.

- **Preparedness**
  Tune in and be vigilant; be ready to act.
- **Action**
  Have the courage to act; be willing to do what it takes.
- **Progress**
  Review your measuring systems and feedback; stay on track.
- **Persistence**
  Keep going, even if it's going badly.
- **Corrective Action**
  If you find yourself off course, make adjustments.
- **Focus**
  Focus on what you *do* want, not on what you *don't* want.
- **Balance**
  Enjoy the journey through all of its twists and turns

Take all of the above ingredients, add a burning flame of desire until you reach the momentum of boiling point, and then remember to always keep the mix simmering, with intense heat as required. Keep adding new experiences because 'it's worth doing well'.

The Strangest Secret

One of the most profound discoveries I made in my studies of success many years ago was when I heard a recording of a speech by Earl Nightingale. If you haven't heard the following speech, I strongly recommend that you listen to it because it just might change your life. It certainly changed mine. Earl's take on success was this:

> "First, we have to define success, and here is the best definition I've ever been able to find: 'Success is the progressive realization of a worthy goal or ideal.' A success is the school teacher who is teaching because that's what he or she wants to do. A success is the entrepreneur who starts his own company because that was his dream – that's what he wanted to do. A success is the salesperson who wants to become the best salesperson in his or her company and sets forth on the pursuit of that goal. A success is anyone who is realizing a worthy predetermined ideal, because that's what he or she decided to do... deliberately. But only one person out of twenty does that!"
>
> **Earl Nightingale – from 'The Strangest Secret'**

Earl went on to talk about how people shelve their dreams and instead of taking risks in the pursuit of them, they conform. He said that the opposite of courage is not cowardice, it is conformity. I won't steal the rest of Earl's thunder. You can listen to the whole recording yourself, but he concluded with the following:

> "Do what the experts since the dawn of recorded history have told us to do: pay the price, by becoming the person you want to become. It's not nearly as difficult as living unsuccessfully.
>
> The moment you decide on a goal to work toward, you're immediately a successful person – you are then in that rare group of people who know where they're going. Out of every hundred people, you belong to the top five. Don't concern yourself too much with how you are going to achieve your goal – leave that completely to a power greater than yourself. All you have to do is know where you're going. The answers will come to you of their own accord, and at the right time.
>
> Start today. You have nothing to lose – but you have your whole life to win."
>
> **Earl Nightingale – from 'The Strangest Secret'**

Figure out what success means to you, grab hold of that ideal, embrace it and live it or strive for it, but as you chase that vision, remember to stop sometimes every day and be thankful for those simple things – that breath of fresh air, that blue sky, that gentle breeze, that smile on the face of someone you have been able to help in some small way… If you enjoy your life, while enriching the lives of those whose life you touch, you are already a success. Here's what 'The Greatest' boxer in the world had to say about dreams and success:

> "Champions aren't made in gyms. Champions are made from something they have deep inside them—a desire, a dream, a vision. They have to have last-minute stamina, they have to be a little faster, and they have to have the skill and the will. But the will must be stronger than the skill."
>
> **Muhammad Ali**

Keeping Your Vision in Perspective

Here's a great little story that was circulating on *Facebook* earlier this year from an anonymous author about some Mexican fishermen. It pokes fun at those business-minded people who can get so caught up in the desire to make more money that the notion of work/life balance becomes something of an afterthought.

An Alternative Philosophy of Life

A boat is docked in a tiny Mexican fishing village.

A tourist complimented the local fishermen on the quality of their fish and asked how long it took to catch them.

"Not very long," they answered in unison.

"Why didn't you stay out longer and catch more?"

The fishermen explained that their small catches were sufficient to meet their needs and those of their families.

"But what do you do with the rest of your time?"

"We sleep late, fish a little, play with our children, and take siestas with our wives. In the evenings, we go into the village to see our friends, have a few drinks, play the guitar, and sing a few songs. We have a full life."

The tourist interrupted, "I have an MBA from Harvard, and I can help you! You should start by fishing longer every day. You can then sell the extra fish you catch. With the extra revenue, you can buy a bigger boat."

"And after that?"

"With the extra money the larger boat will bring, you can buy a second one and a third one and so on until you have an entire fleet of trawlers. Instead of selling your fish to a middle man, you can then negotiate directly with the processing plants and maybe even open your own plant. You can then leave this little village and move to Mexico City, Los Angeles, or even New York City! From there you can direct your huge new enterprise."

"How long would that take?"

"Twenty, perhaps twenty-five years," replied the tourist.

"And after that?"

"Afterwards? Well, my friend, that's when it gets really interesting," answered the tourist, laughing. "When your business gets really big, you can start buying and selling stocks and make millions!"

"Millions? Really? And after that?" asked the fishermen.

"After that you'll be able to retire, live in a tiny village near the coast, sleep late, play with your children, catch a few fish, take a siesta with your wife and spend your evenings drinking and enjoying your friends."

"With all due respect sir, but that's exactly what we are doing now. So what's the point wasting twenty-five years?" asked the Mexicans.

And the moral of this story is:

Know where you're going in life, you may already be there! Many times in life, money is not everything and no matter what you do, you'll end up back where you started.

> *"Live your life before life becomes lifeless."*
>
> **Anonymous**

Loveable Lucidity

- Your dream is your personal blueprint for a successful life, and it is unique to you.

- It could be a huge undertaking, or it could be a collection of small simple things.

- The clearer you can be about what it is that you want and why, the more likely you are to be able to achieve your aims.

- Don't be as concerned about HOW you will achieve it as you are with WHY you want to achieve it (If the 'why' is big enough, the 'how' will take care of itself).

- The more you can build the VISION of what SUCCESS means to YOU (nobody else, just you and WHAT HAVING IT will do for you and for those people who matter to you) the more you are likely to make it happen.

- The WILL or DESIRE to make it happen is more important than the skills or abilities you have – those can be learned or hired.

- It's important to balance your drive for success with a gratitude for what you already have and to remember that time with family and friends should be cherished and not seen as an interruption to work.

- Taking time out for yourself ('me time') is just as important. It will refresh and revitalise you, so in the long run you'll be more creative.

- Remembering to enjoy each day, to catch yourself in the moment and to notice the incredible harmony of nature around you… these things will let you know that you are 'doing life well', and you will find the inner peace that leads to fulfillment.

6

Be Responsible– It's Your Life!

"You are the master of your own earthly destiny just as surely as you have the power to control your own thoughts."

Napoleon Hill
Author of 'Think and Grow Rich'

I hope you'll forgive my political incorrectness here, but I'm about to say something controversial (Please look away now if you are easily offended!).

You are the only one who can get off your own arse!

When you take responsibility for your own life, rather than waiting for your parents, your partner, your boss or anyone else to make things happen for you, that's when you unleash the unstoppable force called your own personal power. "If it is to be, it's up to me!"

Being Responsible for Your Thoughts

Napoleon Hill is a celebrated author of many books about success, motivation and positive thinking. In the quote above, he reminds us that we can shape our own destiny by the way we think. Thoughts are very powerful things. How many times do you witness a game of sport, for example, where one team thinks they can win and the other team begins to doubt whether they can. The second team starts to show it in their body language – their heads drop, they look despondent. Accordingly, their play begins to deteriorate as they lose that mental will to win.

Sure enough, the team who thinks it is losing, and begins to accept that fate, does so.

> *Everything that happens in your life is affected by the way you think. Think empowering thoughts and you will attract the results you desire! Whenever things start to go wrong, I try to stop myself from reacting badly and ask,*
> *"Is thinking this way about this situation, empowering me or disempowering me?*
>
> **Tony Inman**

The first part of this section is something that I cover in my Business Mentoring Group Sessions, so I thought I'd share it with you and add a couple of real life examples.

I don't know the original source, but the concept is a simple one that could have been drafted by a number of people.

Living Your Life Above or Below the Line

Above = Taking Responsibility

Below = Laying Blame/Justifying

People who live their lives above the line accept the principle that they each are responsible for their own lives and will, therefore, shape their own destiny. People who live their life below the line, prefer to blame everyone else for everything that goes wrong and, therefore, absolve themselves from the responsibility of having to take any action to change or improve things.

This reminded me of a tremendously inspirational book that I read a while ago, called *Man's Search for Meaning* by an internationally renowned psychiatrist, Dr. Victor E. Frankl. It is a very moving account of a man who endured years of suffering in a Nazi Concentration Camp in World War II and ultimately survived triumphantly, as a result of his attitude. He asked himself why some people seemed to just give up and die, while others coped with incredible pain, yet they lived.

In a nutshell, he concluded that the ones who lived focused on what they would do after that hell had finally finished and the war was over. They instilled in themselves a belief in their own future and gave themselves a reason to live. No matter how much his oppressors tried to depersonalize his soul, Frankl referred to "the last of human freedoms" – something his captors could never take away unless he let them. You alone retain the ability and the power to "choose one's (your) attitude in a given set of circumstances".

This theory was further supported by studies of the US servicemen who survived being captured and tortured by the enemy in the Vietnam conflict. The survivors refused to let their current circumstances make them live below the line and give up on their dreams. You don't need to be captured though to realize this. Why not go for a walk or take a really good vacation instead? Recharge your spirit and review your goals. Take responsibility, live above the line. By all means, work hard, but also work smart and have some fun.

 Do you take responsibility for your own thoughts?

Being Responsible for Your Actions

One of the key things I look for when interviewing people for a job is whether or not they take responsibility. The staff member who left a previous job because, "The boss was an idiot!" may have a valid point. On the other hand, if the two bosses before that were also both 'idiots', there's a bit of a clue – the common denominator in all three situations was the ex-employee sitting in front of you!

Without wanting to go on too much of a rant, I feel that one of the more insane aspects of today's society is that far too many people are unwilling to take responsibility for their actions. Frivolous legal actions by people with a 'get rich quick' mentality, egged on by 'ambulance-chasing' lawyers have made people live in fear of the perils of accountability. Notice that I'm not saying all people and I'm not saying all lawyers. (I'll talk about generalisations more in the chapter that covers behavioural science and NLP). In the past, if you tripped over something and grazed your knee, you would say, "Oh bother, what a silly person I am for not looking where I was going!" (Actually my language would be a little more colourful I suspect, but you get the idea.) Today, if someone trips, in many cases, they are looking around for someone to blame, and therefore, someone to sue for damages, before their butt has even reached the ground!

This fear of being sued and embroiled in a costly legal battle has caused many people to go to almost outrageous lengths to blame everyone else for almost anything that doesn't go to plan. As an employer of course, I too have had to train staff on being vigilant about leaving themselves or the company open to being sued for some alleged negligence.

One example occurred in the days when I owned the backpackers' hostel business in Perth. On one occasion, when I was away from the business, a young couple checked into a double room and asked the staff member on duty where they could park. My team member advised them that there was unlimited free parking on the street out front and that we also owned a few parking bays in a lane out the back. The lane was still open to the public but was only about a ten metre walk from their bedroom, so they opted to park there.

That night their car was allegedly broken into, and a rather lengthy and suspicious list of items were allegedly stolen. Without saying anything further to us about it, they then tried to sue us on the grounds that the staff member had not warned them that their car might be broken into. Therefore, they claimed we had been negligent, and it was our fault. In fact, the first thing we knew about it was when we received the court summons.

These people were not international backpackers; they were Aussie students. The list of missing items included things like cameras, a wallet containing money, designer label clothing, expensive shoes, expensive camping gear, and so on… To my mind, these were items that I would not leave in an unattended car parked on a public road at any time, but especially if my lockable room was only a short walk away. Fortunately, when checking people in, we also gave them a leaflet which advised that we recommended locking room doors and that we had a safe available in the office in which they could deposit valuables free of charge for safekeeping.

One of my staff members still had to attend court on the company's behalf and present my letter, in which I informed the magistrate that "the only people who were liable for negligence, were the parents of these students for allowing people so stupid to go travelling unaccompanied!" I still believe to this day, however, that the whole matter was a contrivance to extort money from us.

? *Do you take responsibility for all of your actions?*

> *The wonderful thing about taking responsibility for your actions is that it is very empowering because it means that you, and you alone, have the power to change your situation by acting differently.*
>
> **Tony Inman**

Being Responsible for Dealing with Adversity

When my second marriage broke up, I was devastated. It wasn't just the fact that we broke up – it was the way it happened. I won't go into all of the sordid details, but suffice to say that it was a protracted and humiliating break up. In summary, my wife had gone to visit her father in the UK and fallen out with him. Then she had moved in with an ex-boyfriend. One thing led to another and when I realised what was going on I asked her to return home urgently. I forgave her and she stayed with me and broke his heart instead. We went to counselling. She was prescribed anti-depressants but a year later she was at it again with a staff member and it all went horribly wrong. I asked the employee she had been seeing to stay away, as we were starting to get our marriage back on track, but he wouldn't. I was so emotionally screwed up that I seriously contemplated murdering him. In fact, I planned it in fine detail, but I realised that my intrinsic value systems just wouldn't allow me to do that, unless it was a life and death, 'me or him', war situation. I learned that I never wanted to see that 'Dark Side' of my psyche again. We all have it, but some people lose the capability to keep it under control.

It was actually a kind of surreal spiritual awakening, as if I had been tested – pushed to my limit to see if I would crack. In hindsight, it was absurd. I almost lost my sanity for real. I really thought, second time around that I had got this marriage concept right. This was a girl for whom I had been around the world twice, a girl I was still madly in love with, the woman I thought would be sat on the rocking chair next to me on the veranda in our dotage, reminiscing about our adventures. We had even discussed that very scene.

Of course it takes two people to get together and it takes two people to fail to make the relationship work, so this is not about blame. I have seen so many people I know, however, whose coping mechanism is to blame the partner entirely for the divorce.

I will never forget the feeling that it was as if the person I knew and loved had been taken away by aliens and that in her place they had left a cold, irrational creature that behaved completely differently to the girl I had married. She left me to return to England once more, saying that she needed 'to find herself' and left a card on my pillow that she loved me and would return when she had done so. I even continued recording episodes of her favourite TV programme for her.

Within a week of being back in England, she was back with the ex-boyfriend again, though she had drifted in and out of his life so many times that he was an emotional wreck and it didn't last. She proposed spending six months with each of us. My self-esteem was so low that I even considered the idea. When she finally broke the news that she was not going to return this time, I felt destroyed. We had achieved so much together, even just winning the fight to be together after she had been kicked out of the country. I was so low, I actually considered putting myself out of my misery.

"Have you ever felt that low?"

I'll never forget a telephone conversation that I had with my second wife's father. He was always very kind to me. He did strike a chord though when he said, "I do feel sorry for you. At least my wife died, so there was nothing I could do about it. It must be harder for you because your wife has chosen to leave you." He meant well, but the full realisation of that rejection was soul-destroying. Ridiculous as it now seems, putting myself out of my misery fleetingly became one of the seemingly viable options.

 Fortunately for me, I had a resilient streak. Even more fortunately, I have two fantastic children. As I sat in my misery that day another reality hit me: What kind of person would I be to purposely do that to my children? What kind of role model would I be for them? How could I not be there to help them, to see them find their own partners and have their own families?

On top of that, I had a business to run and good staff, whose livelihoods depended on me. Sure, I had lost a second marriage. I had failed in my eyes, but only if I chose to make that my reality. What if I hadn't failed? What if the reality was that it was the end of a chapter and the opportunity to write my own new script for the movie that is my life? And, as you can remember in a previous chapter, I did just that.

Whenever things seem bad, there are always plenty of other people who have it far worse. If you doubt that, go to your local hospital and see what horrors other people have to face every day. You'll feel like a wuss for whingeing. It doesn't make your own 'grazed knee' stop hurting, but it puts it in perspective! Plus, don't forget that I had already tested myself to the point of almost killing another person. Now it was my own life on the line.

I snapped myself out of my pity party and got back to work with a vengeance, determined to rebuild myself and use my business as the vehicle. I can honestly tell you that going through a marriage breakup is no fun at all, but today I am so glad I went through all of that because it shaped my strength of character and my confidence in my own capacity to endure.

Picking yourself up again after you've fallen is when the true test begins.

That's when you realise just how much you have taken your eye off the ball and that your game of business is nearly lost because of it.

> *When you stare defeat in the face, that's when you discover the real strength of your own character, because the only person you can truly count on, the only person who is truly your best friend, in that moment, is YOU.*
> *Trust in yourself and listen to your heart and soul.*
> *Give yourself permission to be your own best friend and you can achieve greatness.*
>
> **Tony Inman**

Of course, in reality, you are not alone. There are always people around you who will help, especially if you are not too proud to ask. Don't underestimate the value of a life coach either. The answers we seek often reveal themselves when we ask the right questions. A good coach will ask you good questions that really make you think. Things and people do not really 'end', they just transform into something else. They literally take another 'form'.

My two ex-wives have both now become 'my old friends', and I get on fine with them both, although I don't see Lesley because she's the other side of the world. Other people come along and take on the roles that those missing people previously acted out. A friend, business sounding board, lover, companion, or whatever the role you appear to have lost when someone leaves can be taken over by another player in the game of life. So when you stop blaming other people for their actions and realise that it is your responsibility to heal yourself and move on, you regain the power you thought you had lost.

You can't control the thoughts or actions of another person. You can only control yours.

You can't make them think what you want them to think (unless you torture them, break their spirit, and brainwash them to take on new identities and new beliefs), but you *can* control how *you* will choose to look at a situation and how you will act. When you take responsibility for the consequences of both your thoughts and your actions, then you are truly free and you know that each struggle has made you stronger.

> "You cannot always choose what happens to you, but you CAN CHOOSE how you will react to what happens to you."
> **Unknown**

With the benefit of hindsight, a huge number of the best experiences of my life have come along after that second marriage breakup. I now know that, had it not happened, I might have missed out on all of them! It seems that not only is life itself created after an intense struggle, so too are your subsequent personal renaissances a reward for surviving life's battles.

Rational Responsibilities

- The winner of the game is usually the one who thinks he can.
- When thinking about a tough situation, ask yourself, "Is choosing to look at it this way empowering me or dis-empowering me?"
- Focus on your goals and your dream. Draw on that energy and enthusiasm to overcome any obstacles.
- Blaming other people can easily become a pattern. If you catch yourself doing that, ask, "What could I have done or what could I do now to change this?"
- "Perception is projection." We can change our reality by changing how we perceive it.
- Give yourself permission to be your own best friend – not only can you survive a bad situation, but you can also bounce back and achieve greatness.
- The true test of your character does not come when all is well in your world – it's when the chips are down that the 'real you' is revealed.
- Don't be too proud to ask people for help.
- Things and people don't end; they just transform.
- You can't always choose what happens, but you can choose your response to what happens.
- Each struggle has made you stronger.
- That which seems awful today may with hindsight yet be a blessing!
- If you can be responsible for your thoughts, your actions, and your attitudes, you will be 'doing life well'. You will remain sane, no matter what is going on around you, and you will be on the path to fulfillment.

7

Get Your Head Straight

"It becomes obvious that if we want to make relatively minor changes in our lives, we can perhaps appropriately focus on our attitudes and behaviours. But if we want to make significant, quantum change, we need to work on our basic paradigms."

Stephen R. Covey

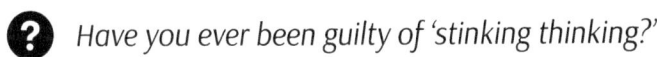 *Have you ever been guilty of 'stinking thinking?'*

The biggest improvement any of us can make is to review the way we think. Our philosophy is the single biggest factor in whether or not we will 'do life well', and the key to a better philosophy is self-education.

Shifting Paradigms

So what is a 'paradigm' you may well ask? A paradigm may be defined as: a set of assumptions, concepts, values and practices that constitutes a way of viewing reality for the community that shares them, especially in an intellectual discipline.

I was impressed with Dr. Covey's book, *The 7 Habits of Highly Effective People*. He holds a Harvard MBA and is a world authority on 'personal and managerial effectiveness'. In this book, he argues against what he calls "The Personality Ethic" – something he sees as prevalent in many modern self-help books. He instead promotes what he labels "The Character Ethic" – aligning one's values with so-called "universal and timeless" principles. I refer to these as 'Universal Laws' or 'Old Truths', and I'll talk more about these in a later chapter.

Covey adamantly refuses to conflate principles and values; he sees principles as external natural laws, while values remain internal and subjective. He proclaims that values govern people's behaviour, but principles ultimately determine the consequences. Covey presents his teachings in a series of habits, manifesting as a progression from dependence via independence to interdependence.

There's an old saying that I've heard in many movies, which goes, "If you don't stand for something, you'll fall for anything!"

 So how do you want to manage your life? Which values are part of your personal belief system?

I challenge you to reflect on what you stand for. If you haven't done so, please take a moment now to write down those values for which you stand. Reflecting on those values may help you to shape your own destiny, because when you understand which beliefs drive you, it will help you figure out the kind of life you want and how you will get there. Sometimes, too, your beliefs may have been formed on incorrect information, and they may well be the ones that can hold you back from achieving your goals in life. I believe that investing the time to really think about what is important to you will make a huge difference to the quality of your life.

I also think that if you run your own business – and I make this point with all of my business clients, even the small businesses – it is vital to allocate time to reflect on and write down what your company's Purpose, Vision, Values and Mission are. If you don't know what you stand for and what your company stands for, how do you expect your staff to know?

'Formal Education' versus 'Self-Education'

One of my personal values is wisdom, so I believe in the importance of education. Having said that, I am also of the opinion that formal education is all well and good. I have nothing but respect for our schools and universities, but also, many of our most successful entrepreneurs have been handed honorary qualifications because they have already become extremely successful without them! It seems, however, that practical hands-on experience, backed up with self-education will bring you far greater results in the long run. The late Jim Rohn is still one of my great mentors because of the books and recordings he has left behind for us to still enjoy and learn from.

> "Formal education will make you a living; self-education will make you a fortune."
>
> **Jim Rohn**

 Are you making time to continue your personal and professional development? If not, what could you study this year that will add value to you and/or your business or job?

If you're not moving forwards and learning new things, you are not keeping pace with the market.

Being Effective

Having just talked about education, it is interesting to note that Sir Richard Branson has expressed that he is happy to be "the dumbest man in the room" because he likes to surround himself with people who really know what they are doing. By enlisting and harnessing the power of intelligent and gifted individuals and creating a team environment where he leaves his ego out of it, he gets everyone having fun while they focus on achieving amazing results. He is a supreme facilitator and that is a major component of his success.

 Who do you spend your time with?

> *The 7 Habits of Highly Effective People*
>
> 1. Be proactive.
> 2. Begin with the end in mind.
> 3. Put first things first.
> 4. Think win/win.
> 5. Seek first to understand then to be understood.
> 6. Synergise.
> 7. Sharpen the saw.
>
> **Stephen Covey**

These seven key elements are pretty self-explanatory, though it is clear that the common links are about sound leadership, empathy and communication skills. He refers to the first three elements as a 'private victory' because they are internal, and numbers four to seven as a 'public victory' because they are external. Another key habit I believe to be true of effective and successful people is that they follow their hearts. They live by their values and because they are aligned with those it enables them to operate at a higher and more instinctive level. Thus, decisions and actions that the less effective people would fear, postpone or avoid are taken easily and more bravely by these role models. That courage is borne of conviction.

Successful people know why they are doing what they are doing.

Professional 'Pearls'

- Everything you know has got you to where you are now. If you want different results, you have to expand your mind, learn new things and think differently.

- Your beliefs and values will shape your destiny.

- The progression to success comes when you move from dependence to independence to interdependence – when you leverage your time and skill by building a fantastic support team.

- Academic education will get you a good job. Hands-on experience backed up by self-education will make you wealthy.

- Learning how to create and communicate win-win outcomes will lead you to effective success.

- Follow your heart and your soul, but feed both with education.

- The more you expand your mind and your consciousness, the more you will be 'doing life well' and the more you will find fulfillment.

8

Sticks and Stones…

"Too often we underestimate the power of a touch, a smile, a kind word, a listening ear, an honest compliment, or the smallest act of caring, all of which have the potential to turn a life around."
Leo Buscaglia

You may have heard this children's saying, but I have a slightly different version for you: *"Sticks and stones will break my bones, but words can truly screw me up!"*

My publisher, Emily kindly reminded me to remove a couple of naughty words from my first draft of this book because she said, "Parents may want their teenagers to read it, so you don't want anything that could upset them."

Well, my friends and fellow parents, I'd really like you to take note of what follows next because as a coach, I spend a lot of my time sorting out issues that adults have carried with them as a result of things that were said to them in a moment of anger, tiredness or frustration when they were children. The spoken word is as irretractable as a naughty picture on the Internet!

The Nurturing Effect of Words – Planting the Seeds of Wisdom and Achievement

Years ago, I read some of the work of the great author, Denis Waitley. I was particularly inspired by his book, *The Seeds of Greatness*, because I was a young parent at the time, with young children, and Denis talked a lot about realising the impact of your words on your children. That really had an impact on me. I made a point of following his suggestions to read them bedtime stories and always tell them that I loved them and how special they were. I missed out on a lot of reading to my daughter, Kim, because of my marriage breakup – though fortunately, she completed a traineeship with me later, so we had time to catch up a bit!

To my first wife, Joyce, telling the kids that they were loved came easily because she was raised in a close knit family in Glasgow, Scotland, who were very open about their feelings. In my case, I had to consciously make a point to remember to tell my children how special they were and how much I loved them, because that was not really done in our family. I'm pleased to say that it was a habit I was delighted to break.

Deep down, it seems that we want to honour our parents by making them proud of us and that this can be a significant source of self-esteem. That's why parents know how powerful it can be when disciplining a child to express disappointment at the child's bad behaviour or poor decisions. Hearing someone say that you have disappointed them is a stinging rebuke indeed. The best parents and the best teachers in schools also understand the power of giving children something to live up to, rather than putting them down. I always remember the words of Dr. Smith, who was the coach of one of the school football teams I played in… Bear in mind that I was, and always have been, 'football mad', so it meant a lot to me.

He said to me, "Inman, I've put you in the team in defence because you're always cool under pressure, so I know I can count on you." That compliment is imbedded in my psyche to the point where it has empowered me to keep pretty calm under quite a lot of pressure in many stressful situations. The teacher probably just thought he was inspiring me to play a good game in that particular football match on that one day, yet he actually inspired me to play a better game throughout my whole life, and not just on the football pitch.

 Are you remembering to plant seeds of encouragement in your daily contacts with people around you?

The English Way

My parents came from an English background where feelings were not really discussed. That was 'the English way' – keeping a stiff upper lip, old chap! My parents had both had challenging upbringings. My mother lost her dad when she was very young and her mum re-married to a man old enough to be her grandfather. She was then shunted around to stay with various members of her mum's family around Chester, and although she was loved, it must have had an effect on her. My father was born in Manchester, and his parents constantly argued and fought. They apparently separated and re-united on many occasions, and he described it as quite a lonely and unhappy childhood. He clearly loved his father, but he felt that his mother was difficult and had given his dad a very hard time.

The fact that my parents were separated by over five years of war is kind of hard to imagine. I also definitely have no concept of what it would be like to find yourself being an aircraft engineer and flight sergeant on Malta at the age of just nineteen, with a team of men reporting to you and bombs landing all around you every day. To then see many of your friends killed in their teens and twenties by a faceless enemy must have been just awful, and I remember him telling me about his memory of the smell of a pilot burning in the wreckage of his crashed aircraft.

Dad survived near starvation, meningitis and several near misses from German bombs, while he and his men kept fixing the Spitfires and Hurricanes – the British fighter planes that were defending the island. Meanwhile, back in England, my mother worked, initially bookkeeping in a hotel (hence, the hotel career later) and then in a munitions factory during the war, living on rations coupons while she brought up my eldest brother, Peter.

Here is a great example of the impact of words. When my father was taken seriously ill on Malta and was sent to the hospital with meningitis, my mother back in Chester answered a knock on the front door one day. A man stood before her clutching a telegram from the Ministry of Defence. Mum read as far as, "Dear Mrs Inman, We regret to inform you…" and she fainted in the corridor. Of course she had immediately assumed from those very powerful and well-known words that this was to be a notification of his death on active service. Fortunately, it turned out to be merely an advice of his serious illness, and since Dad appeared to have as many lives as a cat, he pulled through and later returned home from the war.

From the Mouths of Babes

I read somewhere that the words we hear in our self-talk as adults are often the sayings that we remember spoken by our parents during our childhood. Perhaps that's why we have so many so-called 'old sayings', figures of speech, and idioms. These are sayings and expressions that have been handed down through the generations that help us to understand our national principles and lessons in life. I've already mentioned that the title of this book is a paraphrase of one of my father's sayings that stuck with me from when he used to have me helping him with odd jobs in the family hotels. So, if you want to develop your ability to influence other people, it's important to remember that the right words, at the right time, have a great deal of power.

I was so pleased a couple of years ago when my daughter handed me a birthday card from her and her brother that contained the following poem:

> "You may have thought we didn't see,
> Or that we didn't care,
> Life lessons that you taught to us,
> But we got every word, we swear.
> Perhaps you thought we missed it all,
> And that we'd grow apart,
> But, Dad, we picked up everything;
> It's written in our hearts.
> Without you, Dad, we wouldn't be
> The people we are today;
> You built a strong foundation
> No-one can take away.
> You might be a 'ranga' (redhead)
> And a little over-weight,
> But we love you just the same.
> We've grown up with your values,
> And we're very glad we did;
> So here's to you, dear father,
> From your forever grateful kids.
>
> **Kim and Craig Inman**

It's one of the great joys in life when you look at your children and observe, or when you listen to them speak, and you realise that they do reflect your values.

That's when you also realise how important it is to strive to be a good role model – to be the best 'you' that you can be.

The Impact of Your Words (AKA Influence)

Often you may never know what an impact your words have been on the self-talk of others – whether you have uplifted or destroyed another's soul.

While it is sometimes true that what other people think is none of your business, it is also true that the responsibility for the effective communication of a message lies more firmly in the hands of the speaker than in those of the listener.

Yet another book that had a huge influence on me was Robert Cialdini's book, entitled *Influence – The Psychology of Persuasion*. Cialdini not only gives a fascinating insight into how psychologists have empowered marketers to pitch their messages at consumers, but he also addresses some of the basic human responses in certain situations. For example, if you ever find yourself collapsing in a crowd and you need help, research shows that most people would walk past and ignore you – not necessarily because they might assume you are under the influence of alcohol or drugs, but probably because they would assume that 'someone else' will do something about it. He continued that if you were to call out, "Help me!" Again, very few people would react, for the same reason. He recommended that, if you really do need help, pick out someone specific and enlist their help. For example, it's better to say, "You there, with the red cap on! Please can you help me by calling for an ambulance?!" When you specifically engage someone, they will usually do as much as they can to help, because they feel socially obligated.

The greatest orators throughout man's history have known how to use exactly the right words to influence their audience – sometimes for good and sometimes for evil. Which agenda they have depends on your interpretation of their actions according to your values. I'm sure you know of many politicians, military leaders and sports coaches who have used the very words that it took to inspire and motivate their listeners to amend their own self-talk and change their opinion from, "We might be able to do this…" to "We can do this!"

Those who lived through the era, when Britain was under threat of invasion by Nazi Germany, will never forget the following words, for they galvanised a nation against the forces of evil and tyranny:

> "We shall defend our island, whatever the cost may be, we shall fight on the beaches, we shall fight on the landing grounds, we shall fight in the fields and in the streets, we shall fight in the hills; we shall never surrender."
>
> **Winston Churchill**

If you want to learn how to 'do life well', it's important to learn how to influence and inspire the people around you. It's also a fantastic feeling when you realise that you are inspiring yourself in the process.

Always remember also that words, whether they are used to encourage or to criticise can become a person's driving force. I will never forget a life-changing conversation with my first wife, Joyce. I had battled to improve myself and get better jobs, even taking on a second job, to try to earn more for the family. She kept comparing me with an engineer friend of ours who was working on big projects 'up North' and earning huge money. Whilst my career was going okay and I had been promoted several times, it was never going to be as well paid as his, and the lack of money was causing us to argue. I had been unhappy for over two years, but I did not want to leave my children and break up the family.

Joyce said to me, "You're just a retail manager, and that's all you're ever going to be. The sooner you realise that, the sooner you can be happy in life."

That was the moment when I knew, I absolutely knew in the core of my being, that my marriage was over. I could not stay with someone who had such a different outlook on my potential. Those words burned in my brain and drove me to push myself to prove her wrong. For years, I was angry with her for saying those words to me, but now I'm so glad she did.

Words Create History

One of the interests I had as a youngster growing up on Jersey was in military history. Like most children around that time, it was probably the fact that there were so many gung-ho war movies made, featuring the likes of John Wayne, and the fact that for most of us, our parents had memories of the last World War from their youth. It was also the environment of the island itself, which was steeped in military history. Jersey had been fought over by the English and the French for centuries and was occupied by the Germans in WWII, so the coastline is strewn with a mixture of very old castles and German gun emplacements and bunkers.

Every year, we would be given a day off school to go down to the beachfront at St. Aubin's Bay and watch the 'Battle of Britain Air Display', featuring the Memorial Flight of a Lancaster, Spitfire and Hurricane, as well as modern day aircraft and helicopters. The grand finale was always the breathtaking display of the famous 'Red Arrows' from the Royal Air Force – the best aerobatic team in the world.

I began with making model aircraft, the good old Airfix kits, and that was probably because my father's whole life revolved around his love of aircraft. We used to hang replica models of Spitfires and Messerschmitts from the garage ceiling, simulating the 'dog fights', such as in the Battle of Britain or the Siege of Malta. This interest in military history led me on to war-gaming. My friends and I used to buy metal soldiers from the model shops and by mail order. We would research the uniforms and paint these miniature figurines with minute attention to detail.

This created a great interest in, and love of, books. I have quite a large collection of books on wars, the armies, and their leaders. We re-enacted all kinds of stuff – the Napoleonic Wars, WWII infantry battles, WWII naval battles, WWII desert tank battles, the Marlburian period of siege warfare… We even had a dalliance with Star Trek spacecraft. There were complex rulebooks and well-constructed scenery with plastic trees and farmhouse buildings.

I suppose you could say we were the nerds of our generation, but I can remember spending hours in the library researching German U-Boats or stories like the sinking of the German battleship, Bismarck. Today's youth also play war-games, but it's all on-screen games, like PlayStation or X-Box, and the participants don't do any research.

We once spent a whole week of our summer holidays – a group of five of us in a friend's loft – re-enacting the entire Waterloo campaign. We arrived early in the morning and left as late as we were allowed in the evening, with the mother of the household bringing us food and drinks to keep us going. We were absolutely 'Living the Dream!'

Some of the valuable lessons I learned during that time were about the importance of inspiration, learning about people whose acts of bravery inspired you, friendship, focus, concentration, attention to detail, lateral thinking, research and preparation and working to save money. I noticed and absorbed traits such as leadership, tenacity and commitment, and I learned how to apply the rules of the game to your greatest advantage. Perhaps the biggest lesson of all, though, was the power of imagination.

One of the leaders with whom I developed the greatest fascination was Napoleon Bonaparte. Some British historians paint Napoleon as an evil tyrant and ruthless despot. The British inclination towards 'taking the mickey' out of the French means that he has been lampooned as a comical figure remembered best for the famous line, "Not tonight, Josephine." In contrast, military historians at places like the Military Academy at Sandhurst – one of the world's finest military training centres – analyse the brilliance of his military tactics and use lessons from his battles and manoeuvers to teach today's aspiring generals.

More well-balanced historical analyses show both his strengths and his weaknesses, such as his incredible leadership capabilities and sheer personal magnetism; his absolute commitment to his goals and his life mission; his complete reorganisation of the French civil code, the road-building and the overhaul of the education system which is still used today; his dedication to his family and his desire to leave a legacy for his people and his son.

At one stage, he ruled a vast chunk of Europe. However, in his assault on Moscow in 1812, he made the same mistake that Hitler was later to make: underestimating the ferocity of the Russian winter. That error of over-extension, fuelled by tendencies towards megalomania, led to his eventual downfall. Incredibly, Napoleon achieved so much, yet he only lived to the age of fifty-two.

The overriding assessment is that Napoleon was a warmonger, yet that was very much the order of the day. He rose to power on the back of the French Revolution where people's heads were being chopped off for the daily entertainment of the mob in the village square, so you could hardly expect him not to have been desensitised to violence in a manner far worse than today's television programmes.

So how does my reference to Napoleon fit with you living your life well? Well, it certainly fits with my subtitle that we live in an insane world – insane because of the actions of humanity from the beginning of time. Yet despite the insanity, there has been steady progress by mankind towards discovery and evolution. That all begins with self-discovery and the power of the human mind – a mind which is fuelled by the words you say to yourself and the words used by leaders to inspire their followers.

The Little Emperor of France

Napoleone Buonaparte (sic) was born in 1769 into a poor family on the island of Corsica, part of French Sovereign Territory. He had seven siblings who survived beyond infancy. His father managed to demonstrate somehow to the satisfaction of the royal school at Brienne that young Napoleone (later amended to the more French-sounding Napoleon) and his brother Joseph were descended from a long line of Italian nobility so that they could pass the entrance criteria. Thus, at the age of just nine, Napoleon left his family and went to school in France, where he initially felt terribly homesick and isolated. He was mocked for being an outsider and having an unusual accent in the cruel way that children tend to pick on anyone who seems different.

He soon began to show leadership skills however, particularly in war-games. It is even said that he organised a heroic snowball victory by the juniors over the seniors. Around the age of ten, the story goes that he began to imagine himself one day becoming the ruler of France. That would be akin to a schoolchild from somewhere like the Isle of Skye imagining being King of England or someone from Christmas Island saying they would one day rule Australia. Yet such is the power of self-talk – the words we say to ourselves when we have a conversation inside our own head.

Napoleon studied hard, and he worked his way up through the military. When the moment came to announce his presence, by then he was an artillery captain, and he achieved notoriety for quelling a marauding mob with what became known as the 'Whiff of Grapeshot' incident (for close range impact, instead of using a single, solid cannonball, they fired bags of nails and metal fragments to inflict terrible injuries). He rose rapidly to the rank of a general in the French army, fighting against the Italians and the Austrians. He astounded everyone with his military ability, his courage and his leadership, but most importantly, he steadily climbed towards his childhood dream, also using Josephine's influence in the highest of social circles to build his reputation in court.

In 1804, the unlikeliest of candidates because of his background, Napoleon Bonaparte crowned himself Emperor Napoleon the First of France, renouncing tradition by having the Pope merely bless his coronation, rather than place the crown on the new ruler's head. In that moment, Napoleon fulfilled a lifelong dream. Such is the power of having a dream and working towards it, and such are the power of the words you say to yourself.

Influencing Your Team

The second story I have for you about Napoleon is about his ability to influence his men with his words. The following is an extract from his comprehensive book, *The Campaigns of Napoleon* by the world's leading authority on the subject, David G. Chandler.

> "The routine business of the day completed for the time being, the Emperor would call for his horse and set off accompanied by his 'little headquarters' to inspect some unit or visit a corps headquarters. He was firmly convinced of the importance of a commander in chief seeing and being seen. His incessant inspections, reviews and parades gave him the opportunity of gauging the morale of his men and assessing their mettle. These occasions also enabled him to dispense a little more of the hypnotic attraction he could wield at will over almost all his men. The easy familiarity which he permitted the rank and file made him genuinely beloved; the passing word for a 'grumbler', the rough joke with a sergeant, the summoning of the bravest man in the unit to receive an unexpected reward – these were the means by which he bound the troops to his service and inspired them to suffer ceaseless hardship and to meet the prospect of disfiguring wounds and death with at least a measure of acceptance. Many of his methods were theatrical, and deliberately so, but they had the desired effect. Every visit would terminate with resounding cries of 'Vive l'Empereur!' (Long live the Emperor!) and his habit of apparently taking the men into his confidence, explaining what he was trying to do and the role he was entrusting to them in the execution of his schemes, served to raise morale and increased the likelihood of success. In battle he habitually left command to his subordinates and rarely interfered, but when some particularly crucial attack was about to be launched he would often ride over to the unit concerned, and speed it on its way with some such phrase as 'Thirty-Eighth – I know you! Take me that village – at the charge!' His lightest word of praise was regarded as an accolade by the recipient; similarly, the least expression of his displeasure would reduce a hardened grenadier to tears. Napoleon had few equals in the sphere of man-management."

David G. Chandler

Another key point for me is that Napoleon was a voracious reader of books. It is sincerely my contention that, 'All leaders are readers'.

 Are you committed to some kind of reading programme?

If you were to read just one book per month, over the course of a year, you would have read eleven more books than the average person. If the books are on a specific subject, you would very soon become an expert on that topic! Experts are more empowered, more respected and, in most cases, better paid and more in charge of their own destiny.

> ### Words to the Wise
>
> - The right words delivered at the right time have the power to change lives.
> - Words are the seeds of ideas and accomplishments.
> - Try to give people something to live up to, rather than putting them down.
> - You may never know just how profound an impact your words can have on someone's life.
> - Words evoke memories of pleasure or pain.
> - By changing your self-talk, you can shape your destiny.
> - All leaders are readers.
> - If you want success, study success.
> - The greatest influence you can have on your children is to strive to live by example. None of us are perfect, but if you live life according to your highest values, you will be 'doing life well' and inspiring them to do their best to emulate your example.

9

Behavioural Science and Mind Power

"Thousands of candles can be lit from a single flame

And the life of the candle will not be shortened.

Happiness never decreases from being shared."

Buddha

This chapter really merits far greater analysis in terms of 'Doing Life Well', but for the purposes of this book, my aim is only to give an introduction to the topic for those who have not yet been exposed to any of this research and philosophy.

As I studied for my coaching and NLP certifications, building on over thirty-four years of experience in managing people, my thirst for knowledge of what makes humans tick has only ever been deepened. I've been a student of human behaviour ever since someone gave me a Desmond Morris book, called *Manwatching* when I was about eleven, and I'm one of those people who loves hanging around airports and crowded places, fascinated by the variety of emotions on display. That's why I've been drawn to tourism, coaching and service industries.

Neuro Linguistic Programming (NLP) and What It Can Do for You

What is NLP? To answer that fully would be impossible in the space I have here, so I'll do my best to give you the highlights. You may have read the book entitled

The Secret or watched the movie of the same name. Or perhaps you've heard about the 'Law of Attraction' or terms like 'mental magnetism'. This law states that we literally attract what we think about. Even if you are sceptical about that, please keep an open mind for a moment.

You may also have heard about how we human beings communicate through 'body language' from the works, such as the ones I have read, of people like Allan Pease or Desmond Morris. If so, you'd know that our verbal communication (language) actually only accounts for about seven percent of how and what we actually communicate to other people!

NLP has evolved from studies of human behaviour, studies of our conditioning or programming, and how the way we think governs the results we achieve in life. I was first exposed to how the so-called 'behavioural sciences' applied to leadership and managing people from reading the works of people like Rosemary Stewart and Tom Hopkins. Here's how Wikipedia defines NLP, using the relevant jargon:

> *"Neuro-linguistic programming (NLP) is a controversial approach to psychotherapy and organizational change based on "a model of interpersonal communication chiefly concerned with the relationship between successful patterns of behaviour and the subjective experiences (esp. patterns of thought) underlying them" and "a system of alternative therapy based on this which seeks to educate people in self-awareness and effective communication, and to change their patterns of mental and emotional behaviour."*
>
> *The term "Neuro-Linguistic Programming" refers to a stated connection between the neurological processes ("neuro"), language ("linguistic") and behavioral patterns that have been learned through experience ("programming") and can be organized to achieve specific goals in life.*
>
> *Wikipedia goes on to summarise NLP as "a 'science of excellence', applied within management training, life coaching, alternative medicine, large group awareness training, and the self-help industry."*
>
> **Source: Wikipedia**

Essentially NLP has evolved from the study, theories and practical applications of techniques compiled by some very clever people, originating in the area of the Silicon Valley in California, where huge intellects and free-spirited hippies came together. One thought leader you may have heard of, because he's often on late night television, promoting his transformational DVD programmes, is the legendary Tony Robbins. Years ago, I purchased Tony's series on 'Personal Power' and 'Get the Edge', along with his ongoing CD 'Power Talks'. To this day, I often listen to Tony's entertaining wisdom, whilst I am enjoying nature and keeping fit in my walks around our local lakes in Perth.

Tony Robbins defines NLP as 'Success Coaching' and has devised his own unique slant on things with what he calls 'N.A.C.', or Neuro Associative Conditioning. A highly condensed foundation of his work is that as human beings we are motivated to 'move towards pleasure', but more frequently to 'move away from pain' and that we associate our memories with one or other of those emotions.

> *I'm a great believer in multi-tasking and leveraging.*
>
> *For example, I listen to recordings of people like Tony Robbins when I go for my walks around the lake.*
>
> *It's like hanging out with one of the world's most influential multi-millionaires and picking his brain while you're getting fresh air and exercise at the same time.*
>
> *When you listen to a CD or read a book, in a very short time you get the distilled wisdom that it has taken that person a lifetime to learn. How useful is that!*
>
> **Tony Inman**

My friend, Stan Nelson, of the Streetsmarts Self Defence Tactics Academy recommended the NLP course to me, and it sounded interesting. Thus, I attended the I-NLP Practitioner Programme in Perth with some wonderful trainers, including George Faddoul and Matt James. It was frankly one of the best decisions I ever made. I have always been interested in the subjects of the power of self-talk, the psychology of success, and body language, so this was right up my street. It was very quickly apparent to me that both George and Matt are masters of their craft – they are gifted teachers and absolute gurus of NLP.

> **Here is a modern definition of 'guru':**
>
> a) a teacher and especially intellectual guide in matters of fundamental concern
>
> b) one who is an acknowledged leader or chief proponent
>
> c) a person with knowledge or expertise; expert
>
> **Merriam Webster Dictionary**

Furthermore, Matt, who is from Hawaii is a master of the esoteric teachings of Hawaiian Huna, which assists you in connecting body and spirit. I was so impressed that I travelled to Sydney to do my NLP master qualification – this time with George Faddoul partnered by the equally impressive NLP trainer and poet, Nick Leforce, from California. I went back again to Sydney to gain my NLP trainer qualification and speaker training from George and Nick. The introduction to Hawaiian Huna with Matt James had really intrigued me, so I travelled to Byron Bay in New South Wales for another course in 'Huna – Ancient Wisdom' delivered this time by the extremely wise Dr. Serge Kahili King from Hawaii.

My fascination with behavioural science continued, along with my quest to learn as much as I could so that I might be of use to my clients, as well as learning how to effectively pass that on to them.

I attended a seminar run by two of the best executive trainers and coaches in the world: multi-millionaires, Jeff Slayter and Kane Minkus, otherwise known as 'The Industry Rockstars' or simply, 'Jeff and Kane'. These guys became my mentors, as I completed further NLP studies with them, along with an incredible weekend in Sydney learning about 'Family Systems' and 'Constellation' work from their mentor, Carl Buchheit, from the NLP Marin Institute in California. With Jeff and Kane, I studied for more than a year, travelling regularly backwards and forwards from Perth to both Sydney and Melbourne, to complete my 'Coach's Master Class' certification, 'Industry Rockstar Trainer' courses, and I even enjoyed business mentoring sessions overlooking the beach at Jeff's home in Manley, Sydney. It was truly an honour to mix with top coaches from all over Australia and to learn how NLP truly enhances your understanding of human behaviour.

How NLP, NAC, Huna or Behavioural Science Can Be of Use to You

To start with, I'll give you my view of personal development…

> "The mind is like a parachute…No bloody use unless it's open!"
>
> **Anonymous**

If you can save years of your own time in making avoidable mistakes by learning from other people, people who have done whatever it is that you want to do, then wouldn't you be crazy not to learn from them?

That was a rhetorical question! Some people have formed the misconception that NLP is about manipulating people – for example, that speakers use NLP to mesmerise you into buying their products. Like any knowledge, it can be used for good or evil.

Knowing about nuclear physics, for example, means that you can help people by giving them nuclear power, or you can destroy people by using the same knowledge to build a nuclear bomb. If you're in sales, wouldn't you like to say things in such a way, or use the right gestures to support your proposal, so that people can find less obstacles in the way to buying your product? Well, if that product was one that you knew would help your customer, one that could change their life in a very positive way, and in which you had complete confidence and conviction, wouldn't that be a great 'win-win' outcome!

If on the other hand, you were a dodgy salesperson, trying to palm off that which you knew to be a crappy product or service on some unsuspecting victim, that would just exploit the customer and make you rich from exploiting them. Wouldn't that be a terrible 'I win-you lose' outcome? I find it slightly amusing that an Australian Bank started using the slogan that they had shortened 'Can't' to 'Can'. They will still refuse your loan application if it suits them, but at least they give you temporary hope!

I can put my hand on my heart and say that I have gained something from every course, every lecture, every book, every CD and every seminar. That has a lot to do with the fact that I set my intention to learn and made it my responsibility to extract everything I could that might be useful to me and to my family, friends and clients. Yet sometimes, on the same course, I've heard someone whinge about something, like the air-conditioning, the coffee or one of the speakers whom they didn't like, and they've allowed that inconvenience to ruin the whole learning experience for them. Here's the scoop folks: NLP or any of these 'mind things' are actually explanations or attempted explanations of all of the things that we as humans already do and have been doing all of our lives anyway.

It's scientific, yes, but it's not 'rocket science'. In other words, you don't need to be an NLP expert to know when someone's hacked off with you, even if they don't speak. As a husband, if your wife is giving you the silent treatment, you know she's not happy, even when you have no idea why! You equally don't need to be a 'guru' to notice that someone is delighted to see you even if they speak a different language. So, how can NLP help you?

It starts with having a better understanding of yourself; asking yourself better questions; noticing your own patterns of behaviour in given situations; and realising your strengths to work with and your weaknesses to work on. You learn to change your language and your 'self-talk' so that instead of dis-empowering yourself because of previous mistakes, you empower yourself to do better right now and in the future. As you learn about yourself and how you work, you then learn about other people and how they work. You learn to empower your children, your friends and your staff. You improve morale and you increase effectiveness. You learn to look at things from another person's viewpoint, which makes for better negotiation and the opportunity to create win-win outcomes.

> *Imagine the impact we could all have on the world, if we all understood ourselves and each other, better.*

Imagine the impact that would have on the future of mankind as we begin our journeys to discover new species on different planets. So, in summary, NLP or NAC, or an understanding of 'Behavioural Science' will help you become better in all types of communication.

Huna is a collection of esoteric teachings that is tribal in origin and deeply spiritual. I was amazed and fascinated at how insightful it is and how it helps you harness some of your personal energy and connects your spirit to a kind of higher consciousness. I hope that my over-simplistic explanation doesn't offend the Huna teachers, because I spent five days in a classroom with Dr. Serge Kahili

King writing as fast as I could and trying to learn from all of the exercises, and another day on the road with him, visiting a waterfall and a rainforest, yet I still felt as if I had barely scratched the surface of the knowledge available.

One little example is that the Hawaiians don't have the word 'sorry' in their language. After all, it's easy to say sorry and not mean it at all. Instead, their words translate as, 'Please forgive me.' That requires a response and an acceptance of your offering by the other party so that there is an exchange of energy. If the person doesn't want to accept your apology, there would be a negotiation until a compromise is reached. In ancient times, this would have been overseen by the tribal elders or kahunas. A kahuna is like a guru or expert in their field, so you could have a kahuna in boat-building, a kahuna in crop planting, etc.

Another concept I love about their culture is the concept of the 'talking stick'. He who has the stick has the floor and must not be interrupted. Imagine if that concept were applied in our parliament! So, the key point about learning these disciplines is that it figuratively gives you more tools for your tool box.

 How much would it help you in your business or job if you could understand and communicate more effectively with other people?

I've heard it said that we humans only use about ten percent of our brains, so in my view, anything that can expand that percentage has to be beneficial.

Two of My Earliest and Best Applications of NLP

I used the NLP skills I had acquired on courses to be able to 'anchor', or a way to psychologically link my thoughts to a very empowering moment in my life, which I was then able to put into effect in a very dramatic way.

When my partner Jo's father, Alan Small, passed away, the family asked me to deliver the eulogy at his funeral. My initial reaction was that I would struggle to get through the speech without choking (They do say that a lot of people have such a fear of public speaking that they would rather be the one in the coffin than the one delivering the eulogy!). My concern was less about the public speaking, because I am pretty at ease with that now; it was about wanting to do a good job for the family. Naturally, I was concerned about the extreme emotion of the situation.

Initially, I didn't believe I could do it, so I declined and suggested taking up the celebrant's offer to deliver the speech if I wrote it. A couple of days before the funeral, we had a family brainstorming session on anecdotes, and I crafted a speech, linking the various stories. When I read it out to the family in the safety of their lounge room, they implored me to make the speech in public at the funeral. Having just completed the basic course, I had learned a powerful empowerment technique, so now I began to believe I could do it. In fact, being a visual person, I could see myself doing it in my mind's eye.

When we entered the room and saw the screen filled with a lifetime of images to the right, a sea of mostly unknown faces to the left, and of course, the emotional sight of Alan's coffin in front of me, my heart started pounding like a steam engine. To say I was a tad nervous would be a huge understatement. I used the anchoring technique to slow my breathing and my heart rate, to calm myself, and to change my whole state of mind. As I stood up to deliver the eulogy and faced that crowd, I knew I could do this.

As the words began to flow, I was able to relax and adjust the tempo, the tone and the timbre of my speech. I have to confess to choking very slightly on the final sentence, and in fact, to some people it went unnoticed. I was proud that I had been able to do my best to honour the life of a fine man in a way that gave comfort to his family.

As the procession of mourners approached to pay their respects to the family, some of the group even asked me if I do that kind of thing professionally. I was astounded. Without the NLP skills, I know I would have struggled. In fact, I might well have left the job to the celebrant, who had never even met the man, and that just wouldn't have seemed right to me.

Only a year or so later, my own father, Bill Inman, passed away. I used the same technique to deliver his eulogy. Once again, my heart was pounding in the lead up to the occasion, probably more so, because of my greater personal grief. However, just as I had done before, I used my NLP anchoring techniques and managed to deliver the speech fluently, at a measured pace, and even with some humour. It meant a huge amount to me when my mother, Vera Inman, told me at the wake that Dad would have been very proud of me for the good job I had done in making that speech.

To have been able to sum up a man's ninety years of contribution to this world and do it to a level with which his partner of seventy years was happy, gave me a sense of having been able to honour his memory to the best of my ability. Those two occasions alone have more than justified the many thousands of dollars I have invested in those studies.

Good or Evil? Which One Will Win?

There is an old Cherokee tale of a grandfather teaching life principles to his grandson…

The wise old Cherokee said, "Son, on the inside of every person the battle is raging between two wolves. One wolf is evil. It's angry, jealous, unforgiving, proud, and lazy. The other wolf is good. It is filled with love, kindness, humility, and encouragement. These two wolves are constantly fighting."

The little boy thought about it and said, "Grandfather, which wolf is going to win?" The grandfather smiled and said, "Whichever one you feed."

 Which wolf are you feeding in your mind?

Remember that even when you can't always choose what happens to you in your life, only you can choose how you will react. I just love the wisdom of esoteric tribal teachings. You should always listen to what Grandpa's have to say… I know, because I'm now a Grandpa!

Perception – The Truth Has Many Versions

So we have learned from centuries of study of the mind, and from simple observation of the stories on daily newspapers, that perception is subjective. We all filter our experiences of the world through our own way of looking at things.

What you perceive as theft when someone steals from you, the thief perceives as taking his share. What a court determines is a murder, the murderer sees as self-defence or justifiable homicide. What a movie star or a princess perceives to be an invasion of privacy, a paparazzi photographer perceives as a good photograph that is in the public interest. What you perceive as an incorrect version of the truth, another person insists was absolute fact.

> "History is a set of lies agreed upon."
> **Napoleon Bonaparte**

Thus we must recognise that no matter how much we believe we are right and someone else is wrong, in fact, that belief is founded on a wrong assumption – the assumption that the world operates according to *our* map of the world. The truth is that we are right, for us, according to our values and beliefs; simultaneously, they are right, for them, according to their set of values and beliefs.

If you can take that concept on board, then you have the beginnings of compromise and an understanding of "Live and let live." To put that in NLP jargon, we say, "*There is no reality, there is only perception.*" Hold on, though. Here's the disclaimer! I'm not saying that murderers should not be prosecuted or that society should not have rules. Of course it has to, or we would rapidly descend into anarchy. What I am saying is that if we can seek first to understand the actions of a person even when those actions conflict completely with our view of how the world should work, just maybe we will gradually evolve as a race.

> "The test of a first rate intelligence is the ability to hold two opposed ideas in the mind at the same time, and still retain the ability to function."
> **F. Scott Fitzgerald**

A great example of seeing things from another man's point of view is the notion that to understand him better, you should walk a thousand miles in another man's shoes. The good thing about that is that if at the end of it you still don't understand him, at least by then he's a thousand miles away from you and you have some new shoes!

The Power of Labels

Another aspect of this process of determining how we perceive reality is in relation to the use of labels. I don't mean the things we put on clothes so you know if they fit or how you should wash them without causing shrinkage! Having said that, clothing labels are not a bad analogy. We are all different. People are a complex mix of characters formed by their genetic make-up, their childhood experiences, their family systems, their beliefs, values and habits, yet we so often treat them as if 'one size fits all'.

As soon as we label a person, including ourselves, we pigeon-hole that person into expecting that they will behave a certain way or that they will think a certain thing. So, we have to be very careful about the use of labels, because it can colour our interpretations of who that person is and how they should be treated.

 How many times in life do you base your impression of someone on limited or false information and/or assumptions?

Imagine yourself standing in a supermarket queue one day. It's quite a tight space between lanes and the person in front of you has dithered and dallied, then used the wrong credit card before deciding they didn't want to buy a couple of the items after all. The checkout assistant has remained calm and composed in dealing with the person, but you are late for an important meeting. You are stressed.

Just as you finally move forwards, another shopper runs past you with a bundle in their hands. As they squeeze through the gap, they knock into you, sending you flying and you drop your carton of eggs on the floor.

"Bl@#$y idiot!" you yell at the fleeing yobbo. Consequently, you are delayed and embarrassed when you arrive late for your meeting. You curse the rude shopper and spend the rest of your day telling people about what an idiot he was.

That evening when you turn on your television and catch the evening news, you recognise a picture of the same young guy and you stop to turn up the volume. It transpires that the bundle he was carrying was in fact a small child wrapped in a blanket. The child had fallen out of the special seat on the shopping trolley and had cracked her head on the edge of a shelf. Realising that the wound was serious, the young father had grabbed her, run through the checkouts and had sprinted around the corner to the hospital nearby.

The young father was being proclaimed as a hero, for thinking and acting quickly so that the doctors in the Emergency Department were able to save her young life.

 "Now how do you feel? Has it changed your perception of the situation or perhaps of any random situation you may encounter?"

Labelling Yourself

Consider the labels you allow to be put on yourself. Let's suppose you are labelled as a shy kid by your parents and teachers, so you form the belief, *I'm shy*. Then one day, your teacher asks you to come to the front of the class and read out your homework. You stumble through the words and the other children laugh at you. You are embarrassed, and it is emotionally painful. You draw the conclusion, and you say to yourself, *I messed that up because I am shy*.

Later on, at the school dance, you see a stunning girl (female readers substitute guy here). You want to go and ask her dance, but something stops you. You can't do it because, *I'm shy*.

After the dance has finished, you are angry with yourself. You know you should have asked the girl out, but you didn't. You beat yourself up over it, and it pains you to admit that the reason you didn't do it was because, *I'm shy*. Years later, when the boss asks you to stand up at work and make a speech to the staff, you find a way to get out of it, cringing all the while, annoyed with yourself. You had the chance to make a big impression, but you didn't. You bottled it and wimped out of the opportunity. Why? Because, you say to yourself, *I'm shy*.

So each time, the opportunity comes up to do something different, you don't take action, and you layer on top of the original belief of, *I'm shy*. You now have numerous examples of how shy you were in certain situations, so you are well and truly convinced that you are shy. If people ask you about yourself, you will openly admit to being a shy person. That is 'who' or 'what' you are. You have always been shy. Just for a moment though, consider this possibility…

What if the original story was wrong? What if, on that very first occasion that someone labelled you as 'shy', you were in fact simply quiet, or unwell, or tired, or any number of other things that might appear to someone else as the behaviour of a shy person? If that person had not labelled you as 'shy', it might never have occurred to you to act out the role of a 'shy' person.

Here's the really interesting question… Even if you had thought yourself shy and assumed the role of the shy person in the first couple of instances, what if you had then acted out of character? What if, despite believing yourself to be shy, you had summoned up the courage to behave and act as if you were in fact a confident person? Once you have overcome a belief that is actually limiting your experiences and opportunities, you could be forgiven for wondering why you had ever thought that about yourself in the first place! You are then free to think differently, to behave differently and to enjoy different outcomes.

> *The beliefs you lodge in your brains as a child can still be preventing you from doing things as an adult.*

This is a typical scenario I come across all the time when coaching people. What I often find is that if you can get the client to go back through their memories and re-examine the very first occasion when that belief was formed. By looking at that situation from different angles, the client can often release the emotional charge associated with that memory.

> *Once you have replaced a disempowering belief about who you are, with an empowering belief, you can achieve vastly different results and make your dreams come true.*

 What disempowering beliefs you are holding onto?

Those Who 'Do Life Well' See 'Impossible' as 'A Challenge'

When I was a child in primary school, I remember being given a science project where we had to design a spaceship and make a list of everything that we would need on board for a long space journey. In our minds, we never doubted for one moment that if we could imagine going on such a journey, we could one day achieve it.

Recently, I had the good fortune to hear one of my heroes speak. Sir Richard Branson declared it his goal that every person in the room that day, in June 2013, would have the opportunity to become an astronaut in their lifetime. I believe that it's only a matter of time before we are living the life dreamed of by the creators of *Star Trek* and that, therefore, we will inevitably encounter other life forms out there on one of those billions of planets.

If we are to unite and survive as a race, then we need to develop an ability to resolve differences, to create peace, harmony and tolerance. We must all begin that process internally, in each one of our own minds. Such is the power of the mind and the power of empowering self-talk. Remember that it wasn't so long ago that mankind thought that a human being could not run a mile in less than four minutes. Roger Bannister believed he could, and in 1954, he did. Once he did it, twenty-four other athletes did it in the following year. To date, the mile record has since been lowered by almost seventeen seconds.

> "Whatever the mind can conceive and believe, it can achieve."
> **Napoleon Hill**

 If you knew no-one would judge you, what ideas, concepts or dreams would you dare to allow to occupy your thoughts?

Tremendous Thoughts

- An understanding of behavioural sciences enhances your ability to communicate.
- Our words give us a code to live by.
- There is no reality; there is only our perception of reality.
- When you build the dream, focus on the outcome you desire, and keep working towards it, you will attract the people and circumstances to make it happen
- If you want success, study success
- People do not usually want to disappoint you. They usually want to feel helpful and valued.
- Verbal communication only accounts for seven percent. Learn to observe and to listen to what people don't say as well as what they do say.
- Practice developing and trusting in your instincts.
- Leverage your time and money – learn from other peoples' experience.
- Try to see things from the other person's perspective.
- Always look for win-win outcomes wherever possible
- Watch out for the labels you attach to others and yourself
- If you find yourself experiencing a belief that is stopping you from doing something, examine why you hold that belief and ask, "What if that's not true?"
- Remember that if mankind can conceive it, someone can achieve it.
- Surround yourself with people with the same values as yourself and connect them to each other. The more you create 'win-win-win' outcomes, the more you will be 'doing life well'.

10

That Matter of Life or Death, Plus Using Self-Talk

"If it is to be, it's up to me."

William H. Johnsen

The Importance of Breathing

You may recall that situation I was talking about in the first chapter? I figured it was only fair to not keep you in suspense any longer! So… there I was, scuba diving fifty-five metres below the surface of the Coral Sea, at the bottom end of a vertical swimming pool on the deck of a World War II shipwreck, the *SS President Coolidge*, in so-called 'shark-infested' waters. I had started to cough into my regulator and my breathing rhythm had been completely thrown 'out of whack!' I was also suffering a little, I believe, from the effects of nitrogen narcosis and feeling increasingly anxious.

The visibility below us to the seabed at about seventy metres, was dark and murky. There was an eeriness, and it was somewhat surreal down there next to what was in effect a rusting metal war grave covered in sixty-eight years' worth of barnacles and coral growth, with silence except for the sound of your own breathing… or in my case, coughing. There would have been plenty of sharks around, but we hadn't seen any, and quite honestly, they do not concern me (unless they are a great white, a tiger shark or a shiver of hammerheads). That is to say, that while I am cautious and respectful in the presence of sharks, as I would be with any pack of wild creatures, I am not so much filled with trepidation as I am excited by the photo opportunity that an encounter presents. No, my fear was simply the fact that I could not get my breathing back on track, which is kind of important down there!

I mentioned before that it was like one of those movies where you have a devil on one shoulder and an angel on the other. Both characters were actually me – the dark side of me and the light side of me. Now, some readers here might think that I'm insane, but bear with me. I'm admitting here to having little voices having a discussion inside my head, but I'm sure I'm not the only person who experiences this! If I'm wrong, then too bad – I'll just positively reframe it as, "I walk the fine line between genius and insanity!"

As I struggled to clear my throat and get my breathing under control, the devil began to goad me. The nasty little voice started tormenting me, "What are you even doing down here? You don't belong here. Look, you can't even see the surface. You're starting to choke, and you're losing it. This isn't even real – take that stupid regulator out of your mouth and just breathe like a fish. Better still, it's time for you to panic!"

"Shut up!" said the little angel on my other shoulder. "You can do this. You are an experienced diver. You've done almost 200 dives. Get a grip and calm yourself down. You have handled more stressful situations than this in the past and you'll handle this now." It was at that point that I instinctively did a classic NLP exercise.

My spirit seemed to float out of my body, to a position a few metres away where it could look back down at me. We call it disassociation or dissociation. As I looked back down, I could see myself with my right hand clenched upon my regulator, coughing and struggling to get enough air into my lungs. I could see Jo, looking somewhat concerned behind me. She could tell from the increased number of bubbles pumping out of my regulator that I was having a challenge. Dave was oblivious to my predicament as he was slowly kicking forwards.

When you look at your situation from outside yourself, it all seems much calmer.

When I looked outside myself, I could see an experienced diver coping with a temporary blip. The fact that it was happening about fifty-five metres below the surface was just a detail. A sudden inner peace took hold of me as I looked to the right and noticed a nudibranch sitting on the side of the ship. These are a sort of brightly coloured sea slug, though because of the depth and the lack of light, the colours change to about fifty shades of grey. I relaxed, took deeper breaths, and took my hand off my mouthpiece and grabbed my camera, which has an underwater dive housing.

I took my focus completely off my breathing and directed my attention towards the sea creature. It was as if Mother Nature herself had come to my rescue. As I focused my thoughts on keeping still enough to get a clear photograph, I allowed the part of my brain that normally handles unostentatiously the basic life support actions like breathing to just do what it does best. As I took the photograph, my breathing came back to normal, my heartbeat slowed, and I began to feel better. As we then slowly began to move back up the side of the ship to commence our ascent, the calmness continued to grow as the pressure reduced, which probably had a lot to do with that nitrogen narcosis abating.

Jo told me afterwards that she had been quite alarmed as she had noticed the change in the pattern of my air bubbles, but when she saw me take the photograph, she knew I was okay again. It had been a strangely surreal experience, and I will always be thankful to that little nudibranch. Without his help, I could have been in real trouble down there.

With your self-talk, you have incredible power to overcome the most challenging situations.

A day or two later we were inside the engine room of the *SS President Coolidge*, again at a depth of fifty-five metres looking at the big dials that had given information on engine pressures to the crew back in 1942. We also completed the dive to the stern of the ship at sixty metres. This hadn't been our first experience of deep dives; we had been superbly trained by Neil from *Tulagi Dive* in the Solomon Islands a couple of years earlier, where we had completed many deep wreck dives, culminating with an almost fully intact American battleship with the big five inch guns, the USS *Aaron Ward*. On that dive, we had only had time for about fifteen minutes at deck level before commencing our ascent from sixty-three metres and the many safety stops that made up the rest of the hour long dive. That had also been a dive where we had been pretty nervous prior to it, but had enjoyed the thrill and exhilaration of completing something way beyond our previous limits.

I'm not suggesting that our hobby is for everyone, but I do believe that the real personal growth occurs when you step outside your comfort zone and do something that may prior to that have seemed unthinkable. For some people, it might be taking those first few steps after recovering from an accident. For others, it could be walking up a flight of stairs; for some it could be running a marathon…

Everyone's boundaries are different, but it is when we push through our particular boundary, that we discover the 'sweet spot' – the moment that we realise we are 'doing life well' and living a life of inspiration. The other key point to realise here – that is so obvious that somehow it is often overlooked – is that breathing is really important. That's why practices such as Yoga give it so much attention. If you ever find yourself feeling stressed or anxious, merely focusing on taking a few deep breaths increases the oxygen to your brain and has a calming effect on your being and your sense of fulfillment.

PART TWO:

DOING

Embracing Change And Taking Action

Tony pictured giving a talk on success principles to small business owners.

PART TWO – 'DOING'
Embracing Change and Taking Action

"There is nothing permanent except change."

Herodotus

Part Two is about making new and better things happen in your life. Change can invoke excitement or instil fear. It can cause us pleasure or it can cause us pain. We can perceive change as an opportunity, or we can perceive it as a threat. The one thing we can't do is to bury our heads in the sand and pretend that it will go away!

Ask anyone who has ever run a business or even a sports team, and they will tell you that you cannot just stand still, because your competitors won't! My philosophy has always been this…

> In business, if you're not moving forwards, you're slipping backwards.
> **Tony Inman**

The same actually applies in life. We will talk about this further in the section on Universal Laws and 'The Law of Atrophy'. A muscle not used begins to waste. A mind left unused heads towards dementia.

We always have a choice, even if the choice is to consciously do nothing.

I believe that life is active, not passive. Look at nature, plants, animals, the Earth itself… all are in a constant state of change and evolution. So quite simply, if you want different results to the ones you have been getting so far in your life, you need to embrace change and take action.

11

"Hello, Death, We Meet Again!"

"Know that it's your decisions, and not your conditions, that determine your destiny."

Tony Robbins

It was probably around 1965 on a typical run of the mill afternoon in Jersey in the British Channel Islands. A boy, who was fours year old or thereabouts, was in his bedroom, a sort of attic, on the top floor of the Colesberg Hotel, having just returned from playing in the local park with his nanny. The reason he had a nanny was that his parents owned and managed the hotel and they were very busy people.

The nanny said to him that she would go downstairs to the hotel kitchen and make his tea. I believe it was to be boiled eggs and toast 'soldiers'. The little boy was pleased. He had used a lot of energy running around the park, and he was hungry. He was also quite intelligent, confident and possibly a little precocious.

The nanny switched on the old black and white television set and instructed the little boy to sit down and watch. "You be a good boy and sit there and watch TV, while I go and get your tea. I'll only be a few minutes."

The nanny closed the bedroom door and the boy looked at the black screen and waited patiently for one of his favourite programmes to come on. He couldn't really do anything to cause himself any harm in this safe, little environment, or so the nanny believed anyway. These were the days when television sets had to warm up for about thirty seconds before the picture finally appeared. Any time you are left waiting somewhere, psychologically it can seem as if the time drags endlessly, so the boy soon became impatient.

Nothing's happening, he said to himself. *Silly Jackie must have forgotten to plug it in at the wall. I'm going to miss my programme.*

The little lad jumped out of his chair, lay on the carpet, and looked under the bed. Sure enough the plug was lying unplugged on the floor. Without further ado, he plugged it in, flicked the switch, and returned to his chair. The television seemed to be taking an eternity to come on. Then, as the seconds ticked by, the little boy noticed a smell of smoke. Gradually, the smell of smoke was joined by actual smoke, like the sort he had seen hovering in the room when people smoked cigarettes.

I'll tell you what happened next, a little later on. But first, let's talk about motivation…

12

Kick Your Own Butt

"We cannot solve our problems with the same thinking that created them."

Albert Einstein

I'm sure you can remember a time when you tried to do something, and it didn't work. You tried to do it again, except that you did exactly the same thing, the same way, as you had tried it the first time. You probably expected that somehow, this time, it would work, but once again, it didn't. You may even have tried a third attempt, thinking surely it would work that time.

Perhaps that's why people go on diets, but they eat chocolate cake. They go to the gym, but then always use the escalator. Or maybe that's why they go to a dead end job with minimal prospects and do nothing to improve themselves, yet expect to retire wealthy.

We shouldn't be amazed at mankind's proclivity for repeating patterns that history has shown us simply do not work, yet we are. I suppose the saving grace is that at least it displays an attempt to do something to change the situation, even if it is a pointless attempt – unlike the following story…

Does It Hurt Enough Yet?

One fine sunny day a traveller was walking down a dusty road past a farm by an old country town. He could hear the birds tweeting, and he could smell the bracing country air as he surveyed the grassy paradise around him. Suddenly, his reflective state was interrupted abruptly by a terrible howling noise. He looked around but couldn't see where it was coming from, so he kept walking, concerned at the distressed nature of the sound. Further down the lane, he came to a gate at the farm entrance, where he could now see the farmhouse. In front of the house, he could see a large green kennel with a massive dog's head and two large paws sticking out from the front. He saw the farmer working nearby and waved hello. The farmer smiled and waved back. Suddenly, the awful howling noise struck up again. The traveller realised that it was coming from that dog in the kennel.

"Hi there, sir!" the traveller shouted to the rosy-cheeked farmer.

"Lovely day, ain't it, mister?" responded the local, tipping his hat as a respectful greeting.

"Excuse me, sir, but is that your dog making that terrible noise?"

The dog let out a bloodcurdling howl once more. "Sure is," answered the farmer.

"Well, is he in pain or something? It surely sounds like he is."

The farmer stopped what he was doing and sauntered over to shake hands with the traveller.

"Yes, my friend I'm afraid he is. I've been meaning to fix it, but there's a nail in that there kennel, that's sticking out, ya see? Every time he sits down in that there kennel, he sits on that there nail, and it's a real pain in the butt for the critter."

The traveller was shocked, and he said, "Well, surely he must know what's causing it then, so if he knows it's a pain in the butt, why doesn't he move, sit somewhere else, or do something different?"

"Well, my friend," continued the farmer, "it's really quite simple... That dog's been around folks so long, he's practically human. He's just like us really," continued the farmer. "You see the nail hurts just enough to give the big fella something to whimper and whine about. It just don't hurt quite badly enough for him to actually do anything about it!"

(The origin of this story is unknown, but I first heard it on stage from John Higgs c.1980)

The moral of the story: If something in your life is giving you a pain in the butt, and it's something about which you have the power to create a change, stop whingeing or feeling sorry for yourself, and take action!

If you think you can, you can! Do it now!

So often in our lives, we act just like that dog in his kennel. We whimper and whine to anyone who'll listen to our terrible problems, but in reality, if we just got off our butts and out of our comfort zone, we can take back the power to change our own lives and create our own destiny. Some of the main excuses people give is that they are too old, too tired, and too broke.

That's just baloney! You're never too old. I've been running a City to Surf twelve kilometre run, thinking I'm doing all right for an old middle-aged git. Then I look around and see someone about ninety years old, overtaking me! (Well, not *just* me – I'm not *that* slow!) Tiredness? We all feel that in today's hectic world, but it's amazing how when you set your mind on achieving something and start to take action, the tiredness disappears! I've played sports, and there were days when I didn't feel like training. I was too tired from work. I also found that when I kicked my own butt out through the front door to go and kick those footballs around, I came home feeling fantastic!

If you've been howling and whimpering, you've probably been 'barking up the wrong tree!' That's the kind of work I do for my coaching clients – helping them find the right tree! You *can* make things change. Sometimes you just need to ask yourself some better questions about what you really want and why!

 Which things have you found yourself complaining about on a regular place? What are you planning to do about that?

If You Want to Live Longer, Go on More Holidays!

My whole philosophy about 'Living the Dream' is based on my own practical experience of improving my own life and helping my friends, family and clients to improve theirs. Now this might seem glaringly obvious, but it's nice when you read about scientific research that backs up something you've been espousing for a while. I was glancing at an article on the E-Travel Blackboard website and here was proof that my philosophy stands up to scrutiny. It's all about work/life balance and loving what you do.

"It is a theory long thought true: that taking a holiday was good for your physical and mental well-being. Now, this hypothesis has been backed up by scientific evidence. According to a study conducted by tour operator Kuoni and Nuffield Health, the UK's largest healthcare charity, holidays contribute to lower blood pressure, improved sleep quality and better stress management – all significant factors in helping people live longer. Setting out to establish whether the 'feel good factor' generated by vacations was based on physical and scientific fact, the 'Holiday Health Experiment' also found that the positive effects of taking a break continued for at least two weeks after returning home.

Participants of the study were split into travel and non-travel groups, with the travelling group sent on vacation to Thailand, Peru or the Maldives and the other group ordered to stay at home and continue working; they then underwent before and after stress-resilience testing, psychotherapeutic examinations and full health assessments.

Among its key findings, the study found that the blood pressure of holidaymakers dropped by six percent over the test period, while the blood pressure of the non-vacationers went up by two percent. The study also revealed that holidaymakers saw a seventeen percent improvement in sleep quality, with non-vacationers experiencing a decline of 14 percent in sleep quality. Additionally, the stress resistance among vacationers rose by twenty-nine percent, compared to a seventy-one percent fall in the scores of the non-holiday makers.

Talking to the results of the stress tests, Nuffield Health Medical Director (Wellbeing) Dr. Lucy Goundry said, 'The results clearly demonstrate that on holiday our resilience to stress improves. Becoming more resilient to stress is hugely important as most of us will return back to stress when our holiday ends but being more resilient to it helps lay the foundations for improved productivity at work, better energy levels and ultimately happiness.'"

Source: http://www.etravelblackboard.com/article/139811

What Else Would Motivate YOU?

I gave you that article because I like to add weight to my contention that holidays are very important. Now, I know you might say that not everyone likes holidays or travelling, and that's fine too. I probably developed a travel addiction as a child, because with my dad working for British Airways, we used to enjoy discounted flights, so we went on plenty of holidays. Also, as my mum's family were based around Chester, we would quite often fly up to Manchester from Jersey to go and visit.

As I like to say, our family has aviation fuel in our blood, so we've all had that fascination for visiting other countries and seeing different cultures for ourselves. When I was at primary school, I can remember our teacher giving us school projects to do that involved us researching and writing about countries around the world. We used to frequent travel agencies to obtain travel brochures of places all over the globe. We'd then cut out pictures of tourism icons, elephants, lions, Eskimos, Zulu tribes, anything else you could imagine, and we'd paste them into our scrapbooks, along with our childlike observations of that country. I don't know if teachers still do that today, but it stuck in my memory and fuelled my desire to one day see those places for real. Today, I use a similar principle, along with many other coaches I'm sure, as a motivational tool with my clients.

I recommend that you have a board on the wall somewhere in your house or your office, preferably in an area that you look at frequently. We call this a 'vision board'. On that board, you display pictures of all of the dreams you would like to make come true. Every person's board will be different and unique to you. If your interest is in travel, then think about where exactly you want to go and find some pictures of the place. If your interest and desire is for a new car, then get a picture of that car and put it on the board. If you want to learn to fly, put a picture up there of a light aircraft. You get the idea! Now there are a couple of other things to do here.

If you really want these dreams to come true, be brave enough to put a date next to the pictures of when you will achieve these goals. Notice I didn't say, when you 'hope' to achieve these goals; I said, when you *'will'*. Okay, so here we are setting some goals, and this is where people often get flaky!

Let's quickly look at an acronym that will help you when you are setting your goals. Goals need to be set in accordance with the following formula. If you do all of the below, you will significantly increase your chances of success. Another thing though, once you have put up your board, you must remember to look at it often and keep reminding yourself of how good it will feel when you achieve those goals. I don't know who created the original 'SMART' acronym for it has been used in coaching circles for a long time by many people, but the 'SMARTS' variation was first shown to me by NLP trainer, George Faddoul.

THE 'SMARTS' FORMULA

Goals have a far higher chance of success if they meet the following criteria:

S *Specific (not vague) but preferably simple (uncomplicated)*

M *Measureable and meaningful to you*

A *Attainable, with affirmations 'as if already achieved'*

R *Realistic (no two minute mile runs yet). Give reasons why.*

T *Timed (towards what you want and when by)*

S *Steps required – break big goals down into chunks*

George Faddoul

I can say with complete confidence, because I have done it many times myself, that this process of 'Creative Visualisation' works, if you follow the instructions above and take the necessary action towards achieving your goals.

When I was seventeen, I really wanted a new motorbike. I visited bike shops, did my research and decided upon a Yamaha RD 250cc model. I asked for a copy of the brochure, picked one in the colours I wanted, white with red trims and I found out the price. I looked at that brochure often and I saved my money. I had a little 50cc bike since I had turned sixteen and now it was time for me to get a bigger bike – a 250cc was the biggest we were allowed to ride at that age. I was going to enjoy riding it and feeling like I was a king of the road. Sure enough, I saved up the money and brought myself a brand new bike, within only a few months, even earlier than planned. I was on a high and felt very proud of my achievement.

One more tip, from an NLP perspective, is that you should ideally position your board, up and to the right of where you frequently sit. In my case, it's on my office wall to the right of my desk. The reason for this is that in the majority of cases that is where your eyes travel to when your mind is visualising things in the future. The positioning of your pupils in that direction allows light to refract to the part of your brain that deals with future creation. Some people are wired the opposite way. You can soon find out by having someone ask you some questions that are future time-framed, as well as asking you some that require you to remember the past. For those people whose future is on the left, put the board on the left.

If you have a partner who absolutely refuses to let you put up a board, you could always use the front of your fridge and some magnets. Or at the very least have a scrapbook and look at it every day. The beauty of having it on the wall though is that your peripheral vision will keep instilling those pictures in your sub-conscious mind without you even realising.

The whole process is the same thing that an Olympic gold medallist would do to help them win the race; they creatively visualise themselves crossing the line first in their mind's eye, months before the race even begins. They then build that vision into a burning desire. They see it; they hear the crowd; they smell the flowers on the rostrum; they imagine touching the medal around their neck; they taste the champagne or the sweet taste of success; and lastly, they act as if they already are a gold medallist. You can see now though why 'motivation alone is not enough'.

> *"Motivation alone is not enough. If you have an idiot and you motivate him, now you have a motivated idiot."*
>
> **Jim Rohn**

The other key ingredients are changing your philosophy – the way you think about things; and movement or action, away from the source of your pain and towards the source of your pleasure.

Motivational Mementos

- Don't whinge about things that make you unhappy – do something to change it.
- Realise that if someone else can do a thing, you probably can too. At the same time, don't be disheartened if an eighty-year-old can run further than you. They just might be a retired professional athlete. Focus instead on constantly improving yourself.
- Allocate time to recharge your batteries. You'll return being more effective.
- Set up a vision board of all your dreams – it WILL increase your chances of making them happen.
- Involve all the senses in imagining your dreams coming true.
- If you are in the process of achieving your dreams and goals, you are 'doing life well', and as you progressively complete them, you will feel fulfillment. At the same time, you will realise that it is vitally important to keep on setting new ones.

13

Life Is About Movement

"An ounce of action is worth a ton of theory."

Ralph Waldo Emerson

So, remember the story of the little boy, sitting alone in his comfy armchair, waiting for the old television set to warm up, while his nanny has gone downstairs to the kitchen to make his snack? The wisps of smoke began to increase, and there was that horrible smell of something singeing. The boy had been told to stay there and wait for his nanny to return, but despite his tender years, he had enough common sense to realise that this may be a situation that might allow for a deviation from his normally obedient behaviour.

Something's not right here! thought the little lad. He jumped out of his chair, opened the door, and ran down three flights of stairs to the ground floor as fast as his little legs would carry him. At the precise moment that the boy reached the bottom of the stairs in the hotel hallway, the front door opened and in walked his mother.

"Mummy, Mummy, there's all smoke coming out of my room!" he yelled, breathlessly.

"Quick, Brian, go and check his room!" blurted the mother to her daughter's boyfriend, who also doubled as the assistant manager of the hotel. He had also fortunately entered the hallway at a fortuitous moment, and he ran upstairs, quickly followed by the boy's father. They arrived at the room to discover that the plug that the little boy had plugged in and switched on was in fact nothing to do with the television, but belonged to a heater that happened to have been left under the bed when not in use. The heater, in a confined space, had warmed the mattress to the point where it had begun to singe.

The two men quickly grabbed the mattress, and thinking quickly, they took it to the window on the landing. They opened the window and rather than carry the smouldering fire hazard down three flights of stairs, they threw the mattress out of the window and down into the courtyard below. I'm guessing that they shouted a warning to make sure it didn't land on anyone! As the mattress hit the ground with a thud, it burst into flames. That little boy - you've guessed it I'm sure, was me.

The story has been recounted by my mother so many times. It has gone into family folklore, but the fact remains that had I done as I was told and stayed in that room for very much longer, not only might the whole hotel have caught on fire, but I might have perished in the blaze.

I learned a lesson that day at a very young age, which was that sometimes you need to act on instinct. Sometimes you need to recognise that a situation needs to be changed, and that if you don't do something to change it, there will be consequences.

I remember actually being more concerned that my mother was going to give me a hiding for (a) not staying in the room as my nanny had told me to, plus (b) nearly burning down their whole business! To my surprise, she was instead very pleased, proud and certainly relieved that I had used my initiative, so the expected smack never arrived!

There was another lesson: Sometimes you can let your fears get in the way and allow them to paralyse you into inaction. We'll talk about fear a little further on. I am of course very happy that I found the motivation to change my situation that day, and perhaps that's where I began to develop my trait of calmness under pressure, in that smoke-filled room.

> *"It is not the strongest of the species that survive, nor the most intelligent, but the one most responsive to change."*
> **Charles Darwin**

 Where there's smoke there's fire, so get moving! Where in your life do you need to get things moving?

14

Managing Change and Habits

"A real decision is measured by the fact that you've taken a new action. If there's no action, you haven't truly decided."

Tony Robbins

If you agree that 'Life is worth doing well', then one thing I would whole-heartedly recommend is to work on looking at the concept of change as a good thing. Many people look at it is a scary thing. That's because we humans are very attached to this thing we call a 'comfort zone'. Maybe that goes right back to feeling cosy and safe in the cave or maybe it's a throwback to life in the womb, yet the one thing nature shows us time and again is the need to embrace change, to keep moving, or you will perish at the hands of a bigger,stronger or faster creature and become part of the food chain.

The real magic happens outside your comfort zone.

That's because it's when you are stretched beyond the limits you previously thought possible, that you discover you were in fact always capable of more.

Everything Flows

Firstly, once you have considered the contents of this book, let me wish you the best year of your life so far, along with a few comments about the 'challenges' ahead. In our hectic world where change is the only constant, it is important that we seek out and embrace change as a positive thing, when it is sometimes easy to fall into the trap of being fearful about what might go wrong.

> *"Everything flows, nothing stands still."*
> **Heraclitus of Ephesus**

Think back to 'that person' you were and 'where' you were a year ago, or five years ago, and you will realise that you have already changed. It is inevitable because we constantly face new obstacles and we are constantly offered new opportunities. In many cases the opportunities appear, disguised as obstacles or problems.

The crucial thing is to create some time and space to think and to plan. Dream about the things you want to attract into your life and don't forget to dream 'big' because dreams have no limits. The only limits we really have are the ones we place on ourselves as a result of our own conditioning. Figure out what it is that you need to *do*; figure out how you will become the person you need to *be* in order to *have* the things that you want; and you *make them happen*. Most importantly, then, is to write them down. The act of writing the goals and putting a date by which you will achieve them helps you to make them real and credible to your conscious mind. Break the goals down into manageable chunks and think of some small rewards you can give yourself as you hit the progress targets. Read them out loud to yourself regularly – psychological research has proven that this makes your mind begin to believe that you *can* do it.

Here's an example: A friend of mine wants to lose fifteen kilos in weight – a daunting task and one with which many people in the Western World will start their New Year. Focussing on losing a kilo a week is far more likely to be achieved, perhaps rewarding yourself with a candy bar when you have lost three kilos or waiting until the weekend to have one as a small reward. She has a longer term picture of fitting into a certain dress size by a certain date, so the big picture is there for her to repeatedly visualise. Another crucial element though is emotion, because how we feel is a fickle thing.

By focusing positive emotions on just how great she *will* feel when she is wearing her small dress, how sexy she *will* look, and how much more confident she *will* be, will help her to conquer those days when the spirit may be willing but the conscious will is weak. Knowing and constantly reminding yourself why you want to achieve your goals is the thing that will make you or break you. It's never too late or too early. You're never too old or too young, too bright or too stupid… to go after the things you want for your life and to make them happen.

If you were to set a goal for this year, in a year's time you will still be a year older, whether you did achieve the goal or whether you didn't.

New Year's Resolutions and Why They're Dumb!

I thought I'd better add something to the previous section on the specific topic of the resolutions that people often make at the end of December each year. My research has shown that very few people actually make New Year's Resolutions in the first place, but of those who do, even fewer actually stick to them for more than a few days. If you manage to go the whole of January staying true to your new goal, then you are in an elite group. So why is this so?

Well, just like the 'howling dog' story I told you earlier, most people actually can't be bothered. They may whinge and whine, but they won't make a decision to change. Of those who do decide, they very often make it an unrealistic goal. If you refer back to the SMARTS formula I gave you before, you will see that people make unrealistic demands on themselves. They don't come up with a plan, and they frequently fail to get into action. I'm calling this my DUMB formula.

'D' is for the fact that they Don't focus enough on the Desired result. It also stands for the Determination that they lack. When they have a bad day, instead of accepting that and starting again the next day, they give up and justify their decision that it wasn't really that important to them in the first place.

'U' stands for the fact that they are Unwilling to do whatever it takes. It's important when you want to change something that you develop a plan, give yourself as many support tools as you can, enlist the help of others, and focus on the result that you want, with frequent reminders of how you will feel once you have achieved your result. There seems to be a magic around the thirty-day mark when it comes to setting new habits, whether it's quitting smoking, drinking tea without sugar, going to the gym, or losing weight. If you can get through that first thirty days by getting into a new pattern, it really helps you form the new belief. Here are a couple of observations, however, from what I have learned in studying human behaviour.

Self-talk is extremely important. We discussed this previously in general, but here's something specific on the topic of resolutions. Change your terminology. Instead of making a resolution to 'give up' smoking, make a resolution to 'regain your health' by exercising instead of smoking and by adding something tangible like climbing some stairs without feeling breathless. Instead of 'giving up' chocolate to get rid of that belly and lose weight, make a resolution to fit into some old clothes by making healthier eating choices. Nobody likes giving things up, because psychologically, it feels like we are missing out on something nice. Conversely, we all like to gain something beneficial to us, like improved health, a better physique, and so on.

Remember to always maintain a forward focus. This means keep your eye on the goal ahead, not on the previous standard. This explains the classic yo-yo pattern with weight loss, for example. You one day look in the mirror in horror and you decide that 'enough is enough', and you start a weight loss programme. As you start to lose the weight, usually about five to ten kilos, you look in the mirror and think, *Hey, I look and feel much better*. Now, as the dislike of your poor shape lessens, so does your motivation to keep on doing what is required. That's also when the Universe has this funny way of testing you to see if you were serious or not. You visit your mother, and she hands you a piece of chocolate cake, saying "A little bit won't harm you." That's where you become vulnerable because you lose your momentum.

Weight management counsellors know this, so they sensibly allow you to indulge in some luxury items, but you still keep an eye on the calorie count and cut back something else to compensate. Some programmes even allow you one 'binge' day, where you can have what you want, but the next day, you get back to your disciplined routine. They also take body measurements so that you are not disheartened by a minor weight blip. It's sometimes possible to gain a few pounds when you replace fat with muscle or to have a gain caused by fluid levels.

So, the next part of DUMB is the 'M' is for Momentum and Measurement. The key is to maintain momentum and keep it going until you hit the target. Then it's important to set a new target, even if that target is a maintenance target, such as, "Now that I've hit my target weight, I will continue doing what has worked and I will monitor my weight or the clothes that fit me. As soon as I notice an upward reversal, I will take immediate action to keep it on track." Another key point from the perspective of a behavioural scientist is to change the way you associate to things.

> *"If you change the way you look at things, the things you look at change."*
>
> **Dr. Wayne Dyer**

'B' is for Binding things together. If you can associate pain instead of pleasure with things like smoking or over-eating, your ability to stick with your resolution is significantly improved. That's an area where I would do some Neuro Linguistic Patterning exercises with my clients, to put a new image or a new belief in their minds when they want to form a new habit. If you believe that smoking doesn't really do you any harm and you enjoy it, when you try to 'quit' or 'give it up', you feel like you are missing out on your pleasure.

If you instead associate the pain of missing out on your children growing up because your lungs are filled with tar and you are dying young, the pain of that image makes the cigarette less attractive. Don't focus on that image though or you may attract it! Instead picture yourself, older but happier and healthier, playing with your grandchildren, because you chose to be a non-smoker and thus a healthy person. Unfortunately with smoking, there is the extra difficulty that the nicotine is addictive, but so too are sugar, salt and some fats. That's why it's so important to get all the help you can from your friends and family, to go public with your resolutions, and to have people hold you accountable. Above all, it's crucial to keep your focus on the benefits you will gain from sticking the new patterns required to achieve your desired results.

One example from my youth relates to weight gain. Two of my friends and I had put on weight over the festive period, so we made a bet and made our weight reduction into a competition. We had a weigh-in on January 1st and again on the 31st. We all lost over six kilos because we didn't want to be the one to lose. Consequently, we all won, because we all got back into shape after the Christmas over-eating period. It's important to learn from what doesn't work as much as what does, so watch out for instances where you have fallen into using the 'DUMB' formula.

	My DUMB formula for Not Achieving Your Goals
D	Don't focus on Desired results. Not Determined enough
U	Unwilling to do what it takes
M	Don't gain Momentum. Fail to Measure progress.
B	Don't Bind or associate the goal with something important – the reason why.

Forming More Empowering Habits

Very often we find that the habits we don't want are linked or associated with certain triggers. For example, if you sit down to watch a movie and you consistently feel the urge to start eating popcorn and chocolate, this may because psychologically you have linked the two actions of watching and eating. So why do we do this?

There may be many reasons, but it is largely because we are creatures of habit or rituals. It may be that every time you went out to the cinema as a child, you associated movie with sugary or 'comfort' foods. These types of foods are often also linked with boredom, depression, anxiety, or as some kind of barrier against being hurt emotionally, such as when a relationship has ended.

What then happens is that the 'sugar fix' makes you feel good temporarily, so you associate that food with pleasure. Before you know it, every time you watch a movie, you are stuffing your face because that's what you always do! This may become such a habit that it continues long after the initial cause has become redundant. Six months later you have gained a load of weight and can't think why. After all, you always eat chocolate with a movie!

This doesn't just apply to weight gain; it applies to all areas of life and all kinds of behaviours that have become habitual responses to certain triggers. Someone sends you an email, so you end up surfing the net for an hour and chatting on social media. Someone cuts you off in traffic, so you become abusive and exhibit road rage! Your new boyfriend/girlfriend doesn't answer your text message, so you assume he or she is cheating on you or no longer cares about you, so you send them an abusive text message or, worse still, break off the relationship.

If you step back and look at what's going on or ask your friends or, better still, a coach, for examples of your patterned responses, you may have some surprise realisations. Just be careful if asking your friends, though, because you have to be willing to choose not to be offended if they say something you don't like.

So how do you change when you realise you are behaving in a disempowering way? The key thing is to notice the trigger. If you sit down to watch a movie and you want chocolate, then you have to substitute something else. Perhaps start with a small bowl of popcorn because that's less fattening. Better still, create a healthy snack if you absolutely have to eat something. Consult your dietician on that one! The important thing is to replace the unwanted response with a better response. If you can then maintain doing that for a reasonable period, you will soon have swapped a bad habit for a better one.

What constitutes a reasonable period?

A psychologist recently told me that it depends on how long you have persisted with the old habit. As a rule of thumb, it's usually between fourteen to thirty days. A great example is drinking tea without sugar. If you take sugar, tea tastes awful without out it, but if you can drink tea for thirty days without sugar, you will then find that if someone does add sugar to your tea, it tastes horribly sweet and you will probably struggle to drink it. So a key to changing habits is to identify the trigger, create a new response that leads to the outcome you want, and repeat it til it becomes the new habit. In conclusion then, you will achieve best results if you follow the 'SMARTS' formula and not the 'DUMB' formula. Focus on the desired result, and take massive action to build momentum according to your priorities.

Change Consolidators

- Make a decision to change; become real by taking immediate action.

- Use the 'SMARTS' formula to increase your chances of success. Don't use the 'DUMB' formula!

- Take massive action to build momentum.

- If you have a blip, don't give up. Accept that you are human and start again. The best laid plans rarely go perfectly.

- Change your association with the unwanted habit from pleasure to pain.

- Build and focus upon the benefits you will gain from the new result.

- Enlist all the help you can get – stack the odds in your favour!

- Use the power of creative visualisation to see yourself already having achieved the goal in your mind's eye. If you can imagine it and believe it, you can do it.

- Never beat yourself up for not changing yet. In a spiritual sense, you are already perfect because you are already 'what' or 'who' you are meant to be. The change will occur when you are ready for it to occur.

- Identify triggers that typically elicit a habitual response from you; decide on a more empowering response; and discipline yourself to repeat the new response until you form a new and better habit.

- Choose 'SMARTS' over 'DUMB', and you are more likely to 'do life well'. Knowing that you have changed and evolved will increase your sense of fulfillment.

15

'Carpe Diem' – Seize the Day

"Success is getting what you want; Happiness is wanting what you get."

Dale Carnegie

'Carpe Diem' is taken from a Latin poem by a man known as Horace. The literal translation of it is 'Pluck the day!' or, 'Enjoy the day!' It's a philosophy that I hold dear – to always look for the golden moments that come along each day and that can so easily pass unnoticed. One of the little gems that my coach, Vanessa Dichiera, passed on to me was to keep a 'happiness or gratitude' jar on my desk and to regularly pop into it little notes about the small things that have made me happy or for which I am grateful. I don't always remember to do it daily, so sometimes, I'll write several little notes at once so that it should average one a day. At the end of the year, I can pull out all of these notes and remind myself about all of the wonderful, fulfilling things for which I can feel truly blessed.

Moments of Significance

One night, as I often do, I found myself working til about three a.m. because I wanted to finish something that was of importance to my business and that was essential for my clients. I was also enjoying it. The reason behind why I was left burning the midnight oil was clear to me and ever so valid.

Throughout the day, during the time that I had actually allocated for working on my business, my family had quite simply come first. In the morning I had dropped off my partner, Jo, at her mum's house, who was entertaining Jo's brother, sister-in-law, and two-year-old niece, Madison, who were visiting from Canberra for the festive period. They were off to the Aquarium for the afternoon as little Maddy (as the family calls her and spells it) is obsessed with 'little fishies', thanks to a certain movie about a guy named Nemo. Maddy also appears to idolise Auntie Jo, which I have no doubt is because Auntie Jo makes it obvious that she idolises her cute little niece. Having recently visited both the Sydney and Melbourne aquariums with said family, I figured that I really needed to catch up on my burgeoning, though self-directed workload. As I returned home alone, I made myself a protein shake (part of my health programme!), turned on my computer, and prepared myself to tackle the backlog of 'stuff to do'… That's when my daughter called.

"Dad, what are you up to?" she began.

I explained how I had opened up this window of opportunity so I could catch up on my work, waffling on in great detail in workaholic fashion. Then suddenly, "Why?" became the more obvious answer.

"Craig (my then twenty five-year-old son), Hayden (my then six-month-old grandson) and I (Kim, my then twenty two-year-old daughter) want to come over for a swim."

So that was game, set and match, wasn't it? 'Abracadabra' is an old Aramaic saying, meaning 'Created as I say it'. Hence its application to magic stage tricks. Well, before you could say 'Abracadabra', I had my own moments of magic.

When they arrived, Craig asked for sun cream to be rubbed on his back as he's a 'ranga' (redhead) like me and somewhat vulnerable to the sun's ultra violet. Kim thought it was hilarious to leave him with two large handprints of cream on his back. Probably to most readers it wouldn't seem that funny, but it was one of those 'you had to be there' moments. Luckily for me, I was.

The next moment, I was in the pool lifting my gorgeous grandson into his swim ring chair, watching his beaming smile as his little legs kicked like crazy beneath the surface, like a duck on steroids. It didn't even bother me when my son's dog, who had been left inside as she is not allowed in the strata swimming pool, decided to lift the edge of my lounge carpet and chew the underlay in protest.

A while later, I watched as my son, with his beer in a stubby holder(a true Aussie) hosed down his very hot dog, Roxy, while she tried desperately to bite the water as it came out of the hose. Meanwhile, little Hayden was managing to smear chocolate over the couch, his Mum, up his nose… in fact, just about everywhere

– some even found its way into his mouth! Needless to say, my work was put on hold til they left.

Later that afternoon, as I tried to complete a project, I had to abandon it to drive back up to Hillarys Marina and meet Jo and the clan for dinner at Jo's mum's favourite restaurant. This had been their first Christmas since losing Jo's dad to his battle with cancer, and the sense of a need for family unity was tangible. I watched little Maddy shrieking and giggling with delight as she sat in a playground boat with Auntie Jo and Cousin Troy, while her daddy jumped up and down to rock the boat from astern. I realised that this had been another significant moment in a day filled with significant moments. It is such moments that will be remembered and reminisced over, for years to come by those involved.

Jo stayed over at her mum's house so that she could enjoy breakfast with her niece (Only geography limits these opportunities. They live in Tasmania, and we live in Perth). I returned home to fit in the work I wanted to complete for my clients. When Jo's phone call awakened me the next morning, I was dreaming a strange dream. Rarely do I remember them, but this one had to do with realising that once you die, many of the things, the 'stuff', the valued possessions that seem so important to you now, will be divided up, burnt or thrown away by other people to whom they mean nothing. I thought about our Christmas day family breakfast and how my brother, Peter, had made the effort to fly over from England specially to catch up with our parents, particularly our father, who had been at death's door many times that year, yet was still fighting on. Thankfully, we had those final moments with him.

I'm glad that I could be true to my work ethic and my clients as I completed my tasks that night, but I am delighted that I made the time and space in my life for some far more significant moments. I hope that perhaps as you read this little story, you may consider doing the same and that the years ahead will become filled with 'significant moments' for us all. I love the work that I do. I love where and how I live. I love my family and friends. I'm a lucky man.

> "The first trick to happiness – and success – is to appreciate what we've already got."
>
> **Andrew Matthews**

Here is another quote that I believe sums up very nicely some of the priorities that we might want to consider, so that we make the best of our lives.

> *"Take time to think – it is the source of power.*
>
> *Take time to play – it is the secret of perpetual youth.*
>
> *Take time to read – it is the fountain of wisdom.*
>
> *Take time to love and be loved – it is a privilege.*
>
> *Take time to laugh – it is the music of the soul.*
>
> *Take time to give – it is too short a day to be selfish.*
>
> *Take time to work – it is the price of success."*
>
> **Anon.**

Rhetorical Reflections

- The things that are significant to you may be unique to you because everyone views the world slightly differently, and everyone prioritises the things that they value the most.

- Take time to reflect on what is really important to you – it may not always be the things that you previously thought were the highest priority.

- Ask yourself, "If I knew this was my last day on this planet, would I attach such significance to these so-called 'priorities', or would I take a moment to tell someone how much I loved and valued them?"

- As far as we know, we only have one physical life in our current human forms, so once someone leaves this plane, we lose that physical connection. That's why it's important to make the time count with our loved ones. Cherish those moments as that's part of 'doing life well'.

16

Be Alert to Opportunity

"To hell with circumstances; I create opportunities."

Bruce Lee

Following on from talking about seizing the day, I believe it's just as important to be on the look-out for those golden moments of opportunity. Just like those moments of significance that I mentioned, these golden moments can and are, often easily missed by people. I'm sure that, just like me, you will look back on certain things in your life and say, "I thought about doing/was going to do/or nearly did… whatever, but I didn't." Usually, someone else did!

It might be buying a block of land that was literally 'dirt cheap', taking a job offer, or going on a holiday. You may even recall numerous things that I call the 'shoulda, woulda, coulda's…'. Whatever it was, get over yourself and let it go, because there was a reason why you didn't do it and that reason made sense to you at the time. The reason someone else *did* do it was because it made sense to them to seize that opportunity at that time.

Maybe it's a spiritual belief, but I think that whatever you *did* decide to do instead was exactly the thing that you were *meant* to do. Whatever you feel that you may have missed out on was, in fact, present in your life in some other form. Now let me just elaborate, because you might say, "How can that be? If I didn't buy the block of land, I didn't get another block of land, so that doesn't make sense!" Perhaps not, but it may be that the lesson you were meant to learn was not about the land itself, but about the feeling of owning something significant or about you taking decisive action that would increase your wealth. In other words, it may have been about the energy involved or the teaching you were meant to absorb, rather than the actual object itself.

In my opinion though, life throws opportunities our way all the time, and many of them just blow past us like tumbleweed in a Western movie. So, what I'm saying here is that if you miss that opportunity, another similar one may appear at another time, when you are more ready to embrace it. It's like the old adage, "When the student is ready, the teacher will appear." Nevertheless, some people seem to grab every opportunity and propel themselves to greatness.

 What if you were one of those people who is destined for greatness and the only thing stopping you, is YOU?"

Maybe the reason you are reading this book right now is so that you can awaken that part of you that is just waiting for you to embrace your greatness.

Broadening My Horizons

Here's a quick account of a golden moment in my life that gave me a lot of confidence to do other things in my life.

After over two hours on my own, suspended in the tiny Cessna 152 training aircraft, navigating my way by comparing my map with what I could see over the fields and railway lines of Normandy in North-western France, I was filled with nervous excitement when I finally spotted an airfield in the distance. That airfield was Rennes airport, and I had never seen it from the air or landed there before. It was a defining moment in my life, because this was one of the final stages of gaining my private pilot's licence – a solo cross country flight, landing at the French airfields of Rennes and Dinard, before returning back across the sea to my home base of Jersey – the largest of the English Channel Islands.

For a nineteen year old, I was quite mature and confident. In that same year, I was promoted to a deputy store manager in a supermarket with twenty-three staff members. That was one thing, but flying solo at 2,000 feet over the English Channel, map-reading my way down the French Coast and finding an unfamiliar airstrip was quite another test of self-reliance altogether.

I contacted Rennes Air Traffic Control and was cleared to descend and join the circuit. Although I was still a student pilot, my training had been thorough, and I had picked things up quickly, owing to a lifetime of affinity with aviation. In fact, I had 'gone solo' one fine but grey afternoon a few weeks earlier, on the tiny grass airstrip at Lessay, after just nine hours of training.

Flying solo for the first time had been another truly life-defining moment for me – that heart-pounding instant when your instructor says, "When you land this time, pull over on the side of the runway but keep the engine running." Then, said my flying instructor, John Pedley, "Ok mate, you're ready. Just do one circuit, request a full stop this time, park it over there, and I'll see you in the bar. Enjoy yourself."

I grew up with a fascination for aircraft. My father had joined the Air Force as a mechanical apprentice at fifteen and was fixing Spitfires on Malta, Sicily and in Egypt during the War, before a lengthy career as an aircraft engineer for British Airways in Jersey. My eldest brother became a commercial helicopter pilot, having served with the Army Air Corps, and my sister was a stewardess, also for British Airways. No wonder I loved assembling and painting model aircraft kits as a child.

When I was seventeen, Dad landed me a summer holiday job at a small airline that he had joined while in semi-retirement, called Intra Airways. I had the joyful job of cleaning the aircraft on the turnaround between flights. I had felt important, driving support vehicles across the airport apron, putting locking pins in the undercarriage of the old Dakota DC 3's, wiping oil off the engine cowlings, and directing passengers which way to walk to the terminal building. The downside was in having to empty the bucket from the chemical toilet, but even that unsavoury task did not diminish the joy of working with my father and being 'one of the guys' at Jersey airport. It also made me realise that menial jobs had to be done by someone, and nobody could ever accuse me of asking them to do something demeaning or that I would not be willing do myself if necessary.

So, on that July day in 1980, as I joined the downwind leg of the Rennes circuit and began my pre-landing checks, with my hands on the controls, I felt literally as free as a bird. I think I had goose bumps as the tower controller said, "Golf Romeo November – you are cleared to final." Before I knew it, I was cleared to land. The tyres greased smoothly onto the bitumen, and I taxied my plane to a parking spot in front of the control tower. As I turned off the engine, I actually threw my hands in the air and yelled, "YESSSSS!" at the top of my voice.

I think it was a little from nervous relief as it was from exhilaration. The concentration had been intense, realising that the only person I could count on to find that airfield and bring that plane down safely was me. I had to have my log book stamped by customs officers to prove I had been there, before flying on to Dinard, then back to Jersey. When I gained my wings at the Channel Islands Aero Club in Jersey that summer, I was immensely proud of my achievement.

When I reflect on it though, a large part of my pride stems from the fact that it represented the realisation of a huge dream come true. I had set the goal to obtain my private pilot's licence. I had researched what I needed to do. I had sought the finance required – I took out a two thousand pound bank loan (a lot of money back in 1979). I had enrolled in the course. I had studied the things I needed to study – navigation, meteorology, principles of flight, airframes and aero engines, air law, radio procedures, airfield procedures, flight planning and much more. I had made a commitment to myself, and I had seen it through, overcoming occasional fear and self-doubt, carried with the wind of desire and determination beneath my wings. As a metaphor for life in general, it was a great testament to the power of a dream. Sir Winston Churchill once remarked that, "Nothing can stop the totally committed will." I am a firm believer in his maxim.

> *If you decide that you really want something, and assuming that it fits with your ethical and moral values, then if you commit to its completion, and really apply yourself, you can overcome any obstacle, rise to any challenge and live the life of your dreams.*
>
> **Tony Inman**

We are blessed to live in a free country, surrounded by resources at our disposal if we will but look and ask. We live in a place where the seemingly impossible can be made to happen, and the difficult – well, that just serves to make the challenge worthwhile. So I hope that you have not given up on your dreams and settled for less because opportunity is all around us.

I recommend that you encourage others as you yourself would like to be encouraged because the power of a good support team is not to be underestimated. Rediscover the dreams and goals you may have filed in the 'too hard basket'. What if, just maybe, you could still do them? Great achievements begin with somebody's dream… *Do you still dare to dream?*

The Shoe Salesman

There's a timeless story about a shoe salesman, whose company one day decided to give him a new opportunity. They sent him to Africa to launch their new product range. He was very excited to have been chosen for such a promotion, but within a week of arrival, he was on the phone to his boss back home, sounding very dejected and disheartened. "Boss, I'm sorry, but you may as well bring me back home. This is a complete waste of my time and the company's money. No-one wears shoes in Africa!" The boss agreed to let him come home, as he didn't want unhappy staff.

He decided however, to give another of his salesman a try instead. Within a week, the second shoe salesman was on the phone to his boss, barely able to contain his excitement! "Boss, this is amazing! Quick – send me more shoes! Give me all the stock you've got! No-one wears shoes in Africa!"

The moral of the story is that we can all choose how we look at things in life. Some of us get bogged down in the problems and the obstacles. The go-getters also see the opportunity and the prize, so that's what they focus on. It's never too late to change your personal filters!

 Where in your life could you alter that focus and replace problems with opportunities?

Opportunistic Offerings

- Opportunity is all around us. However, if you're not looking for it or even open to the possibility that it exists, you may just miss it, and someone else will grab it.

- The more you build your dreams, the more opportunities will present themselves.

- Where one person sees disaster, another person sees opportunity.

- In Japanese, the words danger and crisis also mean opportunity!

- Be alert, and be ready! Your opportunity is often disguised as a problem or a misfortune.

- The more you become willing to seize opportunities despite any fears or reservations and run with them, the more you will find you are 'doing life well', and by becoming a person who is capable of achieving them, you will feel a sense of 'fulfillment'.

17

What if This Was Your Last Breath?

"Decisiveness is a characteristic of high-performing men and women. Almost any decision is better than no decision at all."

Brian Tracey

When I took over a Perth-based backpacker hostel business in 1996, a business I was to own for over fourteen years, we dealt with a lot of tour operators, including dive companies. Several of those dive companies offered me the chance to go diving for free, in the hope that by giving me that experience, I would book more customers on their tours. As a child, I used to go snorkelling with my father when on holiday in Majorca, and I remembered being fascinated by all the different, brightly coloured fish in the sea. I also used to enjoy surfing when I was a young bloke and had been taken down to Jersey's world-famous St. Ouen's beach by my father and my elder brother, Geoff, who has always been a surfing enthusiast.

I also remembered as a teenager reading Peter Benchley's gripping novel, *Jaws*, about a great white shark that developed the taste for human beings in an American coastal town. Maybe it was that story that pushed me over the edge, but I had always hated getting water in my eyes, even as a youngster in the school swimming pool. Anyway, somewhere along the way, I had become 'uneasy' about the ocean and had developed some kind of phobia about getting water in my eyes. When I discovered that part of the dive course would involve taking my mask off and putting it back on, underwater, that was enough to convince me not to do it. I would deflect the issue by blaming the sharks and saying, "I've got a pilot's licence, so I'd rather fly over the ocean than be in there with all those sharks." That fear caused me to miss out on a lot of experiences.

Then, in 2005, when I went on my adventure with my Swedish girlfriend, Vicky Bergkvist, and thanks to her, I had the amazing opportunity to snorkel with a whale shark – a beautiful, gentle, plankton-eating giant of the oceans, up in Exmouth. Part of that experience included the surprise of seeing one of the ship's crew shooing away what I could clearly see was a 'proper' sharp-toothed shark below us in the water. Of course, it was only a timid reef shark, but as far as I was concerned, with the limited knowledge I had at that time, it was still a proper shark!

When a four and a half metre, young whale shark finally appeared and I looked into the eye of that amazing creature, I felt a connection with nature like never before. There was a sort of soothing tranquillity about its effortless gliding through the water, and I felt as if it was reassuring me that everything would be okay. That experience made me fascinated with the oceans again, and that was step one. (I have since swum with a whale shark that was seven and a half metres long.)

Step two was when I visited an English girlfriend, Sarah Thompson, in Alice Springs, in August 2005, where she was doing a stint as a country doctor. Ridiculous as it now sounds, Sarah encouraged me to swim across the pool to her and open my eyes under water. There was a horrible moment as I squinted through one eye then the other, with slight stinging from the chlorine. My vision was obviously a bit blurry, but guess what? I survived the experience! My moment of triumph was quickly followed by self-chastisement and self-mockery. *You big girl's blouse!* I thought to myself. All that time, I had resisted something that seemed like a huge obstacle. In fact, it *had* been a huge obstacle, but only in my 'stupid' mind! That was a defining moment because I realised:

Many of our fears are in reality just an illusion created by our own minds.

We are created in fluid and born into the world in fluid. Our ancestors came from the oceans, and we have a natural affinity with the sea. So, in February 2006, we were on a family holiday on Rottnest Island, just off the coast of Perth, Western Australia. Sarah and I took my son, Craig, and my daughter, Kim, for a long weekend experience. I took Kim out snorkelling. She was sixteen and was terrified of the ocean. I held her hand in the crystal blue waters. We saw quite a few fish together – just as I had done with my father many years earlier. Kim liked seeing them. And she was proud of herself for making the effort. However, I'm sad to say that, at the time of writing this book, she is still nervous about both diving and flying.

The following day, Sarah, who was a keen scuba diver, announced that she would be going diving and suggested a trial dive for Craig and me. This was my moment – a massive turning point. Sarah went off with the other experienced divers, while Craig and I descended, accompanied by a watchful instructor. Kim stayed on deck to be chatted up by the crew! Craig and I had a blast, and I knew straight away that it was time to really confront that silly fear.

The next month, I was back at Rottnest Island doing my Open Water Dive Course. I had tackled the issue of taking the mask off in the swimming pool at the safe depth of about one metre. That was fortunate, because the first time I did it, I inhaled water up my nose like an idiot and very quickly shot to the surface! We were trained with absolute German efficiency, by the Schmidt brothers, Florian and Fabien, who made sure we were ready for the ocean.

So, in March 2006, I went on my first dive as a student in the ocean. We formed a circle around the instructor of the day and did various underwater drills. When it came to taking off the mask, I was in severe danger of soiling my wetsuit, but it was all over within a few seconds, and I thought, *That was surprisingly easy!* Then off we went for a look around some of the local underwater scenery in our buddy pairs. I was with a new friend, my Irish dive buddy, Colin Fitzgerald. The instructor checked our air first, and we had plenty.

As we passed through a 'swim-through', a sort of open cave, Colin signalled to me to check how much air we had left. I looked at my gauge, and I thought, *This must be a joke. Someone's played a trick on us!* Mine was in the red, meaning I had about thirty bars of air left. You are supposed to finish your dive with fifty bars left in the tank at the surface. I looked at Colin's gauge and he only had just under fifty bars left as well. What we didn't realise is that when you first start diving, most people breathe a bit heavier than normal, owing to nervousness, anxiety or poor dive skills that cause you to thrash about with your limbs a bit, rather than being relaxed and streamlined.

In that moment I was confronted with a horrible possibility. I was about to run out of air. I knew I could shoot to the surface, but as a new diver, I had no idea how long that would take and if I would make it. I couldn't share my buddy's air because he was low too. That realisation probably didn't help my rate of air consumption too much! I tapped the trainee dive master on the shoulder and showed her my gauge. It was her first dive as a trainee. It's hard to talk underwater, but I could easily see her horrified reaction.

She signalled us to stay put, and she quickly turned to go and grab the instructor who was on the other side of the swim-through, some distance away. As my mind began racing at high speed, I could not help but think, *What if this is it? What if my air runs out and this is about to be my last breath on this planet?*

I'll tell you what happened next in a minute, but first, I want to share with you some concepts that have an impact on all of our lives every day...

18

Harness the Power of Universal Laws

"Watch your thoughts, for they become words.
Watch your words, for they become actions.
Watch your actions, for they become habits.
Watch your habits for they become your character.
Watch your character, for it becomes your destiny."

Lao Tzu

I came across this list of the Seven Universal Laws several years ago and I thought people might find it thought-provoking, because these laws have been around for a very long time. In fact, we find that there is no such thing as 'New Truths' – there are only 'Old Truths' that have been presented in a different way! I don't even know where these actually originated because I have seen them on many websites, and nobody appears to have credited any individual for having written them. Perhaps, that's because they are 'Old Truths'.

The Law of Vibration and Attraction

- Everything vibrates; nothing rests.
- Conscious awareness of vibration is called feeling. Your thoughts control your paradigms and your vibration (which dictates what you attract).
- When you are not feeling good, become aware of what you are thinking, then think of something pleasant.

The Law of Perpetual Transmutation

- Energy moves into physical form.
- The images you hold in your mind most often materialize in results in your life.

The Law of Relativity

- Nothing is good or bad, big or small… until you *relate* it to something.
- Practice relating your situation to something much worse, and yours will always look good.

The Law of Polarity

- Everything has an opposite: hot - cold… up - down… good - bad.
- Constantly look for the good in people and situations. When you find it, tell the person. People love compliments, and the positive idea in your mind makes you feel good. Remember, good idea = good vibrations.

The Law of Rhythm

- The tide goes out… the tide comes in. Night follows day … good times - bad times. Life and business both ebb and flow.
- When you are on a down swing, do not feel bad. Know the swing will change, and things will get better. There are good times coming – focus on them instead.

The Law of Cause and Effect (AKA 'karma' or 'reaping and sowing')

- Whatever you send into the Universe comes back. Action and reaction are equal and opposite.
- Say good things to everyone; treat everyone with total respect, and it will all come back. Don't worry so much about what you are going to get, just concentrate on what you can give.

The Law of Gender

- Every seed has a gestation or incubation period. Ideas are spiritual seeds and will move into form or physical results once they have been nurtured and have had time to grow.
- Your goals will manifest when the time is right. KNOW that they will.

Some Bonus Laws:

The Law of Atrophy

- If you do nothing for very long, you won't just stay where you are, you'll actually go backwards! If you don't use a muscle, it will shrink. If you don't keep your brain active, it will decline. If you don't use skills and knowledge, you will forget.

The Law of Attraction (referred to in the book and movie *The Secret*).

- This is really a renamed version of the 'The Law of Perpetual Transmutation', except there is another part to making this work.
- Thinking about receiving a cheque for one million dollars will not make it appear, no matter how hard you visualise it – the catch is that you have to do some work or take some action as well!

I hope these 'Laws' make you think. They remind us that we can make good things happen in life and, certainly, that we all have the power to choose how we view events and how we will react to them.

Darwin's Law of Requisite Variety

Charles Darwin studied thousands of species on the way to evolving his theories on the *Origins of Man*. In the process, he made this fascinating discovery:

> *"It is not the strongest of the species that survives, nor the most intelligent that survives. It is the one that is most adaptable to change."*
>
> **Charles Darwin**

I generally seek to avoid using the word 'should'. This theory, however, is one of which we should all take note. It applies to us in business, and it applies to us in life. It is at the very core of humanity's existence on this planet, and it is true for the survival of every business venture and every human endeavour.

Understanding Our Universe

- Like it or not, we are all part of a bigger picture. Every 'part' of us affects our 'whole'. In turn, we affect our family and our community; our community affects our nation; our nation affects our world; and our world affects our universe.

- If you cannot change, evolve, grow, keep moving and keep learning, you will eventually fail or perish.

- Follow and apply the Universal Laws – they are the keys to wisdom

- Wisdom and the progress toward it is a key to 'doing life well'.

19

With Each New Breath

"Those who get the most out of life and those who give the most are those who make the choice to act."

Stephen R. Covey

Remember when I was wondering if I was about to take my last breath ever, during my first dive as a student off Rottnest Island…? I had just alerted my dive master that I was about to run out of air. She turned away and went to get the instructor, who was in charge of the dive. My first instinct was to follow her and get to the instructor more quickly; he would know what to do! In that moment though, as I pondered my possibly imminent drowning, the training kicked in.

As with flying, the thing that will save your life in an emergency is to keep calm. I remembered what my original instructor, Florian Schmidt, had taught me: "Stop. Think. Act." I stopped and considered the possibilities. If I followed her, I would be moving and using more air, thus causing me to run out more quickly. My considered action was, therefore, to hold my ground. I knew my buddy, Colin, had a bit more air than I did, though not really enough either. I looked across at the other students a few metres away. They were smaller guys, so their consumption rate would be less. I could share a few breaths off them. We could shoot straight to the surface, but I didn't know if we'd make it. Meanwhile, I focused on trying to slow my breathing and my heart rate.

All of those thoughts flashed across my mind in split seconds. In the next moment, the instructor appeared and signalled, "What's the problem?" I signalled with a cut throat sign and index finger and thumb that I was low on air. As he turned my air gauge to look at it, I felt the air in the tube coming to an end. There was a final suck in of a half breath, and I knew that was it. The dive student's worst nightmare: I had actually run out of air on my first dive!

I rapidly signalled that I was out, and the instructor quickly rammed his spare regulator in my mouth. I was now breathing from his air tank. We went to the surface, and everything turned out to be just fine – though I don't think his boss was overly happy! Nevertheless, I survived running out of air and was reminded of some valuable survival lessons that you can apply to both your life and your business…

Tony's Politically Incorrect Safety Briefing!

- **The Six P's That Will Help You Prevail: Proper Planning Prevents Piss Poor Performance!**
  Always be prepared with adequate training; with the right tools and equipment for the task in hand; with the right contingency plans; and with the right attitude.

- **Stop. Think. Act.**
  In emergency situations, never panic. A person who is panicking is not thinking clearly and is not going to make the right choices. Even though you may be missing the right equipment, if you are thinking clearly, you can explore other options and maybe improvise. If you do decide to panic, please do it somewhere else!

- **Save yourself first.**
  In aircraft safety briefings they tell you, "Put on your oxygen mask first, or you'll be no use to anyone." Of course, save other people too. I'm not saying run away and screw everybody else. I'm saying that you can only help people if you are firstly out of danger yourself. It's one of the main principles of first aid training for that very reason. If a guy is collapsed at work, having been shocked by an electric cable, you make sure it won't shock you too before you help him. Otherwise, there will be two people collapsed and needing help!

- **Learn to trust your instincts.**
  The highest achievers in the world become adept at trusting their own gut feelings. They make decisions quickly, and then turn those decisions into the right decisions. Sometimes you may get it wrong, but it's better than being paralysed with indecision. Sometimes the decision may be to not do anything yet. However, if that is a conscious decision, it is still a decision.

20

Marriage Is Not Necessarily a Life Sentence

"The real act of marriage takes place in the heart, not in the ballroom or church or synagogue. It's a choice you make – not just on your wedding day, but over and over again – and that choice is reflected in the way you treat your husband or wife."

Barbara de Angelis

The fabric of our society has changed vastly in the last century. Women's emancipation and subsequent rise have proven themselves equally as competent as men at developing their careers and earning their incomes independently of the need for a husband. This has changed the Western world. In many cases, women are the major bread-winners in the family, and many men are stay at home carers. A large number of women simply feel that they don't need a man at all.

Yet despite these changing times, there is still a place for the concepts of loyalty and commitment…

The Secret to 70 Years of Wedded Bliss

Many of us would think ourselves lucky to reach seventy years of age in good health, let alone be married for that long. Yet my parents, Bill and Vera Inman of Ellenbrook, Western Australia however, did manage to achieve exactly that incredible milestone in September 2011. There were many times however, in the previous few years when this celebration appeared unlikely to take place.

My father had a fall at the age of eighty-eight, whilst holidaying in Busselton, and he suffered multiple facial fractures and suspected nerve damage that necessitated an emergency flight up to Royal Perth Hospital. I was horrified at the extent of my father's injuries. When I went to the hospital, I could barely recognise him; the bruising and swelling was so severe. The doctors didn't think he'd pull through. Prior to that fateful accident, he was still independent – driving himself to the shops, the bank, and all their medical appointments. It's amazing to think that he survived all the bombings in Malta during the War, but a simple fall could have such dramatic consequences.

My father, who hailed from Cheadle Hulme, Manchester, in the North of England, joined the Royal Air Force at the age of fifteen, and after serving his apprenticeship as a fitter, he married his sweetheart, Vera Wheeler from Chester. Their romance was interrupted by the Second World War though, and he was soon posted to serve in Malta as an engineer, fixing the fighter aircraft, the Hurricanes and Spitfires.

By nineteen, he was an acting flight sergeant, who survived near starvation and meningitis. He even came through polio later on in life. Dad used to tell us as children that we had to eat all of our dinner, because he had been so hungry on Malta that they used to crack open the biscuits and wait for the weevils to crawl out so that he and his mates could eat the biscuits instead (I cite it as a valid reason for being overweight now!). The food shortage in Malta owing to the interception of the convoys of supply ships was nothing compared with the relentless bombing runs of the German and Italian air forces.

On one occasion, my father was walking along the side of the airstrip when he stopped to talk with a colleague, who was working up a telegraph pole. A bomb landed right where he would have been had he not stopped for a friendly chat. On another day, while trying to repair the British fighter aircraft as fast as they were being damaged, their workload led to a need for the engineers to work twelve hour rotational shifts. That night, a bomb landed on the sergeant's barracks and destroyed, among other things, the bed on which my father would have been sleeping had he been off duty. Had either of those bombs had his name on them, none of his five children, ten grandchildren or eleven great-grandchildren would be here today!

The 'Siege of Malta' was later declared to be a crucial factor in the Allies' eventual triumph in the War. The island itself was awarded the George Cross for the courage and determination of the whole community, since between 1940 and

1943, the beleaguered island endured 3,340 air raids. My father participated in the Sicilian and Italian campaigns and in Egypt before the war finally ended.

He and my mother, with their sons Peter and Geoffrey were posted to Aden after the hostilities, where they had a third baby, Michael. The infant unfortunately was diagnosed with a heart complaint, so the family rushed back to England for treatment, but alas, he died, aged only six months.

My father left the RAF and the family moved to settle in the charming British Channel Island of Jersey, and he continued with his love of aviation as an engineer with British Airways, in a career that spanned twenty-six years. At the same time, my parents also ran their own hotel businesses in Jersey, before emigrating to retire in Perth and join Geoff and his family. My parents had two other children, Cheryl and me. We were brought up in the family hotel environment and both later worked in hospitality, with me running my own Perth-based backpackers' hostel business for fourteen years. Peter was the only son to remain in the U.K. The family maintained that aviation link, though, as Peter became a pilot, Cheryl was an air hostess, and I also gained my pilot's licence. Peter's son, Andrew, is a Royal Air Force helicopter flying instructor.

My mother, Vera, is now ninety-four at the time of writing, still lives in their 'Pines Village' retirement home, still looks after herself, and is still very mentally alert. Sadly, my father, Bill Inman passed away three weeks after his ninetieth birthday after two years of battling against the ill health caused by his injuries. At least he fought with determination to celebrate their 70th Anniversary. With four children, thirteen grandchildren and twelve great-grandchildren, Bill and Vera Inman were honoured with messages from HRH the Queen, the Lieutenant-Governor, the Prime Minister and Leader of the Opposition as well as many local politicians.

My mother's secret for a successful marriage is as follows:

> "In all our years together, we vowed never to go to sleep on an argument. We always talked it through."
>
> **Vera Inman**

Living Together versus 'Living Together'

In contrast to my parents, my three siblings and I have all had broken marriages. In fairness, I think that some of the reasons behind that fact include a generational change in attitudes towards the institution of marriage itself. As they jokingly say, "Marriage is a great institution, but who wants to live in an institution?" Okay, that was my little joke. I actually do still believe that marriage can work, but when you look at the alarming statistics of marriage failure, I think the odds of success have reduced significantly compared with those of my parents' generation.

Part of that is because it was 'the done thing' in their day to stay married. 'Til death us do part' meant literally til one of you died. Another part, as I mentioned before, is that thanks to the evolution of equal opportunities in today's society, women no longer depend financially on men, and gender roles and rules have become confusing, with the boundaries well and truly blurred. Today's consumer society operates on a 'throw it away and get the latest model' basis, thus people are less likely to work at it and tolerate each other's idiosyncrasies. If that partner doesn't meet your needs in every way, they can be easily cast aside like a used chamois at a car lot!

In the past, it might have been a lot harder to find a replacement. These days you can just jump online, and there are a myriad of dating websites where you can select a partner that has all the same interests as you – even down to sexual preferences.

I met my partner of over seven years now, Joanne Small, via the RSVP dating website and amazingly it worked. Jo listed her interests as 'Diving, flying and sex!' Prior to that, however, we both dated a few people that didn't work out, so even this shopping menu for relationship bliss has its flaws.

I found fairly quickly that most girls my age share the following attributes: They…

- love a glass of red wine.
- like walking along the beach at sunset.
- want a man who knows instinctively what they want without having to ask.

- want a partner who understands them and will lavish them like a Princess, whilst also treating them like an equal, but at the same time understand their need for independence.

- want a man who knows what he wants and goes after it, as long as that fits with what they want.

- want a man who will give them cuddles and be supportive, but also does his own thing as long as they know what it is and have first approved it.

- want a man who can support them financially, but must also respect their need to own their own money and not have to be accountable to him in any way.

- want him to be assured and assertive in the bedroom, yet not pester them for sex.

- want him to bring them flowers and chocolates but not when they're on a diet, and if he does bring those gifts, they want to know what he's done wrong to warrant it.

- all absolutely insist that he must have a great sense of humour and be able to make them laugh even when they're on their period.

- all agree that their favourite movie is *The Shawshank Redemption*, and they expect him to watch chick flicks rather than stupid football (except for 'Okker' chicks who despise you if you don't like AFL).

- of course, agree that he would ideally be well-endowed, though size doesn't really matter as long as he knows how to use it (except that it *does* really matter). He must also be a lot better than her previous husband, (who was usually a 'bastard'), and he must be willing to let her pay, so she doesn't feel obliged to sleep with him (unless she is going to sleep with him, then he may as well pay for everything!).

For most guys, they want a girl who doesn't whinge and bitch too much, and who 'shags' like a 'two-dollar hooker', but who is ladylike enough to meet his children from his first marriage. She must also understand him a lot better than his first wife (who was usually a 'bitch'), and she must be able to pay her own way (because the first wife usually bled him dry), unless she's going to be awesome in bed, in which case he doesn't mind paying. If I sound cynical to you, then you are probably either still happily married to your first partner and own a house with a veranda and a white picket fence; still live with your mum or you are gay – which is fine by me, but you have probably never dated anyone via a dating website.

One thing to beware with these sites is that not everyone is as noble and honest as you are. Sometimes they tell fibs. Sometimes their photo is not their photo at all, or it's a photo of them when they were twenty-seven and smoking hot. It seems that most people have psychological problems or suffer from anxiety and/or depression (and I'm not in any way demeaning anyone who does!). Some of them *are* axe murderers! It also seems that most people are emotionally scarred or damaged in some way by their previous relationships. Of course, I'm exaggerating all of that because most of us deep down are lovely, 'normal' people who believe in world peace, ending world hunger, and saving the whales. It's just that a lot of people actually do a really good job of hiding their loveliness and... here's a newsflash: there is no such thing as 'normal'!

That's why you'll find it almost impossible (I know because I looked and looked for my parents' milestone) to find a 70th Anniversary greetings card! So how has it come to this? How have we reached such a state in society that most couples can't seem to manage to have the fairy tale romances of yesteryear? Dare I say it? Never mind... another book. That topic could fill volumes! It is, however, an important topic in the context of my goal in writing this one. I've been divorced twice, so I do speak with some degree of authority on how not to do it! Here's my take on the key points of successful relationships.

Relationship Rights vs. Relationship Rites

- Understand yourself first.
  That way, you'll have more of a chance to understand and appreciate a life partner. That's why it's very useful to read some personal development books, relationship books or attend some courses.

- Honest and clear communication is a major factor in making a go of things.
  If you let things bottle up, the problems will fester. People are not mind-readers – you have to explain what you want and be willing to compromise. It's a negotiable contract, which like everything else on this planet, will evolve as you both change and grow – and as your circumstances and life pressures change and hopefully grow.

- Find common ground.
  Ideally, I believe you need some common interests that inspire you both and that you can enjoy together. Otherwise, why are you together?

- Ideally, you both need some 'me' time.
  The person you met and fell in love with had some differences to you and some interests that you didn't necessarily share, which is why you…

- NEVER try to change someone into someone else.
  This usually involves a pre-conceived idea of perfection that we all would like to believe exists. In reality, no-one is perfect (well, not many of us anyway!), so you have to take the rough with the smooth. When you love someone, it should be unconditional. You'll know they squeeze the toothpaste tube in the wrong place, but it's okay because you can focus on the good stuff about your partner. When you fall out of love that toothpaste thing is suddenly a deal-breaker and brings up all the things you don't like about that person.

- If you want to HAVE a better partner, then you have to first BE a better partner.

- Make yourself happy.
  If you want to be happy, then you have to take responsibility for making yourself happy. Sure, your partner can and will help you, but it's your job to make yourself happy, not theirs.

- Be prepared to pick yourself back up.
  If your relationship does break up, and let's face it, with today's pressures, many of them will, the problem doesn't lie in the fact that it broke up. The real problem was if you had no idea that it was coming. That means you need to re-read the points above.

- Stay positive.
  If it does break up, don't seek to pile blame on your ex. Look at what worked well, look at what could have worked better, and resolve to work on yourself. When you've done the work, a more fulfilling relationship will appear. That's why, when you're desperate to find a partner, you could interview a stadium full of them and not meet the right one. When you do the work on yourself and you're probably not looking for Mr. or Mrs. Right, that's when they'll turn up.

- Work on yourself.
  It's just my opinion, but if you'd rather grow old with a companion than alone, at some point, you need to make yourself the kind of person someone would want to be with. If you achieve that, it's one of the traits of someone who is 'doing life well'.

21

Every Step Is Like a Swig of a Sports Drink

"Many drops make a bucket, many buckets make a pond, many ponds make a lake, and many lakes make an ocean."

Percy Ross

One of the traits I've noticed about the people who achieve extra-ordinary results is that they are always looking ahead. I'm not suggesting that you shouldn't take a moment to celebrate your successes – of course, you must or life would be very dull. It's just that when winners win an event, as soon as they have finished celebrating (perhaps with a holiday or a few days relaxing in between), they then look ahead to the next objective. They don't just rest on their laurels.

Running for Fun?

Every year, Perth plays host to one of its biggest community events, the annual 'City to Surf Fun Run'. Raising funds for local charity group, the Activ Foundation, an eclectic mix of runners and walkers, old and young together, make their way from St. Georges Terrace in the City to City Beach on the coast. Originally, the course was a straightforward twelve kilometre stretch, before a four kilometre walk option was added, to cater for those who sought involvement but lacked the necessary fitness for the long haul. In recent years, the event has been expanded to feature half marathon and full marathon options – a massive forty-five kilometres. It truly is a fun event, with many runners sporting fancy dress outfits to brighten the occasion. The finale is somewhat akin to a carnival atmosphere with a fairground and huge marquis banquets provided by Perth's rich mining companies for their staff.

I ran my first City to Surf event at the age of twenty-four, wearing a Target tee-shirt, who were my employers when I first arrived in Perth. Needless to say, having completed both the Guernsey and Jersey half marathons the year before that, I was a fit and relatively skinny young man back then. In those days, the race drew around 4,000 runners. Nowadays, I believe it pulls around 42,000 entrants in the various categories. Since then, I have completed, I think, nine City to Surfs, including the one in September 2013. My partner, Jo, was an excited, second time participant.

Wearing a middle-aged tyre these days, I decided to use Jo's first event as a motivational tool to help me improve my fitness level. To show I was really serious about working on my fitness, I also gave up drinking alcohol for the four weeks leading up to the race (not that I drink much these days anyway.) Despite a few lengthy training stints, I was still not as prepared as I would have liked, but nevertheless, Jo and I made the effort and completed the race in time for a hearty breakfast courtesy of Jo's employer at the time, which was the affluent energy company, Chevron. This year, we ran under the banner of her latest employer, JHG, who were raising money for women's breast cancer awareness. We're now determined to maintain our new habits of going for walks and jogs, and we have set a goal to improve on our time at the next attempt. This fits in well with our goal to complete such goals as the Inca Trek (forty-five kilometres) uphill at high altitude to Machu Picchu, Peru, in 2014.

With our walk to and from the race, plus the race itself, we covered around twenty kilometres on foot that Sunday. We were both pretty stiff and sore by the evening, so we still have a lot of improvement to make, but I am glad to say that we were both exhilarated for sticking to our goals, including a dry month for me.

Keep setting fun goals – they keep you young at heart.

Plus, the act of committing to a pledge you have made to the person in the mirror can be a catalyst to empower you to achieve other goals as well. Every tick off your bucket list is like another swig from an energy-boosting sports drink, preparing you for the next stage of the race.

I highly recommend the idea to my clients (subject to medical clearance of course!). If you're struggling for motivation, then doing it to raise money for a worthwhile charity can help give you that extra impetus (and make it impossible for you to drop out unless you're injured!).

 So, what could you do that would combine improving your health and fitness with helping someone else in need?

Your Bucket List (or Wish List)

The old English expression of 'kicking the bucket' meant quite simply the act of dying. Hence, an expression came into being sometime in the early 21st century from an unknown source, called '*The Bucket List*' – meaning a list of things to do, experiences or accomplishments to achieve before you 'kick the bucket' or 'die'. Those who prefer a more positive slant on the concept call it a 'wish list'.

I prefer the former term because a wish sounds like something that may never happen, whereas doing something before you die suggests that you will indeed take some action. The term became part of modern culture in a big way in 2007 upon the release of the movie, *The Bucket List*, starring Jack Nicholson and Morgan Freeman.

This movie poignantly focused on a couple of terminally-ill patients who decided to embark on the goal of ticking off as many items as they could from their personal lists of unfulfilled goals. The objective of course was made easier than it is for most people because Nicholson's character was a multi-millionaire who could thus afford to travel wherever he wanted and do whatever he wanted, unconstrained by the financial burdens with which most of us are encumbered.

I also remember watching an interview conducted by Australian TV chat show host, Andrew Denton, with Kevin Costner, whose words became lodged in my psyche.

> "I try to live a life and you know, living a life is trying to experience things...
>
> ...In my life, I would like to be 'heroic', because I think that's the place you want to be in your life – you want to do the right thing in your life.
>
> I would like to be smart, you know, 'smarter'. I'd like to read more books. I mean, the things I'm going to regret in this life when I leave will be probably the books I've never read, will be the music I've never heard."
>
> **Kevin Costner**

When I talk about my bucket list, I tend to spout on about the big, scary goals and the exciting adventures, like scuba diving, trekking to Machu Picchu or taking a helicopter ride over the Iguazu Falls, but not everyone is like me. For some people, it may simply be reading a list of good books (I have heaps of them on my list!) or doing something like learning to play a song on guitar.

Our bucket lists reflect our personalities, our physical condition and our priorities and tastes, so everyone's list will be a mixture of items that is unique to them. Many people suppress those dreams because they give up on life and think that such goals are impossible for them to ever achieve. In reading this book, however, I believe some part of you at least is looking for something more than a 'settle for' life. The fact that you have found your way here right now means that you have some unfulfilled dreams inside you! Here's the exciting newsflash for you...

> *When I talk about my 'bucket list', I always think of Scottish comedian, Billy Connolly's stated desire to become 'windswept and interesting'.*
>
> *The more things you tick off your 'bucket list', the more things you can achieve and the bigger your list can be.*
>
> *The reason for this is simple – with each tick on your list, you build your own self-belief and you enhance your charisma.*
>
> *That's why it's so important to remind yourself of your own achievements – to keep a scrap book, a journal, or some photo albums that are devoted to your successes – and remember to look at them often.*
>
> *The more you achieve, the more you think you can achieve. You begin an upward spiral of success, which as you build momentum, becomes an unstoppable juggernaut.*
>
> *Along with reminding yourself of your past successes, which fuel your self-belief, I recommend that you create a vision board of your bucket list items and look at them often. This will build your enthusiasm for the list of things you will do next and in the future.*
>
> *Your personal 'bucket list' is only limited by one thing – your own personal imagination!*
>
> **Tony Inman**

So how do you make a bucket list? It's simple. Either grab a big piece of paper or go to your PC, laptop or tablet, and just start making a list of all the things you'd like to do before you die. Just unleash your mind to write down everything with no regard to whether or not you think it's possible to do. Concern yourself with the 'how to's' later. I'd suggest categories such as places you'd like to visit; things you'd like to achieve (new skills or interests); people you'd like to meet; or even, the type of person you'd like to become.

There's no time like the present, so please go grab some paper now and just let your mind run wild on your 'bucket list'.

Keep writing until you really cannot think of anything more to write down. After you've done that, prioritise them and put a time frame on them. Some of the things will be low cost, or even free – items that you can do soon if you just allocate the time. Others may involve big expense, which may require you to research the costs, then formulate a plan to budget the money and the time so that you can make it happen.

One thing is very clear and proven: If you write down your goals and get specific, the 'how to' will start to become clearer, because you have now set your subconscious mind to work on that question. The biggest questions are, "Why do you want to do that thing?" and, "What will doing that, or having that, do for you?"

> ### *Personal Power Principles*
>
> - With every achievement, no matter how small, you continue to build your personal power and enhance your charisma. You add value to the story that is your life.
>
> - Making a commitment to yourself and fulfilling it increases your faith in your own abilities.
>
> - If you tie in your achievements so that they help others in the process, you will feel even better, knowing that you have touched other lives.
>
> - Ticking off your list is fun and fun keeps you young at heart.
>
> - The only real limits on your potential are those you create in your own mind.
>
> - One thing is certain – we will all kick the bucket one day. Do you want to kick a half-empty bucket, or do you want to fill your life with experiences and joy?

22

Getting on the Bus

"I tell the players that the bus is moving. This club has to progress. And the bus wouldn't wait for them. I tell them to get on board."

Sir Alex Ferguson

When I was a youngster on holiday one time with my parents, I remember spotting a poster in a gift shop that I nagged them to buy for my bedroom wall because it summed me up perfectly at the time, and I was very amused by it.

It read, "Why put off til tomorrow, what you can avoid doing altogether!"

Needless to say, my attitude has improved a bit since then, so if you are a parent of some lethargic teenagers, don't give up on them just yet!

Don't Wait for the Perfect Bus

Dr. Samuel Johnson was a British author who made lasting contributions to English Literature as a poet, essayist, moralist, literary critic, biographer, editor and lexicographer. He has been described as "arguably the most distinguished man of letters in English history" by the *Oxford Dictionary of National Biographies*. Dr. Johnson reminds of the need to avoid procrastination and to be wary of how sometimes a desire to do things perfectly can prevent us from simply getting on with things.

> "Nothing will ever be attempted if all possible objections must first be overcome."
>
> **Samuel Johnson**

Life is actually quite short when you start thinking about all of the things you'd probably like to do during your lifetime if you had the chance. I've always found that if you think about something that you'd like to do, or that needs to be done, and you write it down as a goal or a task to be performed, along with a deadline for achieving it, and then remind yourself of it regularly, there is a far greater chance that you will accomplish it. I always have long lists of 'things to do', but by listing them, I usually do work my way through them – like my goals of flying a Tiger Moth bi-plane or busking on a street corner.

If you didn't do it in the 'bucket list' chapter, find an hour today to sit down quietly and write down all of the things you'd like to do, the places you'd like to visit, the people you'd like to meet, etc. If you have a partner, both write your lists together.

If you're finding yourself struggling already with 'that thing you wanted to do', don't despair. There's good news: Today is the first day of the rest of your life! On the other hand, remember that, Today is the only day of your life! Just be aware that the future is promised to none of us. Please don't dismiss this as pessimistic, but today is actually the only day you've got. In fact right now is the only moment you can be certain of, but in the second it took you to read that statement, that moment has already passed!

There's no point worrying about what you intended to do yesterday, but didn't do, for whatever reason. Yesterday is gone. The present is here right now, so I urge you to embrace it! Life doesn't always go as planned; sometimes a road block means you have to drive down a detour to end up where you wanted to be. For example, isn't it always the case that when you start a fitness campaign, something happens to stop you from doing your exercise that day? Never mind – start again! This time, write it down, and make it 'real'. Don't let a small slip throw you off the path to success!

> "A goal is an objective, a purpose. A goal is more than a dream; it's a dream being acted upon. A goal is more than a hazy, 'Oh I wish I could.' A goal is a clear, 'This is what I'm working toward.'"
>
> **David J. Schwartz**

Professor Schwartz was considered a leading American authority on the topics of motivation and leadership. He was a big dreamer, a big thinker and a big doer. His books, one of which is *The Magic of Thinking Big*, have influenced thousands of people to be successful at whatever is their chosen path.

Start with small steps as the old Chinese proverb says, "A journey of a thousand miles starts with one step." Then, keep going. Have a clear picture of where you are heading, and you'll undoubtedly find the obstacles easier to overcome. Know what it is that you don't want. For example, maybe you don't want to smoke anymore, but keep clearly in your mind's eye what you do want, like a healthier body. No longer will you smoke, but instead, you will have gained fitness and a healthy body in its place. The positive goal toward which you are progressing is always the more important because the sub-conscious mind can't tell the difference between negative and positive.

In the 'giving up smoking' example, it's more important to think about the healthy body you will gain, and plan what other rewards you can have with the money you will have saved by not smoking, than it is to focus on the negative of 'giving up' something you have previously found enjoyable. That positive, or more empowering, focus is what can carry you through the 'weak moments' when the cravings for the old, unwanted habit occur. So write down those goals, look at them daily and get on the bus! It might not be the bus that drops you right to the door-step, but if it's heading in the right direction, grab a ticket!

A Bus Ride Down Memory Lane

One day, out of the blue, an old school chum, Derek Facey, surprised me by 'liking' my 'Tony Inman Living the Dream' Facebook page. I hadn't spoken to him for over thirty years, since we left Victoria College in Jersey, Channel Islands, and I was too busy that day to acknowledge his endorsement. I was then away in Sydney on business and busy on my return, so I forgot to follow it up. A while later, owing to the time zone difference and being eight hours ahead, I was probably one of the first to wish him a happy birthday when I saw his birthday notification appear on Facebook.

Shortly afterwards, though, another school friend sadly informed me that Derek never actually made it to his birthday, having already suffered a massive heart attack on the eve of his birthday. He was only a few hours short of fifty years old. So the lesson is that we don't know how long we've got. Therefore, my advice is don't sweat the petty, trivial stuff that can so easily take over our lives. I'm not saying be an anarchist! Do what you have to do to live a life of decency of course. What I am saying is…

> *Do your best to be kind, be generous, live your life in a way that will inspire others and make each day count.*
>
> **Tony Inman**

At school, I remember that Derek suffered with a stutter and was initially ridiculed for it. I'm sure there were times when I took the mickey out of him too. Children can be more cruel than they intend or realise. He brushed it off, but I'm sure it must have hurt him. I do also remember being friends with him for a while though. I remember catching the bus and visiting his house during school holidays, and he was a good guy from a good family. He usually wore a waistcoat and was slightly eccentric – and eccentricity is a trait I admire greatly!

We never fell out with each other – we simply drifted apart, and I moved to Australia. The funny thing is that once you got to know him, you didn't really notice the stutter so much; you just noticed the person instead. I'll bet if you asked the guys who tormented him back then about this, on hearing of his premature demise, they might wish they had behaved differently back then. Hindsight is a great teacher.

Today's memories are a product of decisions we made in the past.

? *So what decisions are you making today that will shape your future?*

In conclusion, R.I.P., Derek, thanks for 'liking' my page. I hope that you gained something from reading my posts. I'm glad that I knew you and my sincere condolences to your family.

It's been a while since we left that noble school, yet we are still learning lessons from it.

> *"A man who dares to waste one hour of time has not discovered the value of life."*
>
> **Charles Darwin**

Brilliant Bus Rides – Conditions of Carriage on the Journey of Life

- The world carries on, even if you choose not to participate, so join in!
- Circumstances will rarely, if ever, be perfect, so just get on with it! Doing something to eighty percent of your potential is better than doing nothing because you're still waiting for 'it' to be perfect.
- The past is already gone; the future is only a concept; the present is a gift – that's why they call it 'the present'.
- The cure for procrastination is taking action, so take some.
- Whether you do something today or you don't, that is a decision, and your decision will have an impact on your future. That choice is yours alone.
- Get on the bus – 'Life is worth doing, and it's worth doing well'.

23

Don't Let The Bxxxxxxs Grind You Down!

"Impossible is a word to be found only in the dictionary of fools."
Napoleon Bonaparte

This chapter is about listening to advice and in particular about the perils of receiving disempowering advice or the benefits of receiving empowering advice.

Naysayers and Dream Thieves

One of the biggest obstacles we face when we embark on a new project, or want to date somebody new, or are thinking of starting a business… is that very often the people who are closest to us will try to warn us of the perils of this change in direction. Why do they do this, and should we listen to them? These are both valid and important questions.

In the case of our parents, our family and our close friends, their seemingly negative reaction is borne out of genuine concern for your well-being. They are worried about you, and they don't want anything bad to happen to you. As a parent myself, I can definitely state that it is very hard to let your children off the leash or 'cut the apron strings', as the saying goes, but unless you let them go out into the big, bad world, take some risks, and make both good and bad decisions, they will not grow. Of course, you're not going to stand by and say nothing as they head for a disaster, but equally, you have to let them grow up and take responsibility for their own lives. Sometimes, as a parent, you really do have to jump in and say something, but what's most important is that you are there to pick up the pieces when things go wrong, rather than smugly saying, "I told you so."

When friends who are less close, or even acquaintances, dump their often unwanted viewpoint on you, it could be that they too are concerned for your well-being. It could also be for any number of other reasons. They could be jealous, or frequently, it can be that they are projecting their fears and concerns onto you. Someone may say, "I wouldn't be starting a business in this day and age. Everyone is struggling right now!" It could just be that they don't have the courage to start their own business. Perhaps they even started one and failed. Either way, they are really saying, "I couldn't make it work, so why would you be able to?"

I call those people the 'naysayers' – those who filter their view of the world often through a negative looking glass. They have also been referred to as 'dream thieves', because they try to steal your dreams from you.

> *How do you tell the difference between genuine concern and pessimism? How do you know who to listen to?*

In my experience, one way is to ask yourself…

> *What experience does this person have, or what qualifies them, to give me advice on this subject?*

If the topic is you starting your own business, then consider whether this harbinger of doom has ever run their own business and whether they made it work for them. If it's advice about a new romance, consider whether that person has managed to sustain happy relationships and whether they are open to love or closed off and bitter. If it's a decision about a proposed activity or new purchase, consider why that person feels they can dispense advice on that subject.

As a clue, people who make sweeping generalisations like, "Everyone says you shouldn't do this!" or, "Nobody thinks you're doing the right thing!" are often just being prejudiced by their own fears. Ask them, "Who do you mean by 'everyone' or 'nobody?'" Their answer will help you determine the validity of the advice. Don't let their limits become your limits!

I must say that one of the things I have always loved about Australia is that there seems to be a national trait of optimism. It's one of the reasons I moved here. I know that too is a generalisation, but I think it has a lot to do with the weather as well as the strength of the economy. In the U.K., people seemed to be more disillusioned and fearful, so I heard a lot of negativity. There seemed to be a plethora of comments like, "Oh, I wouldn't be doing that!" or, "Oh, be careful… I know someone who tried that, and they went broke! In Australia, however, people seem more open to change and adventure. I hear more encouragement, like, "Good on you for having a go!" or, "That's a great idea. Why don't you talk to my friend, so and so, who can help you with that!"

> "The person who says it cannot be done should not interrupt the person doing it."
>
> **Chinese Proverb**

Find a Mentor (For All Topics)

If you don't listen to the naysayers, then who do you listen to? The best advice I can give you is to seek good advice! Find people who have done whatever it is that you are trying to do and ask them for their advice. The highest achievers in the world today find themselves mentors and coaches. Does the guy who wins the Wimbledon tennis tournament use a coach? You bet he does. Is that coach a better player than him? Not necessarily, but he has the benefit of being the observer. He can see where a change in technique, a tweak here and there, or a better strategy can make a big difference.

This realisation is what led me to become a coach myself. I spent thousands of hours coaching people on their life challenges when I ran a backpackers' hostel for fourteen years. Now I do that for a living. In business, I have bought or set up numerous businesses. I have sold some, and I have closed some down. I've had some wins and some learning experiences. That knowledge and those experiences have allowed me to set up as a business coach and consultant to help other people. In over thirty-four years of management, I have trained, coached and mentored thousands of staff and hundreds of business owners and executives. Despite all of that experience, do I have a coach myself? Yes, I have several coaches and mentors in different areas of my business and my life. You probably can't, and definitely don't, have to do everything on your own!

Surround yourself with a mastermind group of experts – that is a key to success.

Sir Richard Branson says that his goal is to be 'the dumbest person in the room' because he constantly enlists the help of people who are brilliant at what they do. If you want to be the best, seek out the best and model what they do, but adapt it to make it yours. Take their advice, even take advice from multiple experts, and then adapt that advice to suit your personality.

> **Auspicious Advice**
>
> - Listen to advice, but always check whether the source is valid.
> - Don't let other peoples' limits or fears become yours.
> - Surround yourself with a mastermind support team of trusted advisors.
> - Model what successful people whom you admire, do and you will be 'doing life well' according to the things you value.

24

Fears and Failures – The Dream Destroyers

"The most difficult thing is the decision to act; the rest is merely tenacity. The fears are paper tigers. You can do anything you decide to do. You can act to change and control your life; and the procedure, the process is its own reward."

Amelia Earhart

When I ask people about the things they would love to do, but have not yet done, the most common excuses include fears and previous failures at other endeavours. I urge you to remember this important belief that we are taught as coaches:

Your past does not have to equal your future.

Do It Despite the Fear

I was glancing back through another great book I read a while ago by Susan Jeffers, called *Feel the Fear and Do It Anyway*. Susan reminded me again that we are all faced with hurdles that sometimes seem insurmountable, whether it's a job loss, relationship break up, bereavement of a friend or family member, an illness or simply a failure to achieve something that is important to us. It's important to remember that is the way we deal with these 'problems' that defines us.

Fears and Failures – The Dream Destroyers

*Our true character is revealed when we bounce back
from adversity and draw on our inner courage.*

> "Whatever happens to me, given any situation, I can handle it!"
>
> **Dr. Susan Jeffers**

I have learned and experienced many times in my life that things which can seem at the time to be a disaster, or a major problem, were in fact a challenge that would help me to grow or were the seed of an even greater opportunity. With hindsight we can look back and say, "If that seemingly bad thing hadn't happened, then this amazingly good thing might not have happened either." That can be a very comforting thing of which to remind yourself when you are having what may seem like a bad day.

Let Your Light Shine

> "And as we let our own light shine, we unconsciously give other people permission to do the same. As we are liberated from our own fear, our presence automatically liberates others."
>
> **Nelson Mandela**
> **Former President of South Africa**
> **From his 1994 inaugural speech**
> **(written by Author Marianne Williamson)**

President Mandela's inauguration speech captivated the world. As a man who had spent twenty-six years in prison for speaking out against the racist regime of apartheid in South Africa, he did not then speak of revenge for the injustice; he simply promoted peace and harmony. He encouraged people to overcome their fears and be the best they could be.

 Are you allowing your light to shine or are you letting your fears get in the way?

Food for thought: If you are letting fear win, you are denying the world the gift of your talents. Do you realise how unfair you are being on all of those people?

If you can sing, sing! If you can write, write! If you are a great footballer, play football! Here is a definition of fear from an anonymous source that you might not have heard of:

False **E**vidence **A**ppearing **R**eal

Most of the things we are afraid of never even happen! If we are so afraid that we might fail, that we never start, then we have already failed, so we then have nothing to lose by giving it a go! If what we really fear is that we might actually succeed, we will be in the spotlight, and we might possibly embarrass ourselves, then we are not only remaining in our own darkness, we are also keeping everyone else in the darkness as well. Here is the full context, because I believe it's absolutely worth reading…

> *"Our deepest fear is not that we are inadequate.*
>
> *Our deepest fear is that we are powerful beyond measure.*
>
> *It is our light, not our darkness, that most frightens us.*
>
> *We ask ourselves, who am I to be brilliant, gorgeous, talented, and fabulous?*
>
> *Actually, who are you not to be? You are a child of God.*
>
> *Your playing small doesn't serve the world.*
>
> *There's nothing enlightened about shrinking so that other people won't feel insecure around you.*
>
> *We are all meant to shine, as children do.*
>
> *We are born to make manifest the glory of God that is written within us.*
>
> *It's not just in some of us; it's in everyone.*
>
> *And as we let our own light shine, we unconsciously give other people permission to do the same.*
>
> *As we are liberated from our own fear, our presence automatically liberates others."*
>
> **Nelson Mandela**
> **Former President of South Africa**
> **From his 1994 inaugural speech**
> **(written by Author Marianne Williamson)**

What Is Failure Anyway?

You may recall I mentioned earlier that there is no right or wrong – there is only our perception. The same can be said for success or failure. A tennis player could lose the final at Wimbledon and be branded a failure or a loser, but in reality, the person doing the branding is actually defining himself or herself by doing so. If that seems controversial or a bit spiritual, let me explain why…

Just to be at the Wimbledon tournament in the first place makes that runner up a winner, and I have yet to meet a person who has not overcome some kind of adversity in their life. As humans, however, we all judge people. We can't help ourselves. We see the person holding the trophy as the winner and the runner up as the first of the losers, especially in Australia, where children are encouraged vigorously to pursue sporting achievements in their formative years and parents scream abuse at sports officials from the touchlines. Don't get me wrong here. I'm very proud to live in Australia, and I'm a great sports fan and an active participant. I believe that sport is fantastic for children because it engenders many important lessons – lessons in team-building, leadership, dedication, goal-setting, commitment… the list is endless. I cheer for my teams, and when I play, I play to win.

But if I win, does that make my opponents losers? Of course, I enjoy banter like everyone else, and of course, I take the mickey out of my brother-in-law, who is a Liverpool fan, when Manchester United beat them! But if I lose or if my team loses, does that also make me or them into losers? No. The losers are the ones who never try in the first place – not the ones who couldn't do it because of an injury or a disability. I'm talking about the ones who could give it a go, but who let their fear of failure or their fear of success, get in the way of even starting. Even then, I'm not calling them a failure. I'm only saying that they have failed in their behaviour, in that they have let themselves down by not seizing the opportunity to move forwards and empower themselves with the effort.

I'm talking about this because the perception of failure is an issue I still work on in myself. I mentioned that my father used to ask me if I was winning. Winning is important to me, and I still dislike losing. I used to hate it, but I have come to realise that being the best I can be is way more important. I still never like losing a sports contest, but what matters more is whether I gave it my best shot. If I did my best and my opponent was better, then it was obviously the ref's fault!

No, I'm joking, of course. If the opponent was better, then fair play to them. It just means that I need to try harder, to learn new skills, become faster, stronger, whatever it takes. It is in that process that I truly grow. We can learn as much from our defeats as from our victories. Furthermore, without a 'vanquished', there can be no 'victor' and, therefore, no contest.

Isn't that the great thing about the Olympic spirit? We don't just watch the Olympic Games – we are compelled and captivated by the human story and the emotions of the occasion. We know that those contestants have trained for years and have won many heats before they gained the opportunity to compete with the world's best. We celebrate with the winners, and we are saddened for the runners up but inspired by their commitment.

If you saw the event at the Sydney Olympics in 2000, you could not fail to have been moved by the efforts of Eric 'The Eel' Moussambani, who became the slowest Olympic swimmer in history. Coming from Equatorial Guinea, he had only learnt to swim just eight months before the Games. Furthermore, he had not even had a full length pool in his home country in which to train. He was so slow and looked so utterly exhausted as he battled to even complete the race that he received a standing ovation from the crowd. Ironically, he won the heat because the other two starters were disqualified for false starts, though he failed to qualify for the semi-finals as his time was so poor. Did losing make him a loser or a failure? Far from it! His determination, spirit and willingness to face impossible odds made him a crowd favourite and a winner. In 2012, he landed in London as the team coach of the Equatorial Guinea swimming team. No doubt he could let his light shine on the young swimmers he was now coaching.

My take on it: Be the best you that you can be! By doing that, you are already a winner. The trophy is the icing on the cake, but the real victories are when you achieve and notice the duality of the win-win outcome of all participants. Surrender to a higher level of consciousness in that whatever happens, it is exactly the way it is meant to be. The other thing is that the path to success is rarely a straight line. Failures are the feedback we need, so we can do things better and become better. So here's a challenge for you: Think of three things you have been putting off doing or that you have felt afraid of, or uncomfortable about doing. Write them down, plan to do them, and get them done. You will feel so much better for finally taking action. Go on… Do it now!

Reality Revisions

- Most of what we fear never even happens, so we wasted that energy worrying about it for nothing!
- If anything 'bad' were to happen, or even if the worst thing imaginable were to happen, it might actually turn out to pave the way for something better to happen.
- Every time we act, despite the fear, we gain new confidence and inner strength.
- It's okay to be stuck temporarily, but not to stay stuck.
- Success and failure are largely perception anyway. It is possible to 'lose' or 'fail' and yet still be the biggest winner.
- Failures are temporary, and they give us the feedback we need so that we can be better.
- Without experiencing the sourness of defeat, you will not fully appreciate the sweet taste of success.
- If you find yourself making a few mistakes on your quest to fulfil your life goals, you can be reassured that this means you are 'doing life well'.

25

It Ain't So Bad, So Don't Get Mad!

"The best day of your life is the one on which you decide your life is your own. No apologies or excuses. No-one to lean on, rely on, or blame. The gift is yours – it is an amazing journey – and you alone are responsible for the quality of it. This is the day your life really begins."

Bob Moawad

The Passage of Time and Mortality

The one thing that none of us can stop is the passage of time, so why stress about something you cannot change? Well, here we are, just over half a century since I was born – where did it go? If ever had any silly thoughts of dread at the prospect of being called an 'old git' or something equally ageist and demeaning, I have only to think back of a few friends who have not been fortunate enough to live as long as I have, whereupon I can immediately replace that negative thought with a more empowering one.

In my lifetime, I've seen decimalisation, the replacement of 'black and white' TV's with colour ones, and now digital ones. We've gone from computers the size of a room and telephones with annoying ringtones to tiny half-pocket-sized phones that access the internet with annoying ringtones! We've gone from 'no pill' (at least that was my dad's story) to 'morning after' and 'implant' contraceptives. I watched

It Ain't So Bad, So Don't Get Mad!

Sir Matt Busby, George Best and Bobby Charlton pick up the European Cup, and I've seen Sir Alex Ferguson, Ryan Giggs and Gary Neville do the same. I can remember the days when there were ha'penny chews, a can of Coke was sixpence, and kids gave up their seats for adults on buses. Those were the days when drugs were only dispensed by chemists; you could leave your house unlocked; and you could even leave your keys in the car! Those were the days when a naughty kid got a whack from their parents, and the worst swear word a kid would say was 'bloody'. We had respect for our teachers, did as we were told, and grew up with a work ethic. A person in trouble would be helped without a second thought. It was heart-warming to see images of a return to that kind of human compassion and community spirit during Australia's recent floods and bushfires.

Obviously, it wasn't all as rose-coloured as my (one day) spectacles will reveal through the haze of nostalgia, but I certainly feel as if I have lived through privileged times. Bill and Vera (my 'wrinklies') lived through World War II. Dad was starving on Malta while 'Gerry' bombed it twenty-three hours a day. I lost count of the number of times I heard about how they had to crack open the biscuits and let the weevils crawl away, so they could eat the biscuits. Mum had ration coupons in Chester. They starved, so I had to eat everything on my plate (even the green beans) or I wouldn't get my stodgy northern pudding! That's why I've struggled to re-learn that it's okay to not stuff your face with stodge!

As my parents subsequently became hoteliers, who adored escaping for well-earned breaks to fantastic destinations, I have been fortunate enough to follow in their footsteps with a love of travel and tourism. They were also very goal-oriented people with decent, ethical values and, luckily for me, a belief in education. *So what have I learned?* Well, I could dribble on all day – after all, I'm becoming like my mother and find myself explaining to bemused shop assistants why I needed to buy that 'whatever' product, then finding common ground and engaging in lengthy conversations with random strangers! I also have ear hairs, nose hairs and rampant eye brows. Football injuries take longer to heal and just as Billy Connolly (whom I saw in his very first Michael Parkinson TV interview) confesses, I make strange grunting noises when I bend down to pick things up!

Nevertheless, to race towards my conclusions and life-changing, inspirational words of wisdom for you young whippersnappers out there… I still believe that you can choose how you feel about things; you can do things, if you think and believe you can; plus – and this is a biggie – life is definitely too short to take it for granted.

> "Things are to own and people are to love, rather than things to love and people to own."
>
> **Fred Smith**

It is a no-brainer to remember just how important family and friends are to us all. If you don't have any friends – try harder – first, be a friend to others. I'm a firm believer in building a list of dreams and goals and working your way through them.

The only person really ever holding you back is you.

I don't know about you guys, but my 'bucket list' (things to do before you kick the bucket!) of stuff to do is just getting longer and longer. I went from being a guy who couldn't open his eyes underwater to diving sixty metres down to the deck of the World War Two shipwreck of the American battleship USS Aaron Ward in the shark-inhabited waters of the Solomon Islands in the South Pacific.

I achieved a long overdue goal of flying a Tiger Moth bi-plane with the wind in my face. I sold my backpackers business and contemplated buying a resort in either Bali or the South Pacific, but ended up setting up my own coaching and consulting business in Perth instead; and I finally got around to finishing and publishing my first novel –'The Parrot and the Lady' – a spy spoof that became more of a satirical rant against political correctness, set in Vanuatu.

I've done a parachute jump in the Dale River Drop zone and hot air balloon rides over Alice Springs in the Australian Outback, the Valley of the Kings in Egypt and over Parliament house in Canberra. I've fronted a band in Papua New Guinea and I've done acting classes, taken up public speaking and delivered seminars. I've climbed down inside a Gisa Pyramid and up to the top of Uluru (Ayer's Rock). I've also climbed the Sydney Harbour Bridge three times and I've done helicopter rides over the McDonell ranges, the Bungle Bungles and the Twelve Apostles.

I've swum under waterfalls and in outback billabongs and I've run half-marathons and City to Surf Fun Runs. I've rowed boats in underwater caves and I've climbed Mount Kosziosko. I've seen bulls fight, crocodiles jump and snorkelled with whale sharks. I've driven motorbikes, tow trucks and tour buses. I've cable-skied and learnt to sail yachts.

In 2014, Jo and I are planning to do the Inca trail of Machu Picchu (before those unfit grunting noises become too deafening!), visit the Iguazu Falls, Rio de Janeiro, the Amazon and the Mayan Temple of Chichen Itza. I'm going to fit in learning another language or two and all kinds of stuff that will prove that I'm certifiably mad as far as the 'naysayers' are concerned.

I'm not telling you all that to big note myself. Loads of people have done way more than me. I'm just pointing out that:

Life is there to be lived, and before you know it, it can be over in a flash.

The first funeral I ever attended was for the son of one of my friends, Hayley Barber's son, Ashley. He tragically died in a car crash three weeks before his seventeenth birthday. He was a keen surfer, so his service was held on his favourite beach next to his favourite ocean. It was devastating that his life was taken before he could really live out all of his dreams. Then, two of our backpackers, Tim and Jonno, were in their 20s when their car rolled over on the Nullarbor and claimed their young lives. We held the wake at our hostel. The third funeral I attended was for a good friend of ours, Shayne Jensen, who went to bed one night at the age of forty-seven and never woke up. He was two months younger than me.

Jo and I vowed at Shayne's funeral that we would cram in as much as we could, while we could. We discovered during his eulogy that he had been on many adventures in his life – things that we had no idea he had done. We knew that we had to do the same, and we have. In the last few years, I have delivered the eulogy at Jo's father's funeral and at my own father's funeral. At least both Alan Small and Bill Inman lived full and happy lives, mixing adversity and triumph, struggles and good times. Both succumbed to ill health, though my dad was fortunate to see his ninetieth birthday. So whatever floats your boat, don't leave it until it's too late. The things you may regret are the things you didn't do! Definitely, don't let lack of money, the age people say you are, or your irrational fears get in the way.

The Dark Passage of Detail

It's important to have attention to detail, but it's also important not to get caught up in the trap of worrying about every detail. Life is not perfect. The world is not perfect. Change is constant. So as soon as you finish something and decide that it is now 'perfect', a minute later, you'll probably spot something else – some minor change that you could have made, something that you could have done slightly better. One of my past bosses used to call it a 'speed/accuracy trade off'. Sometimes, you just have to accept that it's pretty darned good and keep moving.

Whoa, there… yes, of course, I have to put in my disclaimer here! Certain situations require absolute attention to detail. You don't want the heart surgeon doing your bypass operation to say, "That's near enough." You don't want the aircraft engineer to say, "That plane is almost close enough to being airworthy." Those situations where lives are at risk and the consequences of getting it wrong are huge, of course, require total concentration and attention to detail. I'm talking about the day-to-day stuff here.

> "Ask yourself this question: 'Will this matter a year from now?'"
> **Richard Carlson**

Another of my old bosses, the late Les Woodcock at the Channel Islands Co-operative Society in Jersey, used to apply this criteria to decision-making. It's not an exact quote, but I know he wouldn't have minded.

If a decision is easily reversible, then make it quickly.
If the decision means a lot of work if you get it wrong, then take as much time as you have available to make it the right one.

My Policy of Rigid Flexibility

- Why stress about something you can't change? If you *can* change it, then still don't stress, just do what you can.

- Don't waste time wishing for things to be better. Change is constant. Nothing will ever be perfect, so that makes NOW the perfect time!

- People are to be loved; once they are gone, it's too late (at least in this lifetime anyway and depending on your spiritual beliefs).

- You can't control anyone else, but you, and you alone, are responsible for your own destiny with every thought, every belief and every deed.

- The things you will regret most on your death bed are the things you didn't do!

- In your dreams, anything is possible, so dream big! Then take action to make those dreams come true. That's called 'doing life well'.

26

Touching Hearts and Serving Others

"Every man must decide whether he will walk in the light of creative altruism or in the darkness of destructive selfishness."

Dr. Martin Luther King, Jr.

It's one of the great ironies in life that we help ourselves the most when we help other people first.

Touching Hearts – From Breaking Point to Point Break

In the summer of 2010, George Barr was lying on his death bed and literally thought that it was all over for him. For a middle aged man, he had a very young outlook on life, yet on that fateful day, his heart disagreed. That's somewhat ironic, given that he was, and fortunately still is, one of the most good-hearted guys I am lucky enough to know.

George was working for me in both the Tourism and Cleaning Divisions of my company, Club Red, at the time of his heart attack and has remained a close friend, despite continuing his travels. A little while ago, he wrote down his story for me, to help endorse my life coaching skills for any prospective new clients, who might be seeking background information.

I hope you find it as moving as I did…

From Breaking Point to Point Break
The George Barr Story

Life Coaching – What is it?

This really happened to me, but imagine this as being you…

You're on a plane just taking off from Hong Kong International headed back to Australia. Ahead is the beach, and you're working with a mate you have known for a few years. He owned a good business, a backpackers' hostel – that's how I first met Tony Inman.

On my return from an extended overseas trip, I was going to the backpackers' hostel business that Tony owned at that time to live and do a little part-time work. I got there and started doing the basic routine, and eventually, I was driving great, enthusiastic people to the beach and generally getting immersed in the business.

Tony was keeping a watchful eye on things, and I think that he soon picked up that I was not all on deck health-wise, as I had been helping out with another aspect of his enterprise: the cleaning contracting. I helped out with this occasionally, too, but my standards had slipped due to something I could not personally pin down. I had to admit I was not up to speed. I didn't know what it was. I just was not myself, and I knew it.

Standing in the backpackers one day, I went really cold and had symptoms of a heart attack. One of our mates, being on hand, drove me straight to ICU, and WOW! All the bells and whistles went off. I lay on the gurney signing the paper for the doctor to go ahead with extreme life saving measures like stopping the heart, injections of adrenalin, and God knows what else.

I knew I was as good as dead. I had been down this road before at age thirty-two and recovered. This time, I did not feel confident at all. After all, how can you when red lights are flashing and half a dozen people are looking really serious, and you know it's not a joke? Basically, it's game over.

I actually surprised myself and everyone else I think, as I walked away with this as a memory and a need to recover. This happened twice in the space of two weeks.

So enters Tony… He sat me down and gave me a brief talk, and ahead we went, with me still working but in a supervisory capacity. I had backpackers to do the muscle side and Tony gave me advice on how to keep it organised. He was coaching me as we went along, feeding me the information and advice as required.

Tired and not wanting to be a burden, I actually wanted to crawl into a hole and just go away, as I felt that was it. I had, after all, been technically gone (dead) twice in a month, and I had a new shiny machine implanted in my chest as a medal – my reward from God for not taking up a seat in paradise… yet.

But Tony kept me inspired, mainly due to his own diligence in heading up the numerous branches of his business. What I learned took me forward further than I could have imagined at the time. Initially, I was not skilled in the running of business or dealing with people in that certain way that you need when working at the coal face. I became adept at handling difficulties and difficult people – an essential quality when working with the public or supervising staff.

When Tony sold this aspect of his enterprise, I went road tripping, reasonably well recovered, on a road trip to Broome. On arrival, I headed into a life of beach, sun and surf. Money of course is not in never ending supply, so I went looking for bar work, hoping it would workout at the local pub called the 'Famous Beer and Satay Hut'.

On my CV was mentioned that I had been an approved bar manager at Tony's licensed backpackers. Tony had of course endeavoured to make sure that this part of the business was covered, and I had done the relevant courses and studied for it. So there I was – trained and experienced under the watchful eye of Tony, two and a half thousand kilometres away, looking for bar work.

They actually required a bar manager, and I just happened to be there at that time and place. Now, that is a combination: the life skills that Tony employed and his coaching under the most extreme and difficult circumstances put me there at the right time and place.

I stayed at the job until my feet and surf board were in demand on another part of the continent. Now, that's the life I lead, and it is a life to wish for. Some call it 'living the dream!'

In the last three months, I have surfed more beaches than I could name, driven in excess of twenty thousand kilometres, and have travelled across the Nullarbor twice in as many months. I have great prospects, and no doubt there's a beach or point break waiting for me over the horizon.

Take the hint and get with Tony; his skills are solid… and the life coaching? Well, the facts of my story say it all. If you're at your breaking point, look for your point break. Go surf life, and have Tony assist.

George Barr
'Living His Dreams!'

George's story is an inspiration to us all, and I am proud to count him as a friend.

For me, business was always about the people, and always will be. It's about helping your customers and nurturing your staff. If you don't look after your staff, and put time and effort into developing and training them, you won't have a business. I knew that the last thing George needed was to wallow and feel sorry for himself. I also knew that George was a guy who wouldn't sit still, so we had to keep a very close eye on not letting him overdo it. Fortunately, we got the balance right, and he was able to pick himself up and find a new purpose for his new direction.

I consider myself very fortunate to have been in a position to help George through one of the most significant and challenging times in his life. The irony is that in helping other people, we learn more about ourselves. This is one of the reasons that my mission today is now to help people with business and life coaching, and having reinvented myself on several occasions. It's why I became 'The Reinvention Specialist'. So, thank you, George, for your support and friendship. I have many similar stories of people like George from the fourteen years that I owned and operated my backpackers' hostel business. I'm very proud and happy that I was able to help quite a number of them through various crises and changes in life directions.

The Starfish Story – Making a Difference

This is a story I first heard delivered from the stage by inspirational speaker, John Higgs but its origins are unknown.

A father and his little girl were walking along a beach together one day, enjoying each other's company. At the water's edge, the sand was covered with small starfish who had been washed up in the surf. Unfortunately, they were doomed to dry out and perish in the heat of the glaring sunshine.

"Why are those starfish there, Daddy?" she asked, innocently.

The father explained the imminent plight of the beautiful sea creatures.

"That's really sad!" said the little girl. Without hesitation, the child began to pick up the starfish, one by one and threw them as far as she could back into the sea.

"Why are you doing that, honey?" asked the dad.

"I'm trying to give them another chance to live, Daddy," answered the girl.

"But honey…" he said, "…there's too many of them to save. You can't possibly make a difference."

She turned to her father with a smile as she threw another into the surf. "Well, it sure made a difference to that one!"

The moral of the story: Sometimes it seems like we are wasting our time and trying to turn back the tides of life's challenges. Nevertheless, each one of us can make a difference, in our own special way, just by doing what we can. We can touch peoples' lives in what might be a small way to us, but it could make a big difference to them. Call a friend today, or write a short email. They'll be glad that you did.

Who better to quote on the subject of 'touching hearts' than the lady they called, 'The Princess of Hearts'.

> "Carry out a random act of kindness, with no expectation of reward, safe in the knowledge that one day someone might do it for you."
>
> **Princess Diana**

A Heart-Warming Tale - Making a Dream Come True

In 2006, in a high school basketball game in New York, a coach and his protégé, a young man with autism, made history. Not only did young Jason McElwain have autism, he was only 173 centimetres tall – not really the height for a basketball player. So, instead of playing for the team, he had become the team manager.

Basketball Coach Jim Johnson, at the Greece Athena High School, decided to give young Jason a 'fair go' in the remaining few minutes of the last game of the season. He didn't promise anything, but said he would try to at least let Jason on the court, just to experience the atmosphere of wearing the team jersey on court. The coach, all of the players, and the other students in the audience knew just how much this meant to Jason.

 Do you think he seized his opportunity to live his dream?

He certainly did. On the sidelines, he did everything he could to help and in over three years, he had missed only one game. His enthusiasm was infectious. On the night in question, word got around that Jason might play, and a huge crowd turned up to watch. They even brought cut-outs of Jason's face, ready to raise them if he did make it onto the court. With only four minutes remaining and his team comfortably up by twenty points, the coach summoned Jason. With only three minutes to go, Jason started scoring baskets like a man possessed. He became the highest scorer in the game with six three-pointers and one two-pointer. When the final whistle blew, the crowd ran onto the court and lifted him in the air like a basketball legend.

Coach Jim Johnson said that in twenty-five years of coaching, he had never experienced such an emotional high as he did that night, seeing the popular young man grab hold of his dream with a vengeance.

> *Sometimes, a seemingly trivial gesture or minor accommodation on your part towards another human being can have a profound influence on their life. You may never even know what the consequences of that action will eventually be.*

It was one of the things that I loved about working with people in my time running a backpackers' hostel until I sold the business in 2010 – the opportunity to help people transform their lives with a few questions, a word of advice or simply a bit of encouragement, during the many late night chats with people who were battling with life's challenges. It's the main reason I love the coaching, consulting and mentoring work that I do today. There is no greater buzz than helping someone find the path to achieving their destiny and realising their potential.

Here's a challenge for you – think of three people you could help this week in some way, however small, that might help them achieve their dreams and do what you can. Are you up for it?

The Human Touch

If you have the opportunity to help someone in strife, the ripple effects of that act of kindness could be immense. Do it without expecting anything in return and you will receive far more than you might have expected, at a time you least expect it, in a way you might not have imagined.

Don't be overwhelmed by the fact that too many people need help. Just do what you can, when the opportunity arises.

Be kind to everyone you meet. They are all fighting their own battle and your kindness means you are 'doing life well'.

27

The Jigsaw Pieces of Character

"Nothing in this world can take the place of persistence. Talent will not; nothing is more common than unsuccessful people with talent. Genius will not; unrewarded genius is almost a proverb. Education will not; the world is full of educated derelicts. Persistence and determination alone are omnipotent. The slogan 'press on' has solved and always will solve the problems of the human race."

President Calvin Coolidge

When you connect all of the pieces together, the beauty of the whole picture is there for all to see.

Perseverance and the Law of Sod

I first read one of Dennis Waitley's books about a year after arriving in Australia, in 2005. It was *The Seeds of Greatness*, and it contained a lot of very useful lessons in life, many of which my wife and I applied in raising our two children. I reminded myself recently of one of the key topics in that book that is one of the old truths. It is one that will remain a constant truth:

> *"A key ingredient to success at anything is perseverance."*

The Law of Sod says, "If things can go wrong, they will!" The following is a quote from Dennis's book, which I highly recommend.

> *"Perseverance does not always mean sticking to the same thing forever. It means giving full concentration and effort to whatever you are doing, right now!*
>
> *It means doing the tough things first and looking downstream for gratification and rewards. It means being happy in your work, but hungry for more knowledge and progress.*
>
> *It means making more calls, going more miles, pulling more weeds, getting up earlier in the day and always being on the lookout for a better way of doing what you're doing.*
>
> *Perseverance is success through trial and error."*
>
> **Dennis Waitley**

I am a firm believer in the importance of keeping sharper and more focused on the results you want out of your life, by taking time out to think and reflect on the things that you could be doing better. Travelling to totally different places is one of my key goals in life, but there is a double benefit, because every time I go away, I learn something new about myself in the process. Perhaps for you, the ideas will flow when you are just sitting in the hotel swimming pool, sipping your favourite cocktail. Whatever works best for you... Dream big, and make it happen!"

The Overnight Success Myth

One of the media's favourite labels for people who achieve greatness is to call them 'overnight successes'. In most cases, this is a long way from the truth. I love reading biographies because you find that almost all of these people whom we adore, admire or call our 'heroes' started as ordinary people with extraordinary dreams. Furthermore, they focussed on those dreams, set goals, worked hard and overcame obstacles that would have made lesser people simply give up.

Here are just a few examples:

J.K. Rowling

She is the author of the famous *Harry Potter* series of books, whose career and marriage had failed, and she considered herself "the biggest failure I knew." She submitted her first manuscript of *Harry Potter and the Philosopher's Stone* to twelve publishing houses, all of whom rejected it, before Bloomsbury accepted it a year later. Today, her net worth is estimated at 560 million pounds, according to Wikipedia.

John Travolta

He worked hard for many years as a young actor and dancer before he achieved early success in New York musicals. He then had to move to L.A. to earn his place on TV shows. Then came movie success with *Saturday Night Fever* and *Grease*. Alas, personal tragedy consumed him when his partner, Diana Hyland, died after a battle with cancer. He disappeared into the Hollywood wilderness, but when he got his chance to star in Tarantino's *Pulp Fiction*, he proved to the world he's a true acting legend, and the rest is history.

Craig Johnston

He was a young Australian kid who wanted to be a professional soccer player and had a dream to play for his idols at Liverpool. At the age of six, he nearly lost a leg through illness. At fourteen, he wrote to four English clubs before Middlesborough gave him a trial, and his parents backed him by selling their house to fund his ticket to England. Sadly, he was rejected. He was told to go home and that he was too small to ever be a soccer star. He used to practice kicking a ball against the wall relentlessly to hone his skills. After a brief spell back in Australia, he returned to Middlesborough and gained another trial. He impressed, and eventually, he earned his place in their first team at the age of seventeen. He later joined Liverpool, playing 271 times, even scoring for them in an F.A. Cup Final – the ultimate accolade in English football. He retired early to nurse his sister who was very sick back home, but he will forever be a legend.

History is also littered with those gave up just before reaching the goal. They did a lot of the hard work, but just lacked that last bit of extra self-belief and determination to see it through to the result.

It all starts with a dream, but it needs a commitment to make it come true.

One of the best ways to start is to do what I did, and get away. Travel and connect with nature, and you can clear your head, figure out what you really want and 'why', then work out the 'how' afterwards. My love of travel, tourism and helping people has taken my life down a fantastic path, and I now coach business owners so that they can be more effective and hopefully take more holidays that can recharge the batteries and refocus the soul.

Determination – Climbing Your Personal Mountains

There's an old cliché that goes, "What doesn't kill you makes you stronger." It's a phrase often employed by well-meaning friends and family as a 'pick-you-up' when they try to help you feel better about something that has gone 'pear-shaped'. The trouble is that it is often delivered with a smug, omniscient smirk that far from makes you feel better, but rather, merely makes you want to give your advisor a good slap! Nevertheless, there is some truth to the maxim.

> *We often learn more from the things that don't go as planned than from the ones that do – perhaps one of the biggest lessons being that of persistence in the pursuit of our goals.*

I saw a documentary a few years ago that really moved me. It was about a mountaineer and adventurer called Tom Whittaker whose dream since childhood was to climb what the Nepalese call the 'Goddess of the Sky' – we know it better as Mount Everest. In 1979, though, as a young man, he was the victim of a car accident, thanks to a drunk driver. He suffered multiple fractures of both legs, both of his knees were traumatically injured, both his feet were crushed, and his right foot was torn off. He was so depressed, by the apparent shattering of his dreams and his way of life, that for three months he contemplated suicide.

Then slowly, but surely, he began to do what he could. He took his crutches with him on wilderness trips, and with the encouragement of his friends, he began to rebuild his self-esteem.

No doubt he must have felt at times like his life was destroyed. His passion was climbing and many thought that had been taken away from him. Yet, by 1989, he made his first attempt to climb Mount Everest. Twice, Tom tried and failed to conquer the mountain, but was beaten by the weather. One of these friends, a fellow adventurer named Greg Child, had managed to make it to the peak. In an inspired moment, Greg had taken a stone from the summit and challenged Tom to put it back.

In 1998, Tom decided to have another crack at it. Despite now having an artificial leg; despite contracting altitude sickness and having to go from close to the summit back down to basecamp, get slightly better and go again; despite spending a night in a tent in a howling gale and a snow storm; despite crossing a ladder over a crevasse with sheer drops below him; despite now being fifty years of age… Tom prevailed with absolute determination and focus.

So, our hero returned the stone and brought another back for his friend from the 'roof of the world'. The documentary, *A Footprint on Everest*, was presented on Australian TV by Jim Waley on the *Sunday* programme. With absolutely breathtaking scenery and a heart-warming tale, it won the Teddy Roosevelt Award for Best Adventure Documentary and has now aired in over 150 countries.

> *"In today's world, we are all adventurers, and we are all dreamers. Climbing to the summit of Mount Everest with an artificial foot is the physical and symbolic manifestation of overcoming seemingly insurmountable odds to achieve a dream. It is also the supreme act of persistence and courage."*
>
> **Jim Rennie**
> **From www.tomwhittaker.com**

 So, if Tom Whittaker, a one-legged man, supported with an artificial leg, can climb Mount Everest (forgive the pun), but doesn't that make our excuses in life sound rather lame?

> *"There's an old Tibetan saying that it's better to live one day in the life of a tiger, than 100 days in the life of a sheep."*
>
> **Tom Whittaker**

Develop a Millionaire Mentality

In the book, *The Millionaire Next Door* the authors talk about the inevitability of adversity.

> *"You can't hide from adversity. You can't hide your children from life's ups and downs. The ones who achieve do so by conquering obstacles... even from their childhood days."*
>
> **Thomas J. Stanley & William D. Danko**

We will all have bad days; we will all stumble and fall; we will all have days when we wonder if it's all worth it; we will all feel and wonder, *Why does this happen to me?*

Knowing that everyone else feels this way doesn't lessen your own problems or make them disappear. Knowing that there are always millions of other people who have far worse problems with which to contend than you do may help, but it usually doesn't. For example, as I sit here writing this, I have a sore heel that is inflamed from playing sport. Knowing that someone else is lying in hospital with a broken leg might make me realise that things could be worse. That's certainly a great thought process to adopt as a coping mechanism, but it doesn't stop my heel from hurting.

We would all like to protect our families from adversity; it's what we do. Sometimes, however, we might actually be doing them a dis-service. Stanley and Danko studied the habits of numerous self-made millionaires to see if they had anything extra, a special something that we lesser mortals missed out on during our creation. Of course, there is at least a book's worth of traits and habits, which is why it's well worth reading; however, a key ingredient is the way that these successful people view adversity.

When things go wrong, look at the positives as well as the negatives from the apparent disaster.

"What positives?" you might ask, as you look down at your shattered leg in the hospital bed, for example. Then six months later as you marry the pretty nurse you met in the hospital, you say "It still hurt like hell, but thank goodness I broke my leg or I wouldn't have met Suzy!"

Okay, it could be destiny or a quirk of fate, but how many times have you thought something was one of the worst things that ever happened to you (like losing a job, suffering a relationship break up, etc.), only to find in due course that this was actually a turning point that opened the doors to new and better experiences.

A few years ago, I attended a course where I learned a way of looking at the world called the 'Quantum Collapse Process' (now called The Demartini Method®) with Dr. Pamela Dockery, who was an authorised instructor for the program devised by the wonderful Dr. John Demartini. To summarise a weekend workshop in a few words, when something 'bad' happens, ask yourself what the 'good' or 'potential good' is in that situation. My teacher continued on to instruct that we should then ask alternately, "What is bad about that?" and, "What is good about that?" until we have exhausted all the angles from which to view the apparent adversity. It's an interesting technique, and it does change the way you perceive apparent failures and adversities. I highly recommend Dr. Demartini's courses if you have the opportunity to attend one. I repeated the program with the man himself in 2013 and was very inspired.

So the key point is to always look at things from a different angle. Maybe that's how you'll find your personal pot of gold (or non-monetary equivalent!)

Passion and Persistence – The Tarantino Story

If you want an example of an overnight success, then don't look at *Pulp Fiction* Oscar winner, Quentin Tarantino. Why? Because the Academy Award-winning director was no such thing. He had a dream as a young man, and he followed his passion with unremitting fervour.

A while ago, I came down one day with a mystery bug that left me with barely enough energy to leave my bed in the morning and my couch in the afternoon. Thus, we spent a family evening at home and decided to watch a movie. My stepson, Troy, hadn't seen the movie *Pulp Fiction*, and it had been a few years since we last watched the movie classic, so the decision was a no-brainer. As a writer, I find myself analysing plot structures and subtleties on which other viewers might not 'waste' their time, but to me, it's extremely satisfying. With Tarantino's films, I am always captivated and intrigued. We all enjoyed the movie immensely and laughed out loud at some of the dark humour – with me, who has seen it probably four or five times, laughing just as much as first time viewer, Troy.

Realising that this tenth anniversary DVD came with another disc full of extras, I sat spellbound the following morning watching the in-depth interviews with an amazing cast of accomplished actors and, of course, the director and screenwriter Quentin Tarantino. Most people probably only heard of Tarantino when *Pulp Fiction* took the world by storm, thus making him an 'overnight success'. As in most cases, where these words are dropped in by the media, the man was no such thing. For years, he had struggled as a 'nobody'. Tarantino joked that if you had sent a letter addressed to him at 'The Outskirts of the Movie Industry', he would have received it!

With a passion for movies at the core of his being, he had spent his childhood on self-study of the great directors. His encyclopaedic knowledge of movies, themes, plots, genres, and techniques had earned him a job, working behind the counter in a video store. On the weekends, he would rent video equipment, and to gain the maximum benefit of the rentals, he would work tirelessly from Friday night to Monday morning making what he himself described as 'embarrassingly bad films'. He shot hundreds of hours of movie footage, and he couldn't afford the editing equipment to review it, until a considerable time later.

This was in effect his personal study programme – the apprenticeship that made him ready. The interviewer summed it up as a realisation that 'everything you've learned in your life so far has prepared you for this moment'.

 Have you ever had that feeling?

An incredibly talented expert, his original screenplays were so compelling that one of the producers of *Pulp Fiction* was willing to take a chance on Quentin without having even seen his earlier work, including the lower budget hit, *Reservoir Dogs*. And, the rest is history…

The actors who have worked with him include a star-studded list of names, such as Samuel L. Jackson, John Travolta, Uma Thurman, Harvey Keitel, Robert De Niro, Brad Pitt, and many more. They all proclaim that they would turn up to work with Tarantino in whatever starring, or cameo, role that he asked them to play. Such is their love of his work and his style.

The legend is now also a producer, cinematographer, director, screenwriter and cameo actor in a manner reminiscent of the great Alfred Hitchcock. Tarantino's screenplays are emotive and unconventional, especially with his love of altering timelines to tantalise an audience as his characters' stories inter-weave or run concurrently. The dialogue is supremely realistic and believably commonplace, such as the scene where the two hit men in *Pulp Fiction* are on their way to kill a drug dealer, who has wronged their boss. Travolta's character, Vincent, has just returned from Europe, so on the way in the car, he chats mundanely about the little things he has experienced, such as a cheeseburger being called a 'Royale', or the interpretation of the sexuality of a foot massage. The horrific nature of their job does not alter the humanity of their chit-chat on the way to work.

Quentin Tarantino's acclaimed movies include the following: *Reservoir Dogs* (1992), *Pulp Fiction* (1994 – yes, it was that long ago!), *Jackie Brown* (1997), *Kill Bill* (2003 & 2004), *Death Proof* (2007), *Inglorious Basterds* (2009) and the incredibly powerful *Django Unchained* (2012). In his youth, he was but a poor man, with no car and no money, working in a video store to make ends meet, while sleeping on a friend's couch. What he did have though was a dream, which was, as Tarantino himself puts it, "with no fall back plan." He had a willingness to fail until one day he could earn a living doing the one thing that he really loved.

Whether you personally like his films or loathe them is immaterial, as the man is a rock star of his industry. Slightly eccentric without doubt, but he is a man to be admired for both his passion and his persistence, I thank you, Quentin Tarantino, for sharing your gift with us all. By the way, he also comes in on budget, because he wants "the people who believed in me to get their money back."

Become a Go-Getter – The Blue Vase Award

No, this is not a biblical quote. It's an extract from a quote, taken from a book written back in 1921 about values that I think should still be held dear today…

> "It shall be done."
>
> "Nothing can better summarise the determination, the endurance, the loyalty, the passion, and the personal responsibility of a go-getter. Kindle it in yourself and all shall be done."
>
> **Peter B. Kyne (From The Go-Getter)**

Why a blue vase? you may well ask. Perhaps you've heard of the expression, 'The blue vase award'? Well, you should really read the book – it's only a short one, so it doesn't take you long, but I'll give you a clue…

The Jigsaw Pieces of Character

In *The Go-Getter*, Bill Peck, a war veteran, persuades Cappy Ricks, the influential founder of Rick's Logging & Lumbering Company, to let him prove himself by selling sub-standard wood in odd lengths – a job that everyone knows can only lead to failure. Amazingly, Peck goes on to beat his quota, so Rick hands Peck the ultimate opportunity and the ultimate test: the quest for an elusive blue vase. Peck tackles seemingly insurmountable obstacles and draws upon such admirable values as honesty, determination, passion, and responsibility. The story follows Peck's mission to find the vase and launch his career as a successful manager. I won't divulge the final outcome.

In a time when jobs are tight and managers are too busy for mentoring, how can you maintain positive energy, take control of your career, and prepare yourself to ace the tests that come your way?

Apply the timeless lessons in this compelling parable and you can learn to rekindle the go-getter in yourself. Whenever I come up against an obstacle that stands in the way of achieving my goal, I remind myself of the reason why the goal is important to me. That somehow seems to refocus the creative part of my brain to think outside the box and find another way to succeed. Once you have that mindset, that "It shall be done", it's amazing what ideas are borne and what resilience can be found within.

Bounce Back with Desire

A couple of years ago, my blog of the week was inspired not just by the disappointment of seeing the soccer team I support losing the final of a major tournament, but by seeing the reactions of the coach and his players to that defeat and obvious disappointment.

Love them or hate them – and this club seems to polarise those reactions – our lads were played off the park by undoubtedly the most successful team of the previous three years. To lose in any final of any sport is always a very bitter pill to swallow, because history tends to overlook those who came merely second place, despite the tremendous effort that it took to reach the final in the first place. The emotion displayed during such a competition is the most important things that compel us to watch sport – to capture the essence of humanity, the highs and lows of victory and defeat.

Every final shows the agony on the faces of the vanquished and the joyful excitement of the victorious. The faces of the fans on the terraces emulate those of their heroes in the arena.

During that two hour period, or however long your chosen event lasts, you are uplifted and crushed, sometimes within seconds, as a goal is scored or conceded, and for that brief period of escapism, all of our daily challenges are put aside.

There are a lot of lessons to be learned from sport, which is why it's so great for children to be involved in it at an early age and to be encouraged for their efforts, regardless of whether they succeed or falter. In this instance, my team all acknowledged that they had been beaten by a better side. There were no complaints about referee's decisions, 'what if's' or 'if only's'. They simply said, "We did our best, but they were better. Congratulations to them for it." That kind of reaction is a breath of fresh air, compared with a lot of the excuses we have become accustomed to hearing.

When the coach of the vanquished was interviewed after the match, he said, "There was good evidence we are a consistently good European team, but we were beaten by the best team in Europe, and there is no shame in that. Sometimes you come up against a far better team, and tonight was one of those nights."

The team who won so convincingly are also a young team. Their most gifted star and arguably the best player in the world, is Lionel Messi, who was only twenty-three. No-one could therefore blame the defeated coach, who has already passed the usual retirement age, for deciding that he may as well call it a day. Yet, this man, who like is team, is either loved or hated, dismissed the notion of settling for that easy retreat. Sir Alex Ferguson responded as you would expect from a man who is probably one of the most driven leaders on the planet. When it was suggested that Manchester United can never match Barcelona, then sixty nine-year-old Fergie said, "You shouldn't be afraid of a challenge. It's no consolation being the second-best team. I don't enjoy being second-best. Next season, we must improve even more."

As it turned out, Sir Alex did retire from the game. He did not rest on his laurels, however, and postponed retirement until winning the English Premier League for the thirteenth time, leaving at the top of the domestic game and making it a record twentieth time for the club. Unfortunately, his team was beaten in Europe by another Spanish club, Real Madrid. My message, however, was not about whether he was to succeed or fail – that was immaterial. The point was that he embodied and advocated the spirit of bouncing back from defeat with a desire for improvement, both in himself and with his team.

Craig and His Bicycle

My son, Craig, and I sometimes reminisce about a day in his childhood when I helped him discover how to ride a bicycle. I can't remember exactly how old he was, but he was obviously very small, and like most children, he began riding a bike with trainer wheels on the back to help him remain stable and balanced. Then, one sunny day in the back yard of our family home in Perth, we decided he was ready to be a big boy and graduate to riding a bigger bicycle without the trainer wheels.

At first, I held the bike and moved Craig forwards, running alongside him as he tried to get his balance. Time and again, he would wobble and topple, with me doing my best to catch him and avoid injury. Craig must have expected to just get on the bike and ride it – after all, he had ridden his little bike with the trainer wheels like a little madman! He just couldn't get the hang of this new concept though, and after a few attempts, in complete frustration, he 'spat his dummy', as we say in Australia!

"I can't do it, Dad!' he shouted. "I'll never be able to ride this thing!"

"Yes you can, Craig" I affirmed. "I know you can do it. You've just got to keep trying, and you'll get the hang of it, I promise. Come on. I'll help you."

We went a bit slower with me holding the bike, trying over and over again, each time going a little further, until eventually I let go, and he was able to keep riding across the garden.

"I did it!" he yelled, in complete joy, as his mum applauded from the kitchen window. Within hours, he was tearing around the place, and within days, he was doing tricks on his bike that I couldn't even remember doing! I'm sure Craig fell and grazed his knees many times like we all did, but he always got back up and got back on that bike because now he *knew* he could do it.

Something happens to us as we become adults where we often lose that childlike quality to get back up and have another go. If you think about it, had we not had that inner determination, how would we have ever learned to crawl and then to walk?

Tenacity – An Inspirational Attribute!

While we're on the subject of bicycles, in 2011, I was very fortunate to attend a lecture from a lady who was nothing short of a revelation. I have to confess to my ignorance of the sport of cycling, and that despite watching occasional clips of the Tour de France, I had never previously heard of Marion Clignet. Yet when I read the invitation from WA Epilepsy Association head honcho, Suresh Rajan, I knew we were in for a treat.

Cyclist, Marion Clignet had been crowned World Champion six times, as well as double Olympic Silver Medallist, ten times French national champion and multiple USA champion, plus a world record breaker in a lengthy and illustrious career in the sport – all despite taking medication for epilepsy.

The audience was obviously in immediate rapport with Marion because most of them either suffered the effects of epilepsy, or their lives had been touched by a connection with someone else who has the 'condition'. Nevertheless, it is fair to say that even a person who couldn't care less about the topic would have been moved by Marion's inspirational tenacity to overcome any obstacle put before her. Rejected by the American National Team on the grounds that her having epilepsy might prove a hazard to her teammates, thus effectively discriminated against, Marion accepted an invitation to race for France, courtesy of her French parentage.

Marion also overcame discrimination against her gender in that women do not enjoy anywhere near the level of sponsorship or support as men do, in her chosen sport. Now effectively retired from competing at the top level (she just does triathlons for fun!), Marion revealed how a person with epilepsy can suffer a seizure anywhere, anytime. She explained the absurdity with which first aiders can be trained in how to help people who have suffered heart attacks and have defibrillators often readily available. However, the vast majority of the population has no idea what to do if someone has a seizure, nor is emergency medication readily available!

The message from Marion Clignet was delivered in a witty and spellbinding, yet forthright manner: "Those who face major adversities can realise their dreams and ambitions, and actually having these hurdles can often become the driving motivation behind their successes."

In her book, *Tenacious* with Benjamin C. Hovey, she concluded, simply yet from the heart, "Where there's a will, there's a way."

 This poses the obvious question – If Marion can be a World Champion, despite suffering seizures, can't the rest of us also 'Ride faster, harder and with a smile'?

> **Winning Wisdom**
>
> - If you want to be a winner, you first have to develop the belief that you can be a winner and nurture it until it becomes that you are a winner.
>
> - Winners are willing to delay gratification and focus on the result. If it requires sacrifices in the short term to achieve the result in the long term, then they are willing to pay that price.
>
> - Winners are willing to persevere when others would give up.
>
> - Winners are more willing to fail because they see that as just the feedback they need on the path to eventual success.
>
> - Winners keep their eyes and their hearts fixed on the dream rather than on the obstacles to success.
>
> - Winners are inspired by their dreams, so that passion means they are determined and driven to succeed, and they do not worry about what other people think of their commitment to their dream.
>
> - Winners get knocked down the same as everyone else. The difference is that they just keep getting back up until they win. That's called 'doing life well'.

28

Still Believing You Can Win When Life Deals You a Bad Hand

"Success or failure depends more upon attitude than upon capacity. Successful men act as though they have accomplished something. Soon it becomes a reality. Act, look, feel successful, conduct yourself accordingly, and you will be amazed at the positive results."

William James

We already talked about the myth of the 'overnight success', but what about when you think you're on track to win the game and life suddenly deals you a really bad hand?

 Can you still have faith that you will prevail?

The Oprah Story

Oprah Winfrey has been reported to be one of the richest, if not the richest, and most influential women in the world today. Love her or hate her (though I find it hard to imagine why you would), she has been, and continues to be, one of the most profoundly inspirational characters of our era. Like most high achievers though, Oprah has an amazing story – one that has shaped the great charismatic figure though hardship and struggle.

Winfrey was born into poverty in rural Mississippi. Her mother was single and still a teenager. She was later raised in inner-city Milwaukee. She experienced considerable hardship during her childhood, including being raped at the age of nine and becoming pregnant at fourteen; her son died in infancy. Oprah was then sent to live with the man she calls her father – a barber in Tennessee. She landed a job in radio while still in high school and began co-anchoring the local evening news at the age of nineteen. Her emotional ad-lib delivery eventually resulted in her transfer to the daytime talk show arena. Eventually, she launched her own production company, *Harpo*, whereupon she became internationally syndicated. She built a reputation for creating a more intimate, confessional form of media communication. Thus, Oprah has been credited for popularising and revolutionising the concept of the tabloid talk show.

By the mid 1990's, she had reinvented her show with a focus on literature, self-improvement, and spirituality. Though Oprah was criticised for unleashing confession culture and promoting controversial self-help fads, she is often praised for overcoming adversity to become a source of enlightenment and a benefactor to others.

During Barack Obama's election campaign, by one estimate from a reliable source, her support delivered over a million votes to aid his achievement in becoming the first African-American President. Oprah's programmes have made her an iconic figure across the globe and along with her work for charitable institutions, she has been acclaimed as one of the greatest philanthropists in American History, if not World History.

I am always fascinated and inspired by people who overcome adversity and pursue their dreams with single-minded determination – especially when the achievement of them is of such incredible benefit to so many other people in the world. To think that your own vision for your future can impact so magnificently on the lives of people you may never even meet is truly uplifting.

In Oprah's early days, she used to annoy me when interviewing, because I felt that she wanted to answer her own questions before her guests could! Since then, though, she has learned so much and helped so many; she truly is an amazing and inspirational lady. One of Oprah's key messages is that it is really important to find time to relax and nourish your spirit. Exercise, practices such as yoga or meditation, and vacations really help with this. That's one of the reasons why I'm so committed to including life coaching along with any business coaching or consulting work that I do. To me, your business and your life are holistically and inexorably linked. That's why you have to work on balancing all areas.

A Test of Character – The Freeway Incident

 Imagine the unthinkable were to happen and things were to go about as wrong as they possibly could, how would you react?

Often the answer to that question is impossible to find until you are actually the person who is put on the spot. We'd like to think we'd be brave, heroic even, but would we? As human beings, whenever we feel threatened our DNA automatically brings up a 'fight or flight' response that has been around ever since the days when men ran away from dinosaurs!

That's the whole reason why Occupational Safety and Health regulations need to allow for the majority of people's tendency to panic in a crisis. It's the reason why companies have training and induction programmes – so that people know, at least intellectually, if 'this' happens, we expect you to do 'that'. In times of emergency, though, people often disregard their rational thought processes and respond emotionally, rather than logically.

Training and repetition can play an important role because it increases the likelihood that when we *are* put to the test, we will follow an empowering and useful pattern of response to an emergency, rather than giving way to the emotional and unpredictable response that is founded on our base human instincts. The following anecdote pales in significance compared with many that others have faced, but it can help illustrate the power of keeping faith in your own ability and how your character traits will be revealed when you face the unexpected.

A few years ago I was driving to the Perth International Airport late one evening to do a free pick up for two travellers from England, who had booked places at my backpackers' hostel. As I headed down the front steps of the building towards the company bus, a girl who was sitting on the front steps, stopped me to ask a question. I don't remember the question, but we had a short conversation before I jumped in the vehicle and set off to the airport. As I turned onto the main freeway towards the airport road, I found myself in the only vehicle on a stretch of road, where the lighting seemed unusually subdued. I approached the section underneath an overpass, and I noticed a car parked up on the left side of the freeway, with no driver or passengers in sight.

The centre of the freeway between my side of the road and the oncoming lines was fairly full of natural vegetation – bushes and young trees that would have been planted once the road was constructed. It was quite a wide nature strip. I was driving along, lost in my own random thoughts, when something happened that can only be described as reminding me of a Hollywood blockbuster action movie. Accompanied by the incandescent glow of what seemed like the lights of an alien spacecraft, my peripheral vision suddenly caught site of something large and unrecognisable, spinning through the air, flying above the nature strip, twisting and turning like a stealth fighter aircraft in a dogfight.

In emergencies, our minds go into a super-conscious state, where time seems suspended and you feel as if you are watching a movie in slow motion. It seemed like an eternity til I could understand what my senses were revealing to me, but it was probably only nano-seconds.

The 'spaceship' was in fact, though I didn't know it at the time, a car that had become airborne. It had left the oncoming side of the road and was spiralling and spinning from bumper to bonnet, catapulted through the darkness of the night, uncontrollably flipping like a child's toy that had been thrown across a rumpus room. As it twisted and flipped, bits of metal and glass seemed to be flying off it, and there were unrecognisable noises with each moment of impact with the ground, interspersed with what felt like lengthy moments of silence. I instinctively slammed on the brakes, with my rapid reduction in speed serving only to make the airborne car move in an even more surreal manner.

Within split seconds, that to me were an eternity, the spinning stopped as this chunk of metal took its final flip and smashed down onto its roof, sliding inverted across the road before me, before finally coming to an abrupt halt within about two metres of the abandoned car on the freeway's verge. As my bus simultaneously screamed to a standstill, there was a moment – an utterly indescribable moment of eerie serenity as the chaos dissipated – where some similarity to normality resumed.

I think the vehicle was in fact green, but it was only as I sat dumbstruck at the wheel of my stationary bus that I recognised the lump of metal, not as a spaceship, but as a car that was upside down. I sat for another lifetime in stunned silence, gazing at the metallic mess that was only about two car lengths in front of me.

Things are not always what they seem!

I was suddenly jolted from my dazed state, and I sprang into action. I put on my hazard warning lights and jumped from the bus. I intended to run to the car and look for the remains of the occupants in the unlikely event that anyone could have survived the horror show. Before I had taken about three steps, I saw smoke and steam rising from the vehicle in a message that spelled 'danger'. I immediately leapt back in and reversed to a safer distance from the wreck, imagining that as in something like a *Die Hard* movie, this car would instantly explode into a ball of flame and that I would be inadvertently consumed in the ensuing inferno.

My other instinctive response was to call for back up. I rang the Australian emergency number of '000' as I again alighted to the road. If you've ever answered a phone when you've just been woken up by the call, you'll understand what I mean. It felt like a surreal conversation that bordered on the ridiculous. The voice asked me if I needed, "Police, Fire Brigade or Ambulance."

As I glanced at the smouldering carnage, I replied, "You'd better send all three. There's a car on its roof with smoke coming off it, and there may be people trapped inside."

"Okay," she replied, "Where are you?"

I had been cruising along a familiar freeway, but at night, it all looked the same. Thinking quickly, I said, "I'm on the Graham Farmer Freeway, heading towards the International Airport, but I'm not sure exactly how far down the freeway I have gone. I turned onto it from the Great Eastern Highway though, so it's not far from that intersection."

> *If you don't keep track of where you're up to (in life and in business), what will happen when you suddenly need to know and it's really important?*

The response was so bizarrely unexpected that it will be etched into my brain forever.

"What State are you in?" she said.

I thought, *Surely, she can't be asking about my physical and mental state?*

I think I blurted something like, "I'm sorry, what?"

"What city are you calling from?" said the voice.

"I'm in Perth."

I'm sure she said, "Where?" – which was so absurdly weird.

"Perth, Western Australia!" I answered in a state of disbelief. It transpired that she was in Brisbane, Queensland! I had no idea that emergency services were coordinated from a national centre.

The conversation progressed in an inane and to me, insane fashion, as I had to start all over again, answering questions that were to my mind wasting valuable seconds.

> *When you need to communicate as a leader, never make assumptions about what followers understand!*

Whilst all this was going on, other cars came screaming past, seemingly oblivious to the notion that my hazard lights were flashing next to a road covered in metal and glass fragments with a crumpled car on its roof, oozing smoke from every orifice. I began waving my free arm to signal for drivers to slow down as I continued a dialogue of which the Monty Python crew would have been proud, but they must have thought I was intent on car-jacking them. One 'rubberneck' driver almost clipped the inverted wreck, such was his speed and bewilderment. Bits of glass were sprayed everywhere as two or three vehicles crunched over the debris. I was trying to say, "Never mind all that, just get some help here fast!" but I also understood that the receptionist had to be sure of all the necessary information and that I wasn't some kind of prankster.

"Police and emergency services will be there within a few minutes," she eventually concluded.

An attractive lady ran towards me, wearing her pyjamas and a pair of Ugg boots – clothing that aptly matched the surreal scenario before me. "What do you want me to do?" she asked. Somehow, I suddenly was in charge of the 'incident'.

> *When things go wrong, most people urgently look for leadership!*

She volunteered to bring her car across the verge and put on her hazard lights as well. I agreed this would be really helpful and directed her where to park. Some other people approached me, and I established that a little old lady was in shock. The crashed car had narrowly missed her, and she felt responsible. I dispatched them to look after her and reassured her it was not her fault and that an ambulance would be here soon. I also directed crowds of people to stay clear and safe and persisted in trying to slow down the lunatic passers-by.

As we waited for help, the pyjama lady explained to me that she had only popped down the road to her corner shop for some cigarettes, hence her unusual attire. We laughed about it with that sort of gallows humour that occurs during 'incidents'. Even more bizarrely, a door of the wreck suddenly burst open and a giant of a man clambered out, staggering and dazed from the multiple car spins and flips. He was a huge man, sporting a big grey beard and wearing bikie's leathers with a black leather waistcoat. He had the aura of a stoned bikie gang leader at a Zee Zee Top concert – not that I would actually know, as I have never been lucky enough to attend such an event with such people.

You never get a second chance to make a first impression!

"I've killed my mate," said the man-mountain before sitting down on the verge with his head in his hands.

Judging by the state of the vehicle's roof, neither the pyjama lady nor I could quite believe that a live human had extricated themselves from that mangled mess. Within about fifteen minutes, the scene went from one extreme of 'isolation' to the other… 'chaos'. Emergency vehicles appeared from every direction. From being the 'incident controller', I became 'nobody' as far as the police were concerned.

I watched as the paramedics took one look through the upturned car's side window and cast their verdict. The abrupt look away spoke volumes, and they quickly attached a blanket over the side of the car. Presumably the sight on the inside was something I could be glad not to have witnessed. I also watched as the police chased the burly bikie up the road with a breath tester. They were certain alcohol had played its role in the disaster.

It transpired that this man was actually the passenger. He just thought he had been driving and we had all bought into that idea because the car was on its roof, facing the wrong way and that confused everyone. The fact that it was not obvious which side of the crumpled mess contained the steering wheel told its own story. The two men had allegedly left a pub in an intoxicated state and had been weaving from lane to lane at a speed allegedly estimated by police at around

170 kilometres per hour. The little old lady had changed lanes when she saw their lights in her rear view mirror. They also changed lanes, so she changed back, trying to get out of their way. They simply ran out of road and as they swerved to avoid her, the driver lost control of the car and careered into the nature strip. The speed of impact caused the vehicle to take off and spin in my direction.

The realisation hit me several hours later, after I had checked in the two gents from the airport and gone home to bed, that had I not stopped to talk to the girl on the front steps, that vehicle might well have landed on top of mine. The margin between my survival and my almost certain death was minimal. When I reflected on it all though, I realised that in a few split seconds I had gone from day-dreaming motorist to crash scene team leader, and in a few minutes more to irrelevant bystander, later to become a key witness.

> *None of us know when we will be suddenly thrust into a situation that requires our dormant traits to be revealed or how we will respond if and when they are.*

I simply remember thinking at the time, "There is nobody else. It's up to me. I have to deal with this situation. For some reason, unknown to me, I've somehow been chosen." Numerous other motorists drove past the accident, deciding instead to 'not get involved' and that 'someone else' could deal with it.

 Have you ever felt compelled to just deal with a situation and direct people? If so, imagine what could happen if you 'directed' your own life?

Swim Against the Current

In 2011, Jo and I visited an absolutely wonderful dive site at Sipadan Island, Sabah, off the coast of East Borneo in Malaysia. In fact, the legendary Jacques Cousteau, who is accredited with inventing scuba diving and who certainly brought it to the public arena with his incredible underwater documentaries, named the Island of Sipadan as one of his 'Top Ten' dive sites in the world. We stayed at a magnificent timber village called 'Kapalai Dive Resort' that has been seemingly built on a sandbank.

One morning, we arose early for a dawn adventure at Sipadan. It was not an especially deep dive, around twenty-five metres at most, along a spectacular stretch of coral. The scenery was just spectacular, and the marine life was abundant. There were so many turtles. I almost tired of photographing them (but never would – they are such awesome creatures!). There were massive schools of jack fish, butt head parrot fish (they have faces like buffaloes), barracudas, many reef sharks and a myriad of small reef-dwelling fish. I find the underwater sea world incredibly calming, and I feel a real sense of oneness with nature. It's like some kind of parallel universe where all of these creatures are merrily going about their business, completely unperturbed by the insanity of mankind's existence above the surface.

We were happily cruising along, feeling 'in the zone', when we turned a corner of the reef line. Immediately, we were impacted by a massive current. If you find yourself going with such a current, it is a real adrenaline rush. You feel like you are Superman, flying across the surface of an alien planet, requiring no effort whatsoever. We on the other hand, found ourselves facing the tumultuous rip head on!

Jo and I kicked with all our might, but we were making no headway at all. We suddenly realised that the rest of our group had managed to pull in tight against the reef wall, where they could literally hang on to the reef to avoid being swept away. A local dive master, whom we had engaged to make a video of our experience signalled to Jo to ask if she needed help. Her frantic response left him in no doubt, and he surged towards her wearing the largest fins I have ever seen. Had he been wearing them on the surface, you would have been forgiven for thinking he worked in a circus! Our hero pulled Jo towards the reef, and she grabbed it for dear life.

By then, I was quite a distance away from the group, and I was really struggling. I kicked as hard as I could and was even using my arms in a breast stroke fashion, which you don't normally do when diving. My heart was pounding with the exertion, and my breathing was getting heavier. At this point, I was at about eighteen metres depth – deep enough that you really don't want to be breathing like you have just sprinted. It was beginning to become difficult to get the air into my lungs fast enough.

I remembered my training: 'Stop. Think. Act.' Though I could hardly physically stop, I allowed my mind to mentally weigh up my options. I could stop fighting and let the current take me to who knows where. The chances are I could have eventually escaped the current and simply headed for the safety of the surface. I would however, have been separated from the rest of the group and, therefore, isolated in the event of any equipment malfunctions. The unknown element was that some of these currents can actually pull you down deeper as they follow the reef system. I remembered another such severe current that we had been caught in while diving the Solomon Islands, so I was confident that I could find a way to deal with this challenge.

You can actually often see these underwater currents, because they form a sort of corridor of surreal, shimmering water, and if you move into one from outside it, you can actually often sense a dramatic drop in water temperature inside the vortex. In this case, there was a lot of debris, mostly seaweed and bits of reef.

It suddenly occurred to me to try something. Instead of inflating my buoyancy control device, which would have lifted me towards the surface and away from my support team, I slightly deflated it, which caused me to drop about a metre. I began to make headway as I gradually came into the area where the reef wall deflected the water flow. Using every ounce of remaining energy, I kicked and pulled myself to the wall and clung with huge relief onto a large rock alongside Jo. My heart was pounding, and I thought my lungs were about to explode as I tried to regain my composure and bring my body back to a calm state. Within a couple of minutes, I was able to settle back down and eventually continue and enjoy the rest of the dive. I have to say though that the experience was not one I would care to repeat. Nevertheless, it was a learning experience.

If you suddenly find yourself battling against a current in life and all seems lost or frightening; take a moment, calm your inner self, and take stock of your situation and the options available to you. Then trust in your own instinct, and back your own judgement. You may not always get it right, but you will greatly increase your chances of winning the game. If you do get it wrong and live to tell the tale, reflect on it, and seize the learning opportunity contained within it. That's what winners do!

Poker-faced Pragmatism

- The character you develop in overcoming life's adversities will help you win in business and vice-versa.

- Considering that something may go wrong and imagining and training in how you would best deal with it means that if it happens, your instinct will more likely guide you to follow that training.

- If you can direct a successful outcome from a bad situation, there's no reason why you can't direct a great life for yourself.

- If you can remember your humanity and help people in distress, it will always come back to you in ways you might never imagine.

- When the current is against you, trust in your values and your instincts, and you'll find a way to succeed.

- Being dealt bad hands sometimes is just part of the game. Accept that, survive it, and know that better hands will follow. Learning from adversity is an attitude that winners embrace in order to 'do life well'.

29

The Brighter Side of Life

"1. Find someone to laugh with.

2. Find something to laugh at (yourself is always good).

3. Keep moving."

Alan Alda

It's funny how you feel like you've become wiser as you get older (or at least you think you do), and the things you used to worry about suddenly seem so insignificant in the bigger scheme of things.

Smile Because You Have a Straight Flush

As I exited the room of my father at the nursing home, I wondered what life was all about. To see a once-sturdy and tall man who was known in his younger days by neighbours and friends as a bloke who could fix anything from cars to washing machines, now reduced to a shell of his former self, barely able to lift his frail skin and bone from the wheelchair to the armchair and needing assistance to visit the lavatory, was a sad reminder that our dotage will not necessarily be kind to us.

Even as he reached ninety years of age, Dad was amazingly still a survivor. Having left home at fifteen to escape the on-again off-again bickering of his parents, he joined the Royal Air Force as an apprentice fitter. At nineteen, he met and fell in love with my mother, whom he quickly married after a whirlwind romance. Marriage was the 'done thing' in those days. The advent of world war for a second time had exacerbated the need for people to grab at the chance of happiness, knowing that it might well be an all too short window of opportunity.

Having barely become acquainted, the couple were parted by the exploits of a certain anti-social socialist, called Adolf Hitler. So, our young RAF engineer was off to war and at nineteen, he found himself under a barrage of bombs that rained down for twenty-three hours of the day on the Mediterranean island of Malta. The convoys that carried life-sustaining supplies to the isolated fortress were mostly sunk en route by bomber planes and U-boats. Residents and servicemen alike were starving as the island's resources dwindled. My father told stories of cracking open the biscuits on the table and allowing the weevils to crawl out so they could eat what was left. My siblings and I thus suffered the childhood conditioning of having to eat every morsel that was on our dinner plates, because, "We were starving on Malta, you know".

One day, my Dad, now a young Flight Sergeant, was walking along the site of the airstrip and stopped to talk with a chap doing repairs up a telegraph pole, when a bomb landed right where he would have been, had he not paused to chat. On another occasion, when the workload of trying to repair fighter aircraft as fast as they were being damaged, led to a need for the engineers to work twelve hour rotational shifts, a bomb landed on the Sergeant's barracks and destroyed, among other things, the bed on which he would have been sleeping, had he been off duty.

The barrage was incessant and the casualties among young friends were horrific, yet the herculean efforts of my father and his peers in holding the fort against overwhelming odds were incredible. The 'Siege of Malta' was later recognised as a major contributor to the victory in the North African war theatre and the eventual triumph of the Allies. The island itself was awarded the George Cross for the courage and determination of the whole community. My Dad and his mates kept the hurricanes and the spitfires going so they could defend the island and do their best to protect the supply convoys from the German bombers. Between 1940 and 1943, there were 3,340 air raids on the beleaguered island.

The toll on the health of the young men was merciless. My father survived polio and meningitis, in addition to near starvation, thanks to the dedication of the hospital staff in Malta.

When he was gravely ill and pronounced critically so, the air force decided that his wife needed to be informed of the seriousness of his condition. The fellow who delivered the telegram to my mother's house in Chester had a bit of a shock when she fainted in front of him. She had only read as far as, "We regret to inform you…" when the colour drained from her cheeks and she collapsed.

My mother still has that telegram, framed as a reminder of how close he had come to becoming a statistic of the war effort. Other framed accolades include telegrams from the Queen and the Prime Minister of Australia, congratulating them on their 70th wedding anniversary in 2011. My mother, Vera is ninety-four as I write this and still lives in the retirement village that was fortunately about a two minute walk from the nursing home. It was only my Dad's illness that separated the pair, who had raised a large family and run tourism businesses together in Jersey, while he also worked as an Engineering Supervisor for British Airways. He had a fall during the night, while on holiday in Busselton at the age of eighty-eight.

Collapsing head first into some furniture, the injuries were terrible. He suffered numerous facial fractures, appalling bruising and abrasions and apparently some nerve damage during the impact. Lying in a pool of blood and inhaling a fair bit of it did not aid his struggling lungs, which had already contracted partial emphysema. Dad had been a heavy smoker in his youth, apparently having started the bad habit in an attempt to minimise hunger pangs on Malta.

Prior to this incident, Dad had still been driving to do the shopping and banking, living an independent life with his wife.

After all he had been through in his life, he had even survived a previous fall two years earlier that could easily have seen off a person in their forties. With bleeding inside the skull, causing pressure on his brain, we had all thought he was a 'goner' then. Yet the habitual survivor had pulled through, to our disbelief. This time though, when he was flown up to Perth by the Royal Flying Doctor Service, he was almost unrecognisable.

As I saw him lying unconscious with a neck brace, an oxygen mask, and a face that was swollen like he had been battered by a gang armed with baseball bats down a dark alley, I feared the worst. A year later, after many comings and goings from almost every hospital in Perth, he eventually moved to the high care facility. He was able to only drink thickened liquids and would fall asleep during conversations (Perhaps we visitors simply were that boring!).

Mum told him he had to get well for their 70th wedding anniversary in September. He replied that he didn't think he would make it. We all doubted whether he would, yet we had learned not to bet against him. In contrast, one of my nieces was due to give birth at that time, and my own daughter, Kim, had brought my first grandson into the world. Thus continues the cycle of human existence – as one life reached its twilight, new lives heralded a new dawn, born into a totally different world.

In Dad's youth, they had ration coupons, bombs falling around them, friends dying next to them, enforced separation from those they loved, hardship and struggle. Today's pampered generation are blissfully unaware of concepts like delayed gratification, sharing limited resources, or putting the needs of others ahead of their own. As my father deteriorated towards his end, my girlfriend's son, aged almost eighteen at the time, complained bitterly that his iPhone 3 was 'shit', with the inference that he was hard-done-by when his mother had gifted him her phone upgrade, because he should really have got the iPhone 4. I remember shaking my head in disbelief, not just at this one spoilt adolescent, but at a generation who just doesn't 'get it'. That's probably as much our fault as theirs, because we had it so much easier than our parents did. Maybe I didn't quite 'get it' til I hit my milestone of turning fifty. I did my best to make small talk and cheer up my father, while he suffered the indignity of gradual bodily decline; maybe it was then that I had begun to 'get it'.

Now I realise how lucky I am, and how lucky we all are, to live in a free country, where we can voice our opinions; in a land of opportunity for those who are willing to work; in an environment of abundance, surrounded by a wealth of talent; free to enjoy our unlimited potential, constrained really only by those limitations we put on ourselves.

Men like my old dad sacrificed some of the best years of their lives to resist the shackles of tyrannical despotism, so that we could enjoy the best years of our lives in relative freedom. Luckily, he had what some would call 'a good innings'. Back in 1961, my father was spoon-feeding me my dinner as an infant. In 2011, in the hospital, I was spoon-feeding an eighty-nine year old. We had come full circle. From my perspective, I realise that we are indeed lucky. I live a fortunate life, and I intend to live that life to the full. I will cross as many items from my personal 'bucket list' as I can.

One of the happiest things I recall from the otherwise sad decline of my father was the way he and Mum would reminisce on all of the amazing experiences they had shared through their lives together. They would chuckle and smile as they bickered about whose memory was most accurate about the details of their rich life stories.

For fourteen years, I ran a backpackers' hostel where I met over thirty-five thousand young people from all over the world. I was lucky enough to be able to help a lot of them in lots of ways. I now plan to continue helping others through business, life coaching and through voluntary work, helping others to learn from my life's experience of small victories as well as my setbacks and hopefully to overcome a few of the barriers to success.

As I prepared for the inevitable, some of my father's many words resonated loudly in my memory, such as, "If a job's worth doing, it's worth doing well'. I am so grateful to my Mum and Dad. I love you both and appreciate everything you have done for me over the years, though I probably still don't fully appreciate everything. I'm increasingly reminded of many things that I learned from my parents, and hopefully, I will have the chance to pass on a few pearls of wisdom to my children and grandchildren.

 What will you do with your opportunity?

> *Your future will be determined by the decisions and actions you take today. Your destiny is yours to shape. Make the most of the journey, because you never know how long it will be.*

My father lived just long enough for their 70th wedding anniversary and his ninetieth birthday. He did that through sheer will power and determination. Three weeks later, his time was finally up.

Choose to Be Happy

Here is a small excerpt from a book by Andrew Matthews, an amazingly talented guy whom I have been privileged to hear and see presenting on stage many years ago in Perth. Andrew has written numerous best sellers, including *Being Happy*, *Making Friends*, *Follow Your Heart*, *Being a Happy Teen*, and *Happiness in a Nutshell*. His books have been translated into thirty-three languages and are bestsellers in sixty countries! He is a much sought after speaker around the world on attitude, achievement and prosperity, and I guarantee he will inspire you.

> **What We Have**
>
> *Imagine that we discovered life on Mars – even if it was only a tiny bug, or an ant with one leg... The world would go crazy! Splashed across the front page of every newspaper would be headlines, "THERE IS LIFE OUT THERE!"*
>
> *Scientists would be ecstatic, "Another species!"*
>
> *Now, here's what's strange... 27,000+ of the earth's species of birds, plants, animals and insects became extinct last year. The story never made the headlines. Our tigers and pandas and frogs are disappearing. Meanwhile, we look for signs of life in outer space!*
>
> *How often do we overlook the great things we have – and go looking for new stuff?*
>
> *We do the same thing in relationships!*
>
> *When we finally realise what we had, it's gone...*
>
> *The first trick to happiness – and success – is to appreciate what we've already got."*
>
> **Andrew Matthews, from his book Happiness Now**

Here is an old proverb that sums up 'happiness' quite well:

> *"If you want happiness for an hour, take a nap.*
>
> *If you want happiness for a day, go fishing.*
>
> *If you want happiness for a year, inherit a fortune.*
>
> *If you want happiness for a lifetime, help somebody."*
>
> **Old Proverb**

In my experience, people live happier lives if they live according to their values. It's worth taking the time to figure out what those values are!

> ## *Happy Having Hads*
>
> - This moment right now just became that moment just then, so count your blessings because the 'Good Old Days' are happening right now.
>
> - It's important to keep your sense of humour, especially when things go wrong, because it helps keep you sane. If you can laugh in the face of adversity, things never seem as desperate.
>
> - Take time to reflect and be grateful – you'll find that you SO MUCH to be grateful for. Even when things go wrong, be grateful it wasn't as bad as it could have been!
>
> - You can be happier if you focus on what you do have rather than whining about what you don't have.
>
> - The same can be said for meetings and parties – focus on the people who HAVE turned up, rather than whingeing about the people who didn't.
>
> - Read books and stories and watch movies and shows that make you laugh. Laughter is good for the soul and it's widely believed to be good for the body.
>
> - Surrender to a higher consciousness that in fact 'Things are exactly as they are meant to be!' (Even if the reason doesn't yet make sense to you – maybe it will do later on.)
>
> - Live in alignment with your values! That's a key part of 'doing life well'.

30

Be the Change You Want to See

"The only way to deal with an unfree world is to become so absolutely free that your very existence is an act of rebellion."

Albert Camus

In Thailand, when they train baby elephants not to escape, the handlers tie one of their legs, roped to a post in the ground. They can only walk a rope length away before it tightens and they can go no farther. As the elephants grow older and stronger, the handlers replace the rope with flimsy twine. By then the elephants have become so conditioned to the fact that it is impossible to go beyond that limit, even though the twine would not withstand their mighty strength, that they no longer try to escape because they have given up on the possibility.

 Is there any area of your life where YOU have simply given up on the possibilities?

Are You Willing to Do What It Takes?

I so often hear people saying they would really like to do something, or be something, or have something, but within a few minutes you realise that for them, that elusive thing will only ever be a pipe dream. That is of course, unless something changes…

Usually, the 'something' that needs to change is the person themselves. Now some would argue of course the old saying that, "A leopard can't change its spots." Well, even if your name is 'Jackson' and you're a world famous singer, you can't change the colour of your skin, but can you change your mindset? The answer has to be 'Yes!'

Barring physical impediments, the rule of thumb is that if someone else can learn to do a particular thing, you probably could too. One of the key reasons why most people don't succeed, is that they are quite simply not willing to do what it takes to achieve the result.

If you want to learn to play a guitar for example, you have to practice playing guitar. If you want to be great at it, you have to play til your fingers are sore. Then you keep on practicing despite the pain. When the Beatles returned to England from Germany, they were billed as 'the band from Germany that was an overnight success'. In fact, they were the band from Liverpool who took the opportunity to go to Germany and who played in seedy Hamburg bars until their fingers bled. The reason why they were willing to do what other bands were not was that perceived band leader, John Lennon, later revealed their dream to be 'the best band in the world'. So they had a big dream – a compelling or burning desire, in fact – but they were also willing to do what it took.

Most people don't even dare to dream, or they talk about their dream with a resigned 'someday maybe' attitude. When I work with business clients, I only work with people who are willing to take action. Here's the key point:

> *Whatever your dream, look at someone who's done it and look at what they did. Study what they did, and model what they did. If they did it, you probably can too.*

What's also pleasing is that even if you don't quite make it, you usually end up coming across a better alternative opportunity than the ones you have now, and you can look yourself in the mirror, knowing that you 'gave it a go.'

Mahatma Gandhi's Legacy

A seemingly innocuous, petite man who grew up in a little known region of India was amazingly to become one of the greatest political figures the world has ever known. Mahatma Gandhi studied law in England before going to South Africa, where he spent twenty years opposing discriminatory legislation against the Indians who had been settled there, courtesy of the British Empire. He began to pioneer a concept of resistance to the authorities through mass non-violent civil disobedience.

> "Be the change you wish to see in the world."
>
> **Mahatma Gandhi**

When he returned to his homeland in 1914, he led the same kind of uprising against the British rule of India with mass non-violent protests. His main goal was to free his country from oppression, tyranny, discrimination and excessive taxation. In addition, he wanted to emancipate women, alleviate poverty, end the caste system and ultimately establish an India that was free from the Empire and allowed to govern its own destiny.

In 1930, he led a 320 kilometre march to the sea to symbolically collect salt in defiance of a government monopoly. He was arrested, not for the first time, after the famous 'Salt March', but his persistence and belief in his dream of a free India was finally rewarded in 1947 when the country officially became an independent nation. Sadly, his attempts to heal the rift between the rival religions of Muslim and Hindu led to his assassination in 1948. Nevertheless, his passive but stubborn heroism made him a role model for other great leaders, including American civil rights campaigner, Martin Luther King, Jr., and South African freedom champion, Nelson Mandela.

Gandhi disproved the South American freedom fighter, Ché Guevara's theory that you can only create massive political change with the use of violent force. His argument was that peace, love and belief in a just cause were far more potent weapons.

So it seems that in order to effect change, whether it is on a massive global scale, a massive national scale or a massive personal scale, you need to be willing to first open your mind to seemingly unrealistic possibilities, because the 'History of Mankind' has shown us that change begins with a concept, an idea or a vision of how what 'may be possible' can be transformed into what 'is possible'. This change can only occur if your mind is open to new possibilities.

In the words of an old saying of unknown origin: "The mind is like a parachute – no use unless it's open!"

Exemplary Evolution

- If you want better results, you have to take better action.
- If things are not going to plan, first check if your thinking is correct, then check if you are doing the right things.
- To have the change you seek, you must become the person who deserves it.
- People follow leaders who lead by example. One day, who knows? Great leaders around the world might be following your example because you were 'doing life well'.

31

The Twists and Turns of Life

"With every experience, you alone are painting your own canvas, thought by thought, choice by choice."

Oprah Winfrey

In the last chapter, I mentioned about your mind needing to be open like a parachute. This story really explains why that's a key to a better life.

Be Prepared for Unexpected Twists

One evening around the summer of 1994, I was at a party with a bunch of mates having a few drinks, when we began discussing some exciting things we'd always wanted to do. One of our friends, whose nickname was 'Pearler', began telling us about his recent experience of doing a parachute jump. That was all it took. Somebody suggested that we should all go and do a jump and the 'Dutch courage' kicked in. I'm usually up for most things, so of course I said I was in.

The next day I thought, *What have I done? Why would anyone jump out of a perfectly serviceable aircraft?* but there was no backing out! A weekend or two later a whole group of us drove out to Brookton, South East of Perth, to the Dale River Drop Zone. We were not doing a tandem skydive where you are attached to an instructor and to a large extent find yourself as a kind of involved spectator. Instead, it was a static line jump, where you climb out of the aircraft and you alone are responsible for deciding whether your chute will safely bring you back to the ground. In order to be able to make that decision, it is mandatory for you to sit through parachute jump classes for about six hours, covering everything from how to exit the aircraft to remembering to keep your legs together if you find yourself about to land astride a barbed wire fence!

The training also included a sort of simulated jump where you strap into the equipment and hang off something akin to a swing set frame. I can tell you that it is not the most pleasant experience for a guy as the straps go between your legs and rather tightly either side of your manhood. Because you are suspended rather than falling, this means that the straps take your bodyweight and have a tendency to crush the 'family jewels'! We all came through this ordeal and concentrated hard on the safety briefings, especially with regard to the deployment of the parachute.

Once your primary chute opens, you then have only ten seconds to decide if that chute is good enough, mainly meaning that it is not twisted, and that it will do the job. If not, you pull a chord which disconnects that chute and opens your secondary chute. It is preferable to use the first one because that opens up to a canopy style parachute, rather like a hang glider, whereas the second one is a round chute that is far less manoeuvrable.

The chosen aircraft was a four-seater high winged Cessna, except that the only seat belonged to the pilot. Three parachutists and the instructor squeezed inside on our knees. The instructor and the pilot were the only ones with normal facial expressions and pallor. The rest of us looked distinctly pale and nervous. In my plane was a girl we didn't know, my housemate, Glen Riggs and me. Glen was as white as a sheet, and I'm sure I was as bad. Kneeling down in a cramped position, wearing a sort of boiler suit and protective helmet, with the weight of the parachute pack on my back on a hot day was very uncomfortable. The old plane seemed to take an eternity to climb above the airstrip to the jump height of three thousand feet. Any thoughts I had of changing my mind were ruled out by the fact that I was in the front, so I had to go in order for those behind me to be able to exit. As it turned out, the girl changed her mind and backed out of the jump, but Glen did follow my example. As the warm sunshine beamed through the window of the cockpit, I was sweating profusely and becoming increasingly nervous.

Suddenly, the instructor tapped me on the shoulder. It was time for me to go. There was no door on the plane, just a gaping void where you would normally expect to find one, with a spectacular countryside vista below us. As I put my hands on the door frame and my foot out onto the step below it, the eighty miles per hour wind hit me in the face. I reached out to the wing strut, grabbing firmly with both hands and stood on the wheel of the plane. As I then stepped off the wheel and hung from the wing strut, the full realisation of my situation now kicked in. I remember saying to myself something similar to, *Oh goodness me! Whatever are you doing? You could climb back in and land this plane yourself, you foolish chap!*

I gripped that wing strut with every muscle and sinew in my being screaming at me not to let go. As I looked below me though, I noticed a forest approaching ever rapidly. The logical part of my brain informed me that if I didn't let go sooner rather than later, I could well find myself landing amongst those unforgiving trees and that would not be pleasant. I glanced across at the instructor, and she was giving me the signal to let go. I was supposed to adopt the skydive position with arms and legs spread wide as I counted to ten, before making my decision about the effectiveness of my parachute. Instead, as I let go of the strut and began to plummet towards the ground, I suffered from sensory overload, causing a sort of black out, and I apparently went into pretty much a foetal position!

My momentary disorientation was broken with a jolt as the parachute opened, courtesy of the static line that pulls it open from the aircraft. I was in a cold sweat as I regained my senses. My eyes were initially watering because of the breeze, and I felt an overwhelming sense of gratitude that my parachute had opened. I was still alive, but would I remain so for long? Then my training took over – time to check the chute. I looked up above me and realised to my horror that my lines were all twisted and tangled! My life was in my hands, and there was nobody else who could help me…

If you're wondering whether I survived or not… I'll tell you in a minute!

32

Empower Yourself or Be Overpowered

"Any area of your life you don't empower, someone else will overpower you."

Dr. John Demartini

To turn your life around and reinvent yourself as the person who may previously have only existed in your wildest dreams may require a huge leap of faith. If you can find the will to back yourself, that leap could become a lengthy flight. The following is a terrific example.

Demartini's Gift of Empowerment

Dr. Demartini was once, in his own words, a bum – and he was a bum who had reached rock bottom. All his life, he had been told he would amount to nothing. After eating and drinking all kinds of wrong things one day, he almost died in a tent on a surfers' beach, but he survived and vowed that instead of being overpowered, he was going to become way more than his previously illiterate self. Today, he is considered one of the world's leading authorities on human behaviour and personal development. He is the founder of the Demartini Institute – a private research and education organization with a curriculum of over seventy-two different courses covering multiple aspects of human development. His trademarked methodologies – the Demartini Method and the Demartini Value Determination – are the culmination of thirty-nine years of cross-disciplinary research and study. His work has been incorporated into human development industries across the world.

Dr. Demartini travels 360 days a year to countries all over the globe, sharing his research and findings in all markets and sectors. He is the author of forty books published in twenty-eight different languages. He has produced over fifty CDs and DVDs, covering subjects such as development in relationships, wealth, education and business. Each program is designed to assist people to activate leadership and empower themselves in all seven areas of their lives: financial, physical, mental, vocational, spiritual, family and social.

I caught up with him at a recent event in Perth, entitled 'Business Breakthrough'. He thanked me for coming and complimented me on my tie! In just a few seconds, he gave you the feeling that you were the most important person he had met that day. Now that is a gift to which we should all aspire! I told him that it was an honour to meet him. Of course, I went on to repeat his weekend workshop, The Breakthrough Experience®. If you ever get chance to attend one of his seminars, I highly recommend it. He is one of the most inspirational speakers I've ever heard because he reinvented and empowered himself to empower others.

Choose to Win Your 'Game of Life'

Like many Australians in 2012, I was drawn to my television to watch some of the world's greatest athletes push themselves to achieve results beyond what was previously thought possible. The Olympic Games, of which this was the 30th Olympiad, are in this day and age almost unavoidable, even if you are a person who bizarrely hates sport – which of course, I'm not.

I have played a myriad of sports in my lifetime, though not to any level that even approaches Olympic greatness, but I love it. I'm one of those reasonably good all-rounders. At school, though I could easily have been put off the whole idea…

Rather like the story of 'Tom Brown's school days', my young primary school friends and I were mercilessly sent out into the snow and freezing rain, shivering in our skimpy singlets, our plimsoles being swallowed by particularly squelchy mud in the grassy green fields surrounding our Victoria College Preparatory School in Jersey, Channel Islands. Those so-called cross-country runs are etched into my brain as stark reminders of the 'tough love' brand of education of yesteryear.

Nostalgia is a quirky thing though, because I now look back on those days and those experiences as 'character-building'.

Unless you could prove you were dying of something like bubonic plague, the teachers accepted no excuses, and especially not inclement weather conditions! For me, it was like torture, yet for some gifted individuals it was their chance to shine. Some children found that they had an unusual ability to gallop across those pastures, dodging the cow pats and leaping over barbed wire fences, somehow skipping across the muddy pools without sinking in, while others lost their shoes and socks in the quagmire. These gazelle-like athletes blazed their way back to the school field and the comforting finish line, probably having time for a hot shower and a cuppa while I was still trying to navigate my way through the field with the bull in it as I squelched from the mud in my shoe! It is in those moments of triumph where people like that find an ember of possibility, that maybe, just maybe, they could excel at that chosen sport.

Hockey was another of those sports invented by sadists, though they forgot one important detail in their grand design – that the freezing cold was your ally, because when your opponent's stick slid up your stick and rapped you on the knuckles, you didn't feel the pain. Well, not as much anyway, or at least until you had your hot shower and all of the bruising started to come out as the circulation returned to your almost-hypothermic body!

Anyway, back to my point… Some of these people ignited a passion for a particular sport. In our house system, at our somewhat elite institution, competition was not only encouraged, it was demanded. The will to win was instilled, and people were trained to continually push the boundaries so that those embers of possibility became burning cauldrons of desire and resolve. We competed relentlessly with other schools, and with each other, and achievements were acknowledged at school assemblies.

> *The Human Connection in the Pursuit of Excellence*
>
> *The will to win is intense among the Olympic athletes who grace our screens today. What you see is not the result of some hobby. Rather, it is the result of years of intense passion to achieve a dream, years of sacrifice, years of commitment, to strive to be the best in the world at whatever it is that they do.*
>
> *That is what captures our interest and indeed our imagination, seeing in their faces the joy of victory or the agony of defeat. That saga, even at this extreme level of excellence is one to which we can all relate, even at our most basic and ordinary levels, for we 'relatively average' mortals also experience pleasure and pain in all of our endeavours.*
>
> *It is in fact a globally televised magnification of the experience of being 'human'.*
>
> **Tony Inman**

Here is the interesting twist, however…

Each one of us has a choice in our lives.

We can choose to at least strive for excellence, because even in falling short of that goal, we would probably still improve and grow from the effort. Or we can choose to lead a life of quiet desperation – a life of 'woulda, coulda, shoulda's…' and 'If only's…' We may not all be Olympic Gold Medallists, but we can all choose to be better, faster, braver – just a little better than last time, and in the effort we can all be winners. We can also encourage each other, so that in those moments of doubt and uncertainty there is always someone to offer a helping hand, a kind word or a smile of support. The Olympics are so inspirational because they remind us of the great qualities that lie within us all. Admittedly some people hide those qualities so well that you could be excused for thinking them absent, yet still they are there. They just need to be appreciated and uncovered.

So I say, 'Enjoy the games!' but remember also that the 'Game of Life' continues for us all, perhaps not with medals always up for grabs, but we can all still be winners at whatever we do. Whether your game is to be a great athlete, a boss, a mother, father, employee, spouse, whatever…

> *You have the choice – the choice to settle for*
> *less or the choice to strive for more.*

Remember that every choice you have made in your life so far has got you to exactly where you are right now. What you do next is also a choice.

How About That for a Leap of Faith?

For English speaking people, the name 'Felix Baumgartner' sounds a little quirky, which fits quite nicely with why his name will be remembered for a very long time. Millions of astonished TV viewers around the world watched in October 2012 as the forty three-year-old Austrian thrill-seeker took a huge leap of faith to plummet over 39,000 metres (128,000 feet) from his helium balloon above the Earth. This was no random act of attention-seeking frivolity, however. In making the jump, Felix became the first human being to break the 768 miles per hour sound barrier in freefall. In fact, he reached a top speed of 1,340 kms per hour (833 mph).

> *"If something goes wrong, the only thing that might help you is God. The only thing that you hear is yourself breathing."*
>
> **Felix Baumgartner**

The risks don't even bear thinking about. Had Felix's specially designed $235,000 pressure suit failed in the stratosphere, his blood would have boiled. Had it failed during freefall, his heart would have stopped and his eyeballs would have burst. The bottom line is that failure for Felix would almost certainly have meant death.

The obvious question people asked Felix was, "Why did you do it?"

"For the same reason people climbed Mount Everest," he replied.

This world record breaking leap of faith also provided vital scientific research as mankind continues the quest to explore life opportunities beyond Earth. Baumgartner was covered in monitors that will provide invaluable information about the effects on the human body for scientists and spacecraft designers, who need safe escape options for passengers in the future. It did not escape my attention that Red Bull sponsored the Stratos capsule from which Felix jumped. They are making a habit of supporting adventure sports and are a great example of how companies can align their effective marketing with missions that advance humanity.

I don't get the impression that this will swell Felix's head too much though, as he made this wonderful comment, "Sometimes you have to go up really high to understand how small you really are."

It makes you think though doesn't it?

 If Felix Baumgartner can take a leap of faith like that, with those kind of potential risks, where in your life might you risk taking a teeny bit bigger leap of faith and empowering yourself in the process?

Leaps of Love

- Look for the good in people and find something nice that you can say to them. Be sincere in your compliment, and people will not only feel empowered themselves, they will link that good feeling with you.
- Take responsibility for your life and realise that you are in whatever position you are in because of the choices that you have made thus far.
- That realisation will then empower you to choose whatever changes you wish to make to that situation and to know that you *can* change it.
- When you choose to have a bigger dream and to push the boundaries of what was previously thought possible, you actually have the power to impact on the entire human race!
- If you don't empower yourself, remember that 'Nature abhors a vacuum', so you will, by default, empower someone else in your place!
- You can only truly love and appreciate others, when you love and appreciate yourself, so learning to love yourself is 'doing life well'.

33

Twist or Stick

"We will act consistently with our view of who we truly are, whether that view is accurate or not."

Tony Robbins

In the game of life we take chances – some we win, some we lose. Jumping out of a plane was one of those chances that could easily have resulted in 'game over'. I wasn't ready that day, in Shakespeare's words to "shuffle off this mortal coil," even though I had written a new will the night before!

Freedom from Entanglements

So, back to my foolhardy decision to jump out of a perfectly serviceable aircraft! I had just mentally overridden the muscle memory in every fibre of my being to do the unthinkable and let go of the aircraft's wing strut. As I plummeted to the ground, experiencing a sensory overload blackout, my chute abruptly jolted me back to a state of consciousness.

Looking up at the tangled mess of lines connecting my body to the parachute that had not properly deployed, I now had less than ten seconds to make a life or possible death choice. The wind was making some strange flapping noises as the chute struggled to do its job. I had not yet had the benefit of the 'Stop. Think. Act.' training that we receive in scuba diving, but I did have plenty of emergency situational training when I gained my private pilot's licence as a nineteen year old. My mind was racing as I fell ever closer to the ground below. We had also prepared for this in ground training school and on that horrible 'nut cracking' swing set!

I had to attempt very quickly to untangle the lines or make the decision to jettison that parachute and hope that my secondary chute fared better. I firmly grasped both supporting straps with my hands and pulled down on one side, kicking as I did so to create a counter-movement in the direction opposite to the line tangle. As I began to spin, I literally untangled the lines. As they did so, the air rushed up into the fabric, I stopped spinning and my parachute unveiled in a magnificent display of colour. Suddenly, I stopped sweating. I knew I was in a much safer situation, and I felt like James Bond descending to the mountain castle base of his nemesis.

With the tangled lines now untangled, I focused instead on obeying the signals from my ground instructor, who had a big white arrow that he pointed to show me which direction I should aim for. Turning with a canopy chute is the closest thing to flying like a bird that I have so far experienced. The only sound was the wind flickering in the canopy, the occasional flap of a bird's wings nearby, and the sound of my own heart beating. I felt so alive. The ground rush was exactly that – a sense that the ground is rushing up to meet you as the adrenalin surges through your veins.

I landed reasonably well as I flared out, but with the grass being wet, my feet slid, and I fell quickly onto my backside, albeit in a very safe manner. I had survived, and more importantly, I had conquered another fear.

In that moment, and for a long time afterwards, I felt that if I could do a parachute jump, I could do anything! I had trusted in my inner voice – the one that told me, *It's okay, you can do this!* My preparation had been thorough, the training had covered the contingencies, and my self-talk pulled me through the challenge.

If you can learn to see yourself as a confident, competent person who can handle *whatever* challenge you face, then when you are tested, you will act in keeping with that viewpoint, and the things that make you feel entangled will soon drop away.

34

The Power of Leverage

"Man can either buy his wisdom or borrow it. By buying it, he pays full price in personal time and treasure. By borrowing it, he capitalizes on the lessons learned from the failures of others."

Benjamin Franklin

After I sold the last of my tourism businesses in 2010, I found myself at a career crossroads and really wasn't sure what I wanted to do next.

The Reinvention Specialist

I went to the local swimming pool one afternoon and sat in the spa, relaxing in the warm bubbles, lost in my own thoughts. As often happens, another bloke sat in the spa, and we started chatting. When he asked what I did for a living and I mentioned that I had run a few different small businesses, it was as if I had opened the flood gates. This gent began asking all sorts of questions. He had been considering setting up a business for himself as a lawn mowing contractor, and the types of questions he asked, to me, seemed very obvious. He asked me things like, "Do I need to register a business name?"; "How do I do that?"; "How do I set up a business bank account?"; "Do I need an A.B.N.?" …and so on.

It suddenly dawned on me that the answers were only obvious to me because of my business experience, but to him, it was a whole new world. I began reflecting on the possibility of coaching people in small businesses, but I had also thought about coaching people on their life issues. I cast my mind back through all of the years in the backpackers' hostel and all of the late night conversations where people really appreciated the opportunity to pour out their troubles and have some objective input into their future options. One of the amazing things about travellers is their willingness to be open with people very quickly. It's as if the time it would normally take to build friendships is somehow accelerated because they realise that time is very limited and that within short time frames, the group will disperse around the world and may never see each other again. The impact of social media has enabled people to stay in touch so much more easily, but there is still a degree of effort required. It's staggering to think though that in 1996, when I first started there, the internet was scarcely known to people. People used to hand write a letter to their family overseas and would borrow our office fax to send them a copy!

I thought back to one young Kiwi lad, whose name I think was Joey. He had been going through some family drama back home and had started talking about it. I listened and asked lots of questions, and we worked out some strategies for him. A day or two later, he came to me one morning and said, "Hey, Tony, I just want to thank you so much for what you said the other night. It really helped me a lot, and I feel a lot happier about the whole situation, eh"

He had talked with his family and they had managed to patch up a lot of their differences. The only thing was that I really couldn't remember what it was that I had said that could have made such an important impact on his thinking. Maybe it was just that I listened and cared.

That was only one example, and if I thought long and hard, I'm sure I could fill a few volumes with stories because it was all about the people. People are fascinating. We are such a mixture of hopes, dreams, fears, love, confusion, jealousies, hatred, anger, sorrow, pain, joy… the list is massive, and the challenges are many. What I love though is seeing people's potential, especially when they struggle to see it in themselves. If you can nurture that; if you can encourage them; if you can inspire them; if you can equip them with the tools and techniques to achieve their potential; then how much of a ripple effect can you have on the world?

When you study the examples set by people like Nelson Mandela, Mahatma Gandhi, John F. Kennedy and others, you start to realise the power of worthwhile dreams and goals and how you can inspire others and leverage your time and your ability to effect change by sharing your vision for a better world. If you look at the mass appeal and high esteem in which we hold our sporting heroes like Michael Jordan, Mohammed Ali, David Beckham and others, you can see how people can emulate their success, learn from their failures, study their techniques and styles and duplicate the best parts to drive human beings on to even higher levels of performance.

If you consider the incredible performances given by actors such as Robert De Niro, Al Pacino, Helen Mirren, Cate Blanchett, backed by great directors like Steven Spielberg, Martin Scorcese, the Coen brothers, Francis Ford Coppola – there are too many to mention, and I know you will have your own favourites – you can see how Hollywood and other great movie production areas can deliver stories, experiences, the history of mankind, interpretations of our evolution along with projections of what may or may not eventuate in the future. Then there are the musicians of all categories from the Beatles to Beethoven, Billy Joel to Barbra Streisand – people who can make us laugh, make us cry, make us distraught or inspired.

I have talked about the famous, but there are many in ordinary everyday lives who have the power to inhibit our growth or propel us to greater heights, from our parents, our teachers, our friends, our enemies, doctors, nurses, fire crew and police – all of have lessons for us to learn.

If you consider the huge volume of information that we now have at our fingertips at any given moment, the technology of today has created an insane amount of noise. We have hundreds of social media outlets and thousands of apps for smart phones and tablets. When I was a child, a computer took up a whole room, and you had to get out of your chair to change television stations or change the volume. Today, we are bombarded with emails, with mass consumerism, with home shopping, with discount vouchers… and so much more.

We can take a photograph on our phone and send it to a friend on the other side of the world in split seconds along with our views on everything from politics to the state of Mum's cooking. We can leverage our time and our expertise in ways that would have made the ancients turn in their graves.

Yet, despite all these advances, people are still people. If anything, they have more hang ups than ever before, because the speed of change and progress seems to make most people feel inadequate in some ways, whether it's not having the right job, the right sized business, the right clothes, car or other material possessions, the right weight, the right attitudes – in some way, just about everyone feels like they have not achieved what they should have.

Governments manipulate us with even more propaganda than ever before because technology allows them to do so. Big corporations rule the world and the power brokers use their influence to manipulate governments to amend the rules to suit their shareholders. I see and I hear all of this noise and confusion – that's why I call it an insane world. How can it be sane when we have all of this progress, yet there are still wars, famines, illness, and destruction of our eco-systems?

So who do you listen to if you want to make sense of it all? I read, listen to and, where possible, meet the kind of people who can help make sense of it all. I listen to business and life coaches, philosophers and professors. I try to keep my businesses in balance and my life in balance. I do yoga. I stop and think. I read and I write. I exercise. I enjoy nature, and I travel to explore different civilisations, cultures and attitudes. I have studied aspects of psychology, NLP, family systems, the esoteric teachings of Hawaiian Huna, behavioural sciences and, of course, soccer! In summary, I may only have a short time on this earth, but I want it to count for something.

The best way to achieve that, I believe, is to leverage my time and leverage my resources. I can't do it all on my own – nobody can. What I can do is expand my philosophy and my knowledge and hope to distil those learnings and use them to enrich others. If by reading this book, you find one new idea that can make a difference in your life or in the lives of people you know or even people you have yet to meet, then I have achieved something of significance.

Please take note, when a fifty-two year old writes a book, it has taken them at least fifty-two years and nine months to learn the stuff they have written about. So, when you read that book, you have just leveraged the few hours it took you to read it to gain fifty-two years' worth of lessons of good and not-so-good ways of doing things. It is then up to you to use for yourself and your loved ones that which is useful and empowering to you and to reject that which is not.

> *"You'll be the same person in five years as you are today, except for three things – the books you read, the tapes you listen to and the people you meet."*
>
> **Charlie 'Tremendous' Jones**

That is how you leverage your time and your expertise, and that is why I do the work I do.

When I started in coaching, I was concerned that I might not have enough experience and felt compelled to spend a year doing every course I thought would help. I sat down for a coffee one day with a man who had been a coach and consultant for several years already and expressed my concerns. That man was David Deane-Spread, and he asked me how long I had worked in retail management alone before I had started my own businesses. It was about twenty years. He asked how many staff I would have coached, trained and developed throughout that time. The realisation hit me as he knew it would. He cited a book called *Outliers: The Story of Success* by Malcolm Gladwell, in which he introduced the '10,000 hour rule', claiming that if you have done something for more than 10,000 hours, you are to be considered an 'expert' in that field.

David and I soon worked out that I had done way more than 10,000 hours of coaching, training and developing people in retail alone. Then there were the eighteen years running my own businesses, with hundreds of staff. If you then multiply that by the knowledge I have gained according to Charlie 'Tremendous' Jones' theory, then I am sufficiently qualified to help people transform their lives and their businesses. Thus, I encourage you to seek out mentors in every area of your life and your business.

I don't mention all of the above to big-note myself but to make the point that you, the reader, can multiply your knowledge, your expertise and your time-effectiveness to an unlimited degree. All you have to do is find a reason why. The other key point is to surround yourself with what my networking specialist friend, David Bearsley calls 'The Power of Many' – a support group of likeminded people, or what author Napoleon Hill called 'a Mastermind Alliance'.

Critical Concepts

- You may not yet see yourself as an expert but if you know much more about something than someone else does, to them you ARE an expert.
- Therefore, seek out people who know more than you. To you, they are an expert.
- Time is the one resource you cannot regain – a second lost has gone forever, so don't waste it. If you are slacking off, relax and consciously rest without feeling guilty – you obviously needed it. (No, I'm not condoning 'sickies' – that is called unfairly wasting the boss's money!) If you are working, work hard, but better still, work smart!
- It is obviously important to learn from your mistakes. It is even smarter to learn from other peoples' mistakes!
- Seek out coaches for every area of your business and your life. Even coaches have coaches! A coach is not as emotionally involved or attached to the same things as you, so they can see the little things that can make the big differences!
- Always ask yourself, 'How could I have done that easier, better, smarter, quicker?'
- Knowing your reason 'Why' will help you seek smarter and more efficient ways of getting there, and you'll be 'doing life well'.

PART THREE:

HAVING

Finding Peace, Balance and Fulfillment

'King of the World' - Tony happily re-enacts the Titanic pose at the wreck of HMAS Perth near Albany WA.

PART THREE – 'HAVING'
Finding Peace, Balance and Fulfillment

"When you arise in the morning, think of what a precious privilege it is to be alive – to breathe, to think, to enjoy, to love."

Marcus Aurelius

Part Three is about having the results you want in life – about recognising that you have them and about appreciating what you have. When I first began my coaching consultancy, I agonised over whether to focus on business coaching or life coaching. Some clients engaged me to do life coaching, and we found ourselves sorting out their business matters. Other clients engaged me to tackle business growth, and we found a need to sort out their life first. I soon realised that, in fact, my point of difference was to be able to jump comfortably between the two areas and to integrate them for my clients.

I also had the feeling that everything I had done in my life thus far had prepared me for this role and this moment. To use Steve Jobs' great analogy, I could "connect the dots backwards" that led me down this path. Now, I was starting to connect both my clients' dots and my own dots forwards as I designed the kind of lifestyle that I wanted. Of course, there could always be more money, more time, more travel, more holidays, but you have to balance the whole spectrum. On the whole, I feel blessed to have a great life. It's okay to want more – that's what drives us. It is, however, your responsibility to be happy now, wherever you are and whatever is going on. I'll explain the 'how' in a moment.

I have a wonderful grown up family with my son Craig, daughter Kim and partner Marty, and a gorgeous grandson, Hayden; a fantastic partner and stepson in Joanne and Troy; and I have an awesome collection of friends, who are way too numerous to mention. My mother is still going strong at ninety-four, and my brothers, sister and extended family are all also terrific people. Jo and I design wonderful adventures, often based around our love of scuba diving and travel.

PART THREE – 'HAVING'

We play lots of sports, including volleyball and beach volleyball. I still play soccer, and we do yoga classes and go for lots of walks around beautiful lake areas. For creative reflection, I love playing guitar and singing, and I really enjoy writing. My business interests are growing steadily, and I feel calm, happy and blessed.

This didn't all happen by accident though. It's a situation I've worked hard for and I've created over a period of time. I've certainly worked very hard over a long stretch, and I've had some pretty major challenges to overcome. I have, however, stuck with a system, which is based on the anonymous 'Be. Do. Have.' coaching theory.

The following diagram is my illustration of my 'Transformation Model'. Put simply, the reason my life is the way it is today, is because of what I have learned and who I have become on the journey to this point. I have applied the teachings I have devoured from some of the world's leading coaches and transformational thinkers. I love helping people; I love seeing them grow and get results; and I love the energy that comes with the enthusiasm of their success. I have learned many things from many great and talented people, and in a way, I feel as if I have therefore become a conduit to pass on those lessons to my clients, my family and my friends.

When my time comes to transform into whatever energy form comes next, I believe I will have made a contribution that is meaningful, and I am happy for that. Until that day comes, I hope my candle can continue to burn brightly as I certainly still have a massive 'bucket list' that seems to grow more than it shrinks, and I love that. None of us will achieve everything we set out to, but I'm sure going to give it my best shot. So this section of the book is about finding your peace, your balance, and your fulfillment. Thank you to everyone who has played their part in my journey so far.

Inman's Transformation Model

The following image is my visual model of how we go about achieving the results we really desire in our lives.

INMAN's TRANSFORMATION MODEL

©AD INMAN 2013

- HIGHER VISION
- HAVE — REWARDS
- WHO — I WILL BECOME!
- EXPAND MY PHILOSOPHY
- IDENTITY — WHO AM I NOW?
- VISION
- RESULTS
- ACHIEVE GOALS
- TOUCH LIVES
- SYSTEMS & STRATEGIES
- MODEL SUCCESS
- MISSION
- PLAN
- VALUES & PURPOSE
- GIVE
- SUCCESS
- DO — TAKE ACTION
- BE — THE BEST YOU

"The success is in the journey and in the people whose lives you touch along the way. The success is in who you become rather than in what you have as a result."

Tony Inman

35

So Have You Found Your Why Yet?

"The two most important days in your life are the day you are born... And the day you find out why."

Mark Twain

The clues to finding your life's purpose will be found in noticing and examining the things you naturally enjoy doing and that you gravitate towards.

Your Two Most Important Days

You may never have heard of Samuel Langhorne Clemens, but he is better known by his pen name of Mark Twain. He was an American author and humourist. He is most noted for his novels, *The Adventures of Tom Sawyer*, and its sequel, *Adventures of Huckleberry Finn* – the latter often referred to in literary circles as "The Great American Novel." He is also held in high regard for his many profound quotes and observations on life. Twain was born during a visit by Halley's Comet, and he predicted that he would "go out with it" as well. Intriguingly, he died the day following the comet's subsequent return. I find it interesting to reference Mark Twain's quote to an ancient Egyptian tomb that I visited at Abu Simbel.

The twin temples were originally carved out of the mountainside during the reign of Pharaoh Ramses II in the thirteenth century, BC, as a lasting monument to himself and his Queen Nefertari, to commemorate his alleged victory at the Battle of Kadesh, and to intimidate his Nubian neighbours. However, in 1968, the entire temple was relocated, numbered stone by numbered stone, onto an artificial hill made from a man-made dome, high above the Aswan High Dam reservoir.

The relocation of the temples was necessary to avoid their being submerged during the creation of Lake Nasser – the massive artificial water reservoir formed after the building of the Aswan High Dam on the Nile River. Abu Simbel remains one of Egypt's top tourist attractions. What is particularly amazing is that they originally constructed this tomb with hand tools, yet they angled the floor upwards and the ceiling downwards towards the back of the temple, creating a sort of zooming effect. On the back wall of the inner chamber, they drew the four gods, plus the Pharaoh himself, the 'God on Earth'.

They aligned it all so that twice each year a beam of sunlight goes through the front door, through the public chamber, through the High Priests' chamber and into the Pharaoh's sanctum, illuminating the face of the Pharaoh – once on the anniversary of his birth and once on the anniversary of his coronation. Were those guys amazingly clever or what? Perhaps those were the days, as per Mark Twain's quote, when the Pharaoh was born and the day he found out 'why'?

 Have you found your 'why' yet?

The Sum of a Man's (or Woman's) Life

If you want a lesson in making your life count for something, try writing and delivering a eulogy. It's not my intention to darken your day. In fact, read on, and I hope you'll find my message will have the opposite effect. Nevertheless, in May 2011, I had to do exactly that, at my own father's funeral, Bill Inman. Raymond Inman, known by his preferred name of Bill, passed away three weeks after his ninetieth birthday and eight months after his seventieth wedding anniversary. It's the second eulogy I had spoken – the former was at the funeral of my girlfriend's father, Alan Small. On both of these occasions, I realised that the legacy you leave behind consists of four things:

The Legacy You Leave Behind

1. **Your Family**
   It took the passing of my father for me to realise what a loving, caring bunch of people my family actually were, because like so many families these days, we have allowed our busy lives to get in the way. My siblings and I have all devoted our careers to service-providing industries. Our children have all done the same.
   Note: Think about the role model you want to be.

2. **Your Relationships**
   In both cases, I was staggered at how many people either turned up to pay their respects, or took the trouble to send their condolences.
   Note: Think less about what you want from others, and think more about what you can give.

3. **Your Experiences**
   Actor Kevin Costner said in an interview, "A man's life is the sum of his experiences." Well, both of our fathers lived incredible lives, travelling the world and living their dreams, while they quietly got on with their work and provided for their families.
   Note: Don't live a settle-for life – design your life the way you want it to be.

4. **Your Messages**
   The words you spoke to your partner, your children, your grand-children, your friends… in fact, anyone with whom you connected – those words that made a difference to peoples' lives, whether verbal or written are the greatest legacy you can leave. Your deeds may also serve as an example and perhaps as a source of inspiration to others.
   Note: We live in a transparent world where your every move can be scrutinised and where people can assume your 'hidden agendas' based on their own values. Reflect on your words and deeds, and ask if the life you live is one of which your children and your loved ones would be proud. Of equal importance is to look in the mirror and ask that person, "Are you proud of your thoughts, words and deeds?" The more easily you can answer, 'yes', the more you will be 'doing life well'.

   Tony Inman

I have recently learned a little about quantum physics with Dr. John Demartini and a little about Hawaiian esoteric spiritual Huna teachings with Dr. Serge Kahili King, and I find a common theme in the belief that we are all connected – to each other and to planet Earth and all of its creatures. We are also all made up of goodness and badness, lightness and darkness. In fact, things are neither one nor the other, unless we make them so by our own perception of reality.

In my eulogy for my Dad, I used the following quote:

> *"We are not human beings having a spiritual experience, but rather we are spiritual beings having a human experience."*
>
> **Dr. Wayne Dyer**

Tony Robbins (famous inspirational author and speaker) says, "Nothing in life has any meaning except the meaning we give it. If you don't like the way you feel, choose to create a new meaning." When all is said and done, one day, we will all transform from our physical form into whatever you believe comes next for you. I'm reminded of the stirring words of the Scottish warrior in the movie *Braveheart*...

> *"Every man dies; not every man really lives."*
>
> **William Wallace**

Our two fathers really lived. So, I ask you sincerely, think about what you stand for, whom and what you are passionate about and what meaning you would like your life to have for those who follow and care about you. Don't sweat the small stuff. Be glad that you have another day on this Earth – another day to influence the people with whom you connect, smile more often, and seize your day.

 If you had to write your own eulogy or pick the words for your own tombstone, what would you want it to say?

I know that might seem a little depressing in one sense, but on the other hand, it helps you get focused on what is really, truly important to you!

Pondering Your Purpose

- If you haven't yet thought about what you want to do in your lifetime, then think about it now – and write down the answers! Then there's much more chance that you will achieve it!

- Don't worry right now about *how* you will achieve all of these things – you can figure that out later or ask someone who knows!

- Make sure that you progressively do all the things you want to do, while you still can!

- Think about what you'd like to be remembered for – that's your legacy.

- Think about whom you wish to become and what you'd like to be known for while you're still here – that's how you'll 'do life well'.

36

Keeping the Wind Beneath Your Wings

"Follow your instincts. That's where true wisdom manifests itself."
Oprah Winfrey

There will be times in your life when you feel as if you just can't see the forest for the trees. You know there should be more to life. You know that you are capable of more, but you just can't see the next move.

I hope that this book has encouraged you to feel that when it's really important for you to make the right decision, you can trust your own intuition.

Embrace the Winds of Change

The engine rumbled into life as I turned the ignition key of the gleaming white Piper Cherokee Archer – a four-seater touring aircraft that belonged to the Channel Islands Aero Club. My three passengers beamed with excitement as I received permission from Jersey Air Traffic Control to line up for take-off. It was a fine summer day with lovely flying conditions, and we were bound for a small French town on the Cherbourg peninsular called Lessay. The town is famous for a large annual fair, and that was the reason we were flying there.

In truth, we didn't really need a specific reason. The real joy was just getting up in the air and experiencing that thrill of escaping the daily grind of the island, feeling that freedom of being as free as a bird and travelling somewhere different. Jersey is a delightful jewel in the English Channel between England and France, and I will always be nostalgic about my birthplace. However, like anywhere in the world, you eventually feel the urge to go somewhere else and explore new territory.

France offered us a significant contrast, and it was right on our doorstep. From coast to coast, it was a mere twenty miles, so our flight from Jersey to Lessay only took about twenty minutes. It had become a pretty regular event for me to pop over to France for a coffee, a lazy lunch or a day at the beach. My friends and I relished the opportunity to so quickly find ourselves using another language, using different currency and enjoying different cuisine. I think I could have happily lived in France. I love their laid back culture, well outside of the bustling cities anyway, where they happily take two hours or more over lunch, while chatting with their friends and enjoying fine wines. They seem to have found that sense that life is to be savoured and not rushed.

The ocean below, though welcoming on a warm day, was a dark contrast to the clear blue skies above as we meandered to the French coastline, cruising at around two thousand feet above sea level. I had never been to Lessay before, so as a private pilot, I always had that sense of excitement and wonder at seeking out an unfamiliar airstrip, picking it out in the distance. The dual attraction in this case was the opportunity to visit the largest open air market in Europe.

The French have a disconcerting habit of sticking their airfields in the middle of a forest and not always making it a very long airstrip either, thus leaving little margin for error in your approach – whether you descend short or land too far down the runway, you could easily find yourself smashing into trees, which would not have a happy ending.

I followed the usual airfield circuit-joining protocol and was cleared to final by French Air Traffic Control. I had completed all my pre-landing checks, lowered my air speed and extended the flaps on the wings. It was all looking great. Suddenly, something extremely unexpected happened. We hit what I later discovered was a phenomenon known as wind shear. This is a strange atmospheric condition whereby winds can change direction and speed abruptly, thus having a significant effect on the flight path of a light aircraft.

If you have sufficient height it is not usually too much of a problem. In fact, light aircraft are more than capable of handling quite severe stresses caused by weather conditions. In this case, however, I was on final approach, in the last stage of my descent at a very slow airspeed, so this situation was potentially very dangerous. I suddenly found that my aircraft was being sucked down towards the trees.

Of course I was rather taken aback by this, and a quick glance at my passenger next to me, who was not a brave flyer to start with, confirmed that he was clearly breaking out in a sweat. The trees were looming ever closer, appearing to fill the whole front window of the plane with green foliage.

If I didn't do something, and quickly, we would probably all be dead. There was no time to think it through. It was time to go with my instincts!

What happened next…? I'll tell you in a minute!

37

Operating on Instinct and Being Congruent

"Trust instinct to the end, even though you can give no reason."
Ralph Waldo Emerson

I have studied success for over thirty-four years now, and I've developed a fascination for getting to the bottom of the enigma of what makes a human being stand out from the crowd.

High Achievers

I've mentioned many of the composites of success in previous chapters, facets such as:

- The importance of having a dream that is broken down into written-down achievable goals

- Stubbornness and persistence in the face of adversity

- An enhanced vision of what 'can be', rather than settling for what 'is'

- A willingness to go the extra mile and do whatever is necessary to get it done and make it happen

- Charisma to attract, engage and use the leverage of a team of loyal followers and advisors, and the leadership qualities to keep that team motivated and inspired

- The intelligence to establish smarter systems and the means to measure whether the project is on track
- The ability to focus on getting results and leverage their time and expertise
- Seeing setbacks and failures as the feedback they need to do better
- A sense of inspiration to transform a vision into a non-negotiable mission

In this book, I've added quotes from many of the world's most successful people. Those people are proven to have achieved greatness, because history records the facts of their accomplishments. Yet each and every one of us can be a high achiever in our own way, in our own lives, among our own friends and families.

If you have raised a child, helped the sick or the elderly, counselled someone in distress, inspired someone else to succeed at something they thought impossible, then who's to say you're not a high achiever in your own way? It really is all a matter of subjective perception. 'Sure!' the sceptics might say, "But what is it that really sets apart the people who achieve more than the average Joe?"

That answer is also subjective, so I'll give you what I think it is – which is just my opinion, though it's an opinion based on a lot of study and observation. I believe that all of us have far more potential than what we actually use. A lot of that is because we let our 'stuff' get in the way, and by that, I mean our limiting patterns, our learned responses, our lack of self-confidence, etc.

One of the key things that sets 'higher achieving' people apart is that they have learned to trust their instincts more often, and the more often they do trust their instincts, the easier it becomes to do so and the sharper those instincts become.

> *"The very essence of instinct is that it's followed independently of reason."*
>
> **Charles Darwin**

The other factor is that by connecting with their own internal link to a higher consciousness, the more they are congruent with their higher core values.

> *Simply put, in my opinion, high achievers know why they are doing what they are doing and that it aligns with their core values and their chosen mission.*
>
> *Thus they can more easily and more frequently trust their gut instincts, which will often prevail over logical reasoning to achieve exceptional results.*
>
> **Tony Inman**

Just to put in a sensible disclaimer here, I am not advocating reckless abandon. To use one of my heroes as an example, a person like Sir Richard Branson will move swiftly to follow his instincts, which he has learned over time to trust. Nevertheless, he would also back up that action by surrounding himself with the smartest people he can find to give him the best advice available. These people would do the research and go to work on proving or challenging the viability of the 'gut instinct' ideas. If in the process, the numbers just don't stack up, despite the emotional attraction of the idea, the chances are that an objective and considered decision will be reached. Time and again, however, Sir Richard's hunches and self-belief have proven to be correct, and his team go about making the 'impossible', possible.

Instinct is like a muscle, the more you trust it and use it, the stronger and better it will grow.

Ask Yourself Better Questions

Something I have truly gained from the works of the world's leading transformational coaches and thought leaders, like Dr. John Demartini and Tony Robbins, is the concept of learning to ask yourself better questions. When you are listening to your inner voice – you know, the one that asks you things like, *Are you crazy? What makes you think that YOU can do this?* one thing that you can really start to do more and more, until it becomes a new habit, is to ask yourself better questions. By better, I mean more empowering, more useful and more constructive.

For example, instead of asking...

❓ *Why does this (perceived bad thing) always happen to me?*

You could change that to…

❓ *What could I do to make sure that I make this (perceived better thing) happen for me more often?*

We are actually driven by the questions that we ask, so if we begin to ask more empowering questions, we will actually start to see hugely different results to those we have previously achieved. It's not so much a question of 'positive thinking', which can be helpful, and it's not just a case of looking for the positives in every situation, though that undoubtedly helps too. It's about accepting that a situation or an outcome simultaneously contains both 'positive' and 'negative' aspects and that both are valuable. Even something we view as negative now could later on turn out to be the best thing that could possibly have happened to rock our world. It's more about asking yourself how you *can* achieve what you *do want* more often.

The mind is an amazing energy source, most of which we don't use, but what we *have* learned is that when you operate at a higher level of consciousness, (i.e., more in alignment with values that are part of a more significant, more ethical and often more altruistic purpose), and we ask the questions of ourselves that will lead us to invoke greater powers, such as the Law of Attraction, our minds will help us to achieve extraordinary results.

Instinctive Intelligence

- Instincts are like muscles - the more you trust in them and use them, the more you will develop them.

- Accept that all situations are neither 'good' nor 'bad' unless we perceive them and label them that way.

- Learn to ask yourself more empowering questions that will focus on getting the results you DO want and your sub-conscious mind will go to work on ensuring that you will HAVE better outcomes and you will be 'doing life well'.

38

Defying Logic

"There will be a few times in your life when all your instincts will tell you to do something, something that defies logic, upsets your plans, and may seem crazy to others. When that happens, you do it. Listen to your instincts and ignore everything else. Ignore logic, ignore the odds, ignore the complications, and just go for it."

Judith McNaught

I promised I would tell you what happened next with my 'wind shear' predicament as I approached the Lessay airfield in North-Western France. The small four-seater Piper Cherokee was being sucked down into the trees by a force of nature, and my three passengers and I would more than likely be about to reach an untimely demise. The foliage filled my windscreen, and there were only seconds in which to make a life or death decision.

When something is coming towards you and you are about to collide, your natural reaction is to turn away. In a car you would probably turn the steering wheel without thinking if you thought the brakes would not do the job. In an aircraft in flight, unless you are in a Harrier Jump Jet, capable of stopping in mid-air, braking is not an option. Your first reaction, therefore, would be to pull back on the control column and pull up the nose of the plane. I didn't think, or at least if I did, it must have been as fast as lightning. I immediately reacted according to my gut instinct, in complete contradiction to that human impulse reaction.

Instead of pulling back on the column, I pushed the column forwards and pointed straight at the trees while simultaneously ramming on full power with my right hand on the throttle. With his sharp intake of breath and physical bracing, I could sense my passenger alongside me thinking that I had gone completely crazy as we initially appeared to plummet so close to the foliage that we could make out the twigs on the branches.

What had triggered my instinct reaction, I can only presume with the benefit of hindsight was the quality of training that I had received from my flying instructor – a truly gifted though slightly crazy and eccentric pilot, Jon Pedley. Somewhere in my training, Jon had drummed into me that the attitude of the nose of the aircraft controls air speed, while the power of the engine does not make the plane go faster in the air as a primary response – it actually controls your height. Therefore, the effect of my actions was that although the plane was pointed more downwards towards the trees, thus increasing my air speed towards them, by increasing power at the same time, I caused the plane to lift upwards and over the trees to safety.

As soon as I was clear of the huge obstacle, I cut the power again and brought the aircraft down for a safe and smooth landing on the runway, as if nothing out of the ordinary had happened. My passenger later confessed that he thought we were all about to die and that he had thought me insane when I pointed the plane down at the trees.

The reality was that a plane is at its most vulnerable either just after take-off or when it is on approach to land. The reason is that you don't have the height and, therefore, the time to respond to emergencies, nor the airspeed to accelerate out of trouble. By pointing downwards and increasing the air speed, I had prevented the possibility of the aircraft stalling and literally falling out of the sky and into the unforgiving trees below. When we say 'stalling' in an aircraft, we are not usually referring to when the engine stalls mechanically, but we are talking in terms of aerodynamics to when the airflow breaks up over the wing. It is the difference in pressure caused by the air flowing over the wing trying to catch up the air flowing under the wing that causes lift.

When you go beyond a critical point, you lose that lift and cease to be aerodynamic. Stall recovery is not a problem if you have sufficient height, but if you stall at below two hundred feet, you may not have enough time to recover. In other words, the plane would be falling rather than flying.

What that means in this story is that I acted on instinct, based on quality training, rather than according to the conventional human reaction of trying to avoid the obstacle. In doing so, in that split second of trusting my instinct, I saved my life and the lives of my three passengers. I was very proud of myself that day and very grateful for the fantastic training that my instructor had given me.

> "Being able to act intelligently and instinctively in the moment is possible only after a long and rigorous period of education and experience."
>
> **Malcolm Gladwell**

39

Inspiration and Joy – It's All Around You

"To give pleasure to a single heart by a single act is better than a thousand heads bowing in prayer."

Mahatma Gandhi

The ability to inspire others is a gift with which all of us are born. Some of us use that gift consciously while others may do so unconsciously. Even in the moment that our parents become aware of our conception, we may have begun inspiring them to be better, to strive to do more perhaps, simply by existing. All too often we remain blissfully unaware that we have inspired other human beings, yet surely there can be no greater joy than to inspire others to greater actions and to know that you planted that seed of an idea or that word of encouragement that uplifted their soul.

The Human Experience That Unites Us All

There are moments in life when we glimpse the human spirit in its purest form. One such moment occurred in 2012 in an English Premier League football (soccer) match between Tottenham Hotspur and Bolton Wanderers.

With no other player near him, a twenty three-year-old Bolton player named Fabrice Muamba collapsed suddenly in the middle of the pitch. The emergency response was rapid, and it soon became apparent that the situation was serious; he had suffered a heart attack. The reaction of the crowd and the players was what was most admirable. Everyone immediately put aside their sporting differences, their regional differences, and their partisan passions to become united in hope – that this young man would simply survive the experience.

For an extraordinarily long time, the players and the crowd were helpless bystanders as the paramedics used all of their skills to try to save Fabrice's life. There was simply an eerie, stunned and tangible silence throughout the stadium. His teammates linked arms, some visibly weeping. When they were finally confident enough to stretcher him from the field to the waiting ambulance, the entire crowd erupted with applause that carried far more respect than the usual cheers to which the athletes were accustomed.

> *"...footballers – for all their wealth, for all the adulation lavished on them, for all their privilege – are simply human beings.*
>
> *Human beings susceptible to the same slings and arrows of fortune as us. They're not immune from tragedy.*
>
> *Last night should have reminded us of that one terrible fact. Idolise them, criticise them, laud them, decry them.*
>
> *But remember, they are the same as every man, woman and child that loves this beautiful game."*
>
> **Andy Dunn**
> **Journalist – *Daily Mirror Sport UK***

At times like these, we are reminded of our humanity – that deep down we all face our own human struggle for existence and that deep down, we have more in common than we often acknowledge.

Fabrice's father was a political refugee from Zaire, so you can imagine his pride that his son would succeed in sport to the point of playing football for a top English team, as well as representing England as an Under-21 International. Imagine now the pain and fear of a father waiting to see if his son would make it through the day, as he lay critically ill in hospital. Plus, there was the added shock that this could happen to someone who was a professional athlete. From all of us in Australia, we sent him best wishes, as we would do for all those around the world who are waiting on news of a critically-ill loved one.

Life is all too short so I urge you to make it count.

Do what you love and bring joy to others, just as Fabrice has brought joy to his family and his fans. Fabrice has been living his dream, and fortunately, he recovered, despite having died and been resuscitated five times on the pitch. Alas, on the advice of his doctors, Fabrice had to subsequently retire from the game, but the point was that even in just playing for a Premier League team, he had lived the dream of his childhood and made his family so proud of him.

 Are you living the life of your dreams? Are you inspired by what you do?

Joy Can Be Found in the Simple Things

I have a feeling that my grandson, Hayden, is going to teach me a lot. He's now two years old and full of beans. "Shouldn't that be the other way around? Shouldn't you teach him?" you might well ask. Well, actually, here's the thing…

Something I've rediscovered in my quest for continual improvement as a coach is that the best way to learn things is to teach them. Profound, eh? Think about it though – when someone asks you a question or they have a problem on which they are stuck, you help them discover the solution by asking questions around the issue. Jeff Slayter and Kane Minkus, who are known as 'Jeff and Kane,' are two of the amazing guru coaches under whom I have studied. They describe the process as "Discovering a whole heap of rabbit holes and diving down them until you figure out which rabbit hole is the most important one to the client so that you can keep digging deeper."

As you ask the questions and observe the reactions and responses, it challenges your own thinking too. In fact, the strangest thing is that I keep finding that the very things my clients are asking me about and having problems with seem to be a direct reflection of my own questions. Sometimes, they are current issues, or sometimes, they are issues that I have just finished sorting out myself. In helping my clients, I also crystallize my own thoughts and consolidate my own strategies or direction.

You could actually conclude that we see life as a reflection of ourselves, because all of our beliefs and habits are shaped by our experiences and our familial structure, so we filter everything we experience through our own unique view of the way the world works – what we students of Neuro Linguistic Patterning (NLP) call 'Our Map of the World'.

George Faddoul, another of my great NLP mentors said, "We should never be astonished at anything that happens in life." Now that's a deep topic for another day, but the point is that the lessons are there, just waiting for us to notice them. What started my train of thought was seeing the sparkle of joy in Hayden's eyes as I waved a bottle of water in front of him. We'd just finished our Tuesday evening volleyball game, and the family all stood in the car park chatting under the floodlights. The light was catching the water in the bottle and causing interesting reflections. Hayden was fascinated, and his little face was beaming with delight as he reached out to touch the bottle. It was the same fascination he had when we had put a mirror on the floor for him when he had first started crawling, and he could see another Hayden looking back at him. So there you have it.

*Seek out enlightenment and joy and reach out
and grab it, no matter your age.*

Children aren't cluttered with all of the stuff that we worry about. They just see the joy in the simplest of things. Imagine if we as adults could reinvent ourselves to be that way again…

Remember to be vigilant and actually notice those special moments as they can be a source of great joy and even inspiration.

Inspirational Insights

- Despite all of our differences around the world, we are all united in some way by our own humanity. Sometimes, we just need to look for that common bond.
- Life can be snatched away from us unexpectedly at any time, as can our health. The future is promised to no-one, so don't take it for granted.
- Joy can be found all around us in the simplest of things – we often just need to allow ourselves to notice.
- Some of the greatest inspiration and learnings can occur to us when we are helping someone else to figure things out. Teaching or helping others helps us 'do life well'.

40

What Next? – Winning the Games of Business and Life

"In a time of universal deceit – telling the truth is a revolutionary act."

George Orwell

John Lennon challenged us in one of many immortal Beatles' songs, "You say you want a revolution? Well, you know we *all* want to change the world. You tell me that it's evolution. Well, you know we *all* want to change the world!" The simple fact is that the world is constantly changing. It always has, and it always will.

Change Is Constant – Get Used to It!

Today's world is fast-paced and so full of contradictions, political upheaval and hidden agendas, wars and famine (that should simply not be occurring with today's technology), rampant consumerism and ecological destruction. It is so rich in information and disinformation that we have actually come very close to making George Orwell's vision of the future in the book *1984*, become a reality. As we human beings continue to make the mistakes of the past, despite technological, medical and communications advances, these are the reasons why, in my book subtitle, I have labelled our world as 'insane'.

We might think that as individuals we cannot change anything, that we cannot make a difference, and that our voice would never be heard in the chaos, yet history offers us plenty of examples of people who have done exactly that.

That is part of why I have included so many quotes in this book. I feel that inspiration is all around us, and we *can* push beyond the limitations that we so easily put upon ourselves.

In recent decades, we have seen images flashed around the world in seconds that have stayed with us for years. There have been horrible images. In Vietnam, we saw the little girl running from the napalm bombing. In Afghanistan, Iraq and Egypt, we have seen war, death and suffering. In the U.S.A., those who saw it will never forget the images of planes crashing into the Twin Towers of the World Trade Center.

Yet we have also seen inspirational images. In China, we saw a brave student holding up a column of tanks in Tiananmen Square. In Germany, we saw people tearing down the Berlin Wall. We have seen Steve Jobs of Apple launch the iPad, and we have seen Sir Richard Branson launching test flights of a prototype for a commercial space shuttle.

We have the power to effect change with a ripple that begins with one person declaring 'That is enough. This situation needs to change!' It can equally begin to change when one person asks, "How do we solve this problem?" or, "How do we create a better world?"

No matter whether we're trying to achieve global peace, save the eco-systems of planet Earth, and/or end famine, poverty and disease, we all have a little more power than we think. The uprisings of the people seeking political change in Middle Eastern countries have shown us that. The internet, smart phones and social media have changed every aspect of our lives and will continue to do so. I'm just one author with a few, possibly zany ideas, but in this book, I have distilled the wisdom of many great thinkers and leaders taken from many years of study. If only one of these ideas makes a difference in the life of each reader, then imagine the profound ripple effect that could be achieved with even just one book.

It all starts with YOU making some decisions about designing your life in such a way that you can help yourself to find fulfillment, and in doing so, you can restore that elusive sanity that you may have misplaced amid the chaos.

A Mobile World of High Speed Communication

Something that we will all need to embrace rapidly for our survival in the business world is the way we think about the nature of work and how we go about doing our business.

On the 'threat' side of the matrix is the fact that jobs are no longer 'safe'. A recruitment consultant in Perth recently declared, "No matter how long you think your contract of employment is for, the reality is that it's actually at most a month." Subject to disclaimers about length of service and unused leave benefits, what she was saying is that we can no longer expect to stay in the same job for our whole career. The days of seeing old Fred presented with his gold watch for long service are gone. That's not based on any judgment about your perceived loyalty; it's about the rapidly changing nature of work and the way it will be done.

Your job security is going to be based on a combination of your ability to produce and on your knowledge and skills. So if you don't perform and 'achieve the required outcomes', you will be replaced. Equally, if you don't stay current and topical with an active 'personal and professional development programme', you will be perceived as a 'dinosaur', and you will be replaced.

For some of the more mature generations, we have seen a quantum leap in humanity's knowledge and technology. The Gen Y people have grown up with a high-tech world as 'the norm'. Children can figure out how to use a smart phone or a tablet device way faster than their parents, while their grandparents are left nothing short of 'gobsmacked'. The rate of change seems only to be accelerating, so if your plan is to bury your head in the sand and make statements like, "Oh no, I don't use social media. I don't believe in it!" then I strongly urge you to call me, or another life or business coach, because you need to get your head around this.

The mobile phones of today are the 'communicators' that we saw Captain Kirk carrying around in the early episodes of *Star Trek* back in 1966, when I was five years old. We are already talking verbally to computers which can think for themselves and answer us. We are already building robots to do the jobs people used to do. We have already cloned animals and duplicated life forms. Sir Richard Branson is not only developing planes that can fly from Australia to England within a mere couple of hours, he is also asking his experts to figure out how we can colonise Mars. We are probably not far away from Kirk's famous request,

"Beam us up, Mr. Scott", whereupon we will be physically able to be 'transported' or moved across vast distances within split seconds.

These are all benefits on the 'opportunity' side of the matrix, because it means that with access to information, cloud technology and lightning fast communication, more and more people will work from home or from 'mobile offices'. Already, vast amount of work is being done by virtual staff and by bidders around the world via websites, making it a globally competitive marketplace on a scale never seen before. Collaboration and joint venturing are the new ways to move forwards, with work completed on a project and contractual basis. The word 'employee' could well disappear from our vocabulary in my lifetime.

Social media and rapid information sharing mean that the reputations of businesses that have been built over years can be destroyed within minutes, courtesy of a few dissatisfied customers or worse still, ruthless competitors. Equally, reputations can grow faster in days than might previously have taken years. In the Western world at least, almost everyone has a mobile device, uses the internet, and is probably on at least one social media platform. The new business world is built on a return to values. It is built on trust, referral, recommendations and transparency.

Unethical business operators and even politicians may experience karmic meltdowns thanks to judgement by social media, while reporters don't worry about waiting for court judgements – people are tried and sometimes innocently convicted by the mass media. They know that 'mud sticks' in the same way that Orwellian governments know how to discredit their critics and conspiracy theorists.

So what can you do to keep pace? I'd suggest both a business and personal SWOT analysis. That is where you divide a piece of paper into four quadrants (see how I'm showing my age!). Better still, use a computer. Label the four segments, 'Strengths, Weaknesses, Opportunities and Threats'. Then brainstorm everything you can think of to fill those quadrants, for your business and for you personally. Notice that some of our greatest strengths are also our greatest weaknesses. For example, a business run by a strong leader may have that as a strength, but the fact that the business depends on the strong leader for its leadership makes that a weakness.

To keep yourself and your business effective, you need to build on your strengths whilst overcoming your weaknesses; you need to seek and maximise opportunities whilst developing contingencies for the threats. This is a lot of the work that

I help people with, in my capacity as a coach, consultant and mentor because these things are often easier to spot by someone with the advantage of objectivity. To keep your sanity as you negotiate this 'Brave New World', you will need to become a great juggler. By that I mean this…

> *I believe that our ability to achieve the proper work/life balance ratio and the ability to think holistically about our personal and professional 'big picture' is a vital piece of our 'maintain sanity jigsaw'.*
>
> *We need to think strategically and develop consistency in our actions and our management of our personal and our business lives to achieve harmony and fulfillment.*
>
> **Tony Inman**

21 Steps to Creating Lasting Change for Sanity and Fulfillment

These are a few of my ideas and recommendations for creating your own fulfilling life, with supporting quotes from some of history's most influential and inspirational people. Remember that there are no 'New Truths'. We sometimes need to remind ourselves of the things we have always intrinsically known and rediscover our sense of humanity in order to progress as a species.

1. **Stop and think about what you really want – what fits your values.**

"If people knew what they wanted, they would be incapable of failure."

Mark Twain

2. **Re-assess your current plan. Is it working?**

"However beautiful the strategy, you should occasionally look at the results."

Sir Winston Churchill

3. Write down your lifetime dreams – your 'bucket list'.

"The biggest adventure you can ever take is to live the life of your dreams."

Oprah Winfrey

4. Break your list down into manageable goals in all areas of your life.

"Effectiveness is doing the things that get you closer to your goals."

Tim Ferris

5. Put a deadline on your goals if you are serious about making them happen.

"The most important thing about goals is having one. The next most important thing is having them on paper. When I started to write down my goals, and date them, it changed my life dramatically."

Tom O'Toole

6. Know yourself. Work with your strengths; work on your weaknesses.

"Everyone has something buried inside that can make him successful. The trick is to encourage that latent ability to surface and then use it to get whatever it is that will make you happy."

Chuck Norris

7. Seek out mentors and model people who have done it.

"Our chief want in life is somebody who will make us do what we can."

Ralph Waldo Emerson

8. Start a new fitness campaign to create energy.

"The path to success is to take massive, determined action."

Tony Robbins

9. Be brave and start now. Don't procrastinate!

"The key is not to prioritise what's on your schedule, but to schedule your priorities."

Stephen R. Covey

10. Refer to your written plan often and keep making adjustments.

"Life is like riding a bicycle. In order to keep your balance, you must keep moving."

Albert Einstein

11. Never give up, and don't listen to negative people.

"The winners in life think constantly in terms of I can, I will, and I am. Losers, on the other hand, concentrate their waking thoughts on what they should have or would have done, or what they can't do."

Denis Waitley

12. Educate yourself to stay on track. Read. Listen. Learn.

"An investment in knowledge pays the best interest."

Benjamin Franklin

13. Focus on being the best *you* that you can be.

"You gain strength, courage and confidence by every experience in which you really stop to look fear in the face."

Eleanor Roosevelt

14. Set targets, and reward yourself for achieving your goals.

"Life will pay any price you ask of it, if you ask intelligently."

Tony Robbins

15. Enjoy the journey! Keep a record of your successes and be grateful.

"The more you praise and celebrate your life, the more there is in life to celebrate."

Oprah Winfrey

16. Do what you can to serve others. Become a source of inspiration, and be a good friend.

"Life's most persistent and urgent question is, 'What are you doing for others?'"

Martin Luther King, Jr.

17. Find an idea for a mission for your life.

"A man may die, nations may rise and fall, but an idea lives on."

John F. Kennedy

18. Be a force for good (…and sometimes you may have to look hard for 'the good!').

"Great ambition is the passion of a great character. Those endowed with it may perform very good or very bad acts. All depends on the principles which direct them."

Napoleon Bonaparte

19. Take time out to recharge your batteries and stay healthy.

"The deeper you get into yoga you realise it is a spiritual practice. It's a journey I'm making. I'm heading that way."

Sting

20. **Develop self-belief and sane fulfillment by living in congruence with your values.**

"If my parents were still alive, they would be very proud. They gave me a good start in life, the values that have driven me, and the confidence to believe in myself."

Sir Alex Ferguson

21. **Accept that 'This too shall pass'. All things happen for a reason, and that reason may not appear until we have the benefit of hindsight.**

"Everything happens for a reason. People change so that you can learn to let go; things go wrong so you can appreciate them when they're right, and sometimes good things fall apart so better things can come together."

Marilyn Monroe

That's it – a winning hand in card games is '21' so I'll 'stick at 21' for this book!

Start Living Your Dream Life

You may recall that somewhere at the beginning of this book when I began to ask you if you had found your reason 'why', I also mentioned that if you were in any way struggling with that, sometimes the other question to ask yourself is, *Why Not?*

> *"Twenty years from now, you will be more disappointed by the things you didn't do than by the ones you did. So throw off the bowlines. Sail away from the safe harbour. Catch the trade winds in your sails. Explore. Dream. Discover."*
>
> **H. Jackson Brown**

Once you have those answers, ask yourself, *Why not me?* and *Why not now?*

What Will Be Your Legacy?

In 2004, I had escaped the 'real world' for a brief time. I had created time and space to simply run away from the daily pressures, struggles, and perceived injustices by going on a road trip, travelling around Australia with two mates, Brett Kibblewhite and Glen Riggs.

It was a little surreal in that we balanced the simple pleasures of being free with the attachments of a caravan full of 'stuff'. We joked about the fact that Brett hadn't just brought a television and video player, but actually two video players so that he could edit highlights of sporting contests from one tape to another. We took the mickey out of him for it, but we also understood that sporting events, such as football and motor racing, were his passions and that was important.

I'll never forget though a moment when we were in the north of Western Australia, exploring the magnificent scenery of the Karijini Gorges. We stood in wonderment at the Oxon Lookout as the red ochre sand of the Aussie Outback contrasted with the never-ending pale blue sky, devoid of clouds, the faded green foliage of the trees with sun-bleached bark, adjacent to massive, deep canyons carved out of the landscape by the flow of ancient springs and catchments from high ground run-offs that had created waterfalls and mysterious and murky rock pools 250 metres below us.

The silence of this incredible scene was broken when Brett turned to us, drew attention to the insects crawling across the rock face and asked, "Can you imagine what it would be like to be an ant living out here? How insignificant are we?" Of course, we ribbed him for this moment of deep philosophical introspection, yet he had made a valid point.

When we withdraw from the insanity of our fast-paced, noisy world and reconnect with the vast and spectacular omnipresence of Mother Nature, we simultaneously experience a reduction to the ridiculous of any over-inflated sense of importance in the big scheme of things, with a sudden spiritual awareness and connection to the 'Grand Organised Design', that leaves us in wonder at what a miracle each and every one of us are, along with all of the other living elements in our amazing existence. Yet, as humans, this marvel is never enough. Our tiny minds cannot cope beyond 'Cause and Effect' thinking.

We have to search for what came before and what comes next. We cannot bear the thought of a world existing and evolving with us no longer playing a part in it. Perhaps it is when we are faced with our own mortality, provoked either by the loss of a loved one, the witnessing of an event or a place that makes our existence pale into insignificance, or the inspiration of a movie, a book or a show, that we actually create the time and space to really stop and think. When we stop and think long enough, we will always come back to the eternal questions, *"Why are we here? What is the meaning and purpose of our lives?"*

In 2007, I achieved one of my lifelong goals to not only see the Pyramids of Giza, but to enter inside one. I also entered many of the Pharaohs' temples and chambers, including Karnac, Luxor, and the breathtaking Abu Simbel. Men like Khufu and Ramesses II were revered as gods on Earth, yet this was not enough for them. They had to leave a legacy that they hoped would last for eternity, and that as their spirits were reunited with their gods and creators among the stars, their existence in this realm would never be erased from the memories of mankind. I have become fascinated with the thinking of such characters and such civilisations, and next year, if all goes to plan, we will be trekking the Inca trail to Machu Picchu in Peru and gazing on the Mayan pyramid at Chichen Itza in Mexico. Yet most of us will probably not be able to afford to create our own such expensive, symbolic statements to the world, so what can we do?

Recently, I attended a show that combined most of singer and dancer, Michael Jackson's band with the acrobats of the Cirque du Soleil. The legendary entertainer died prematurely, aged only fifty, destroyed by his own retreat into an escapist world of drug-taking. The show, however, was hugely inspirational, thought-provoking and emotional. Whether mankind, with its own fickle addictions to new trends in music and the arts will remember his works forever, remains to be seen. Yet, the show painted Michael as a troubled soul, tormented by a childhood, sadly lost in the pursuit of serving the world with his talents, but nonetheless, a musical genius who evolved from a disco king to a noble and philosophical campaigner, hell-bent on protecting the innocent children of the world from our own rapacious craving for self-interest at the expense of our brothers and sisters. Whether history will instead choose to focus on the ironic allegations of Jackson's sexual abuse against children, for which he was found 'not guilty' in court, yet perversely 'guilty by media judgement', will only be known in decades to come.

Certainly, the impression that this show created was that he was a star who became mortally tormented by his inability to change the crazily destructive nature of mankind. His later musical offerings may yet empower the voices of reason and change – even if, for now, they merely document the absurdity of mankind's predisposition towards war, its abuse of fellow humans, its lack of compassion, and mankind's refusal to learn from its own past …so, my friends, this is why my book title referred to an insane world.

The question then is, how do you find your sanctuary from the noise around you? I don't have all of the answers, alas, but I'd like to paraphrase John F. Kennedy's wonderful words in the presidential inaugural address he gave just seventeen days before I was born.

> *Ask not what mankind can do for you, but what you can do for mankind?*
>
> **Tony Inman**
> **(paraphrasing President John F. Kennedy)**

I have yet to meet someone who does not possess a gift of some kind. Admittedly, some people hide it better than others! Whatever your gifts are though, I implore you to make use of them and ask yourself how, in so doing, you can make an impact on the lives of those around you, in an empowering, positive way. You may not even realise you have done so, but I'm pretty sure that you already have if you take a moment to look.

It is through using our gifts to enhance the lives of others that we leave our own true legacy and in so doing, we will have fulfillment.

41

The Last Word

My publisher queried the unusual number of chapters in this book. "Why forty-one? Why an odd number? That's most unconventional." Luckily for me, Emily Gowor is not your run of the mill publisher. She's as sharp as a tack, and she's out there, so she 'gets me', but I think even Em was surprised and amused by my solution.

You'll recall that earlier on I mentioned the satirical story of *Hitchhiker's Guide to the Galaxy* and how, after years of painstaking research, the answer to the question of, "What is the answer to the Ultimate question of Life, the Universe and Everything?" was given as simply, "42".

Thus, the 42nd chapter of this book belongs to you. That's correct – you heard right. Chapter 42 is a notional chapter in your own notebook, where you write down everything you think, every idea you have gained, every 'note to self' that you have formulated as a result of you reading my work here. That's why in my introduction I said that it has an alternative ending – you have the choice whether to frown, look bemused and do nothing with it, or nod, smile, reflect, plan and take action.

 I know there was a reason YOU were meant to read this book and a reason for the timing of it. It's now your job to figure out what that reason was. Why you, and why now?

In the act of reading my book, it's as if you have walked with me a little way on the path of life, and for that, I humbly thank you. In part, you have heard my thoughts on how I have processed my own highs and lows in life, but you have also heard a lot of the words of wisdom I have gathered during my studies from some of those people whose thoughts and actions have shaped mankind's destiny.

The Last Word

Through their words and deeds, they have left a legacy that continues to influence many lives.

> "What is powerful is when what you say is just the tip of the iceberg of what you know."
>
> **Jim Rohn**

You often may not realise the influence that your words can have on people. I certainly didn't realise the impact of the words of my parents on my life, until we lost my father. That's why I'd like to leave the last of my words in my book to a genuine gentleman who was both a wise man of few words, but words that counted, and a war hero from the 'Siege of Malta', though he would never have seen himself that way. Through my eyes at least, he will always be one of my heroes. These are words that I have paraphrased, to find the title for this book, but I hope they may be of use to you for anything that you attempt in your life, and that, if followed, will help you find fulfillment.

I'll say goodbye for now and leave you with the words of my father, whose real name was Raymond Mallalieu Inman, but preferred the nickname he borrowed from his father, William James Inman– my Dad, 'Bill' Inman.

> "If a job's worth doing, it's worth doing well."
>
> **Bill Inman (1922-2012)**

Tony, aged 20, proudly about to fly Bill and Vera Inman from Jersey to Dinard, France for a day trip in 1981.

42

The Alternative Ending

Author's Note – This is the chapter you can write for yourself in your own notebook – all of the random thoughts, ideas, realisations, goals, resolutions and commitments you may have made during the reading of this book.

Good luck and I hope you'll be back for more in the not-too-distant future.

[Fades to shot of Tony Inman sitting on sun-drenched white sand in front of a crystal blue ocean with his hot girlfriend, sipping cocktails as the waves foam on the exotic beach. He nods and smiles at you as if to say, "Here's to you living your life well. Thanks for joining us. "]

Bibliography

Self-Help, Motivational

Albom, Mitch – The Five People You Meet in Heaven

Allen, James – As a Man Thinketh

Anthony, Dr Robert – The Ultimate Secrets of Total Self-confidence

Bach, Richard – Jonathan Livingston Seagull

Biggins, Jonathan – The 700 Habits of Highly Ineffective People & How You Can Avoid Falling into Them

Bronson, Po – What Should I Do With My Life?

Byrne, Rhonda – The Secret

Calton, Vailima – Get Perky

Carnegie, Dale – How to Win Friends & Influence People

Carnegie, Dale – The Quick and Easy Way to Effective Speaking

Carnegie, Dale - How to Develop Self-Confidence and Influence People by Public Speaking

Cialdini, Robert – Influence – The Psychology of Persuasion

Covey, Stephen R, – The 7 Habits of Highly Effective People

Dale, Arbie M – Change Your Job, Change Your Life

Demartini, Dr John F – The Breakthrough Experience - A Revolutionary New Approach to Personal Transformation

Dyer, Dr Wayne – Gifts from Eykis

Dyer, Dr Wayne – You'll See It When You Believe It - The Way to Your Personal Transformation

BIBLIOGRAPHY

Faddoul, George – How to Get a Bigger Bite Out of Life

Fulghum, Robert – All I Really Need to Know I Learned in Kindergarten

Frank, Milo O. – How to Get Your Point Across in 30 Seconds or less

Galloway, Dale E – 12 Ways to Develop a Positive Attitude

Giblin, Les – Skill with People

Gray, John – Men are from Mars, Women are from Venus

Greive, Bradley T – The Blue Day Book

Hay, Louise L. – You Can Heal Your Life

Heibloem, Peter H – Alpha Mind Power Training

Helmstetter, Shad – The Self Talk Solution

Hill, Napoleon – Think and Grow Rich

Hooper, Doug – You Are What You Think

James, Dr Matthew - The Foundation of Huna - Ancient Wisdom for Modern Times

Jeffers, Susan – Feel the Fear and Do It Anyway

Johnson & Blanchard, Dr Spencer and Kenneth –Who Moved my Cheese?

Jones, Charlie 'Tremendous' –Life is Tremendous

Jones, Charlie 'Tremendous' – Humour is Tremendous

Jones & Phillips, Charlie T and Bob – Wit and Wisdom

Kyne, Peter B – The Go-Getter

Littauer, Florence – Personality Plus

Littauer, Florence – Dare to Dream

Littauer, Florence – How to Get Along with Difficult People

Maltz, Maxwell – Psycho-Cybernetics

Matthews, Andrew – Being Happy

Matthews, Andrew – Making Friends

Matthews, Andrew Follow Your Heart

Matthews, Andrew – Happiness Now

Matthews, Andrew – Happiness in a Nutshell

McGraw, Dr Phillip – Life Strategies & Relationship Rescue

McInnes, Johnson & Marsh, Lisa, Daniel & Winston – How to Motivate, Manage and Market Yourself

McIntyre & Barker, Jamie & Leigh – What I Didn't Learn at School But Wish I Had

Migliore, R Henry – Personal Action Planning

Myers, David G – The Pursuit of Happiness

Pease, Allan – Body Language

Pease, Allan & Barbara – Why Men Don't Listen & Women Can't Read Maps

Peale, Norman Vincent – Six Attitudes for Winners

Peale, Norman Vincent – The Power of Positive Thinking

Pelusey, Jane and Michael - Live Your Passion - How to Live Your Dreams using the Stories of Others

Polston, Don – Living Without Losing

Robbins, Anthony – Awaken the Giant Within

Rohn, Jim – The Five Major Pieces to the Life Puzzle

Ruiz, Don Miguel – The Four Agreements

Ruiz, Don Miguel – The Four Agreements Companion Book

Schwartz, David J – The Magic of Thinking Big

Schwartz, David J – The Magic of Thinking Success

Schwartz, David J – The Magic of Getting What You Want

Skinner & Cleese, Robin and John – Families and how to survive them

Smith, Fred – You and Your Network

Waitley, Dennis – Seeds of Greatness

Waitley, Dennis – Being the Best

Bibliography

Business, Management & Leadership

Adair, John – Effective Leadership

Allen, David – How To Get Things Done

Blanchard & Johnson, Kenneth & Spencer –The One Minute Manager

Blanchard & Lorber, Kenneth & Robert – Putting the One Minute Manager to Work

Blanchard, Oncken Jnr & Burrows, Kenneth, William & Hal – The One Minute Manager Meets the Monkey

Blanchard & Peale, Kenneth & Norman Vincent – The Power of Ethical Management

Blanchard, Hutson & Williss, Ken, Don & Ethan – The One Minute Entrepreneur

Blanchard, Zigarmi and Zigarmi, Ken, Patricia and Drea – Leadership and the One Minute Manager

Branson, Richard – Losing My Virginity

Brech, EFL – Management – Its Nature and Significance

Brown, Margaret – The Manager's Guide to the Behavioural Sciences

Carlzon, Jan – Moments of Truth

Collins, Jim – Good to Great

Collis & LeBoeuf, Jack and Michael – Work Smarter, Not Harder

Drucker, Peter F – The Practice of Management

Drucker, Peter F – The Effective Executive

Elvy, H – Marketing Made Simple

Ferriss, Tim – The 4 Hour Workweek

Fox, Anne – Australia's New Entrepreneurs – How They Succeeded

Gerber, Michael E – E-Myth Mastery

Gladwell, Malcolm – Outliers – The Story of Success

Gowor, Emily – The Unlikely Entrepreneur – A Spiritual Guide to Business and Your Path of Greatest Evolution

Guber, Peter – Tell To Win – Connect, Persuade and Triumph with the Hidden Power of Story

Hardy, Leonard – Marketing For Profit

Heller, Robert – The Business of Winning

Hopkins, Tom – How to Master the Art of Selling

Jones & Cooper, Andrew & Cary – Combating Managerial Obsolescence

Maxwell, John C – The 21 Irrefutable Laws of Leadership

McCormack, Mark H – What They Don't Teach You at Harvard Business School

McCormack, Mark H – The 110% Solution

Mogano M – How to Start and Run Your Own Business

O'Toole, Tom – Breadwinner – A Fresh Approach to Business Success

Peters, Thomas J – In Search of Excellence

Roberts, Wess – Leadership Secrets of Attila the Hun

Stewart, Rosemary – The Reality of Management

Trump and Zanker, Donald & Bill – Think Big – Make it Happen in Business and Life

Tzu, Sun – The Art of War

Biographies & Auto-Biographies

Alda, Alan – Things I Overheard While Talking To Myself

Best, George – Blessed – The Autobiography

Blake, Robert – Winston Churchill

Bower, Tom – Branson

Branson, Richard – 'Losing my Virginity' – The Autobiography

Chandler, David – Napoleon

BIBLIOGRAPHY

Clarkson, Wensley – John Travolta – Back in Character

Clignet & Hovey, Marion & Benjamin C – Tenacious

Cronin, Vincent – Napoleon

Ferguson, Alex – Managing My Life

Ferguson, Alex – Alex Ferguson – My Autobiography

Fox, Michael J – Always Looking Up

Frankl, Viktor E – Man's Search for Meaning

Glover – Wellington as Military Commander

Golden, Anna Louise – the Spice Girls

Halliwell, Geri – If Only

Iacocca, Lee – Talking Straight

James, Clive – Unreliable Memoirs

James, Clive- Falling Towards England

Keane, Roy – The Autobiography

Lange, Larry – The Beatles Way

Law, Jonathan – The Giant Book of 1000 Great Lives

Milligan, Spike – Puckoon

Norris & Hyams, Chuck & Joe – The Secret of Inner Strength – My Story

O'Toole, Tom – Breadwinner

Parker, John – Sean Connery

Parkinson, Michael – Parky – My Autobiography

Perry, Roland – Mel Gibson – Actor, Director, Producer

Stephenson, Pamela -Billy (Connolly)

Stephenson, Pamela – Bravemouth – Living with Billy Connolly

Williams, AL – All You Can Do is All You Can Do but All You Can Do is Enough

Williams, Robbie – Somebody Someday

Money and Financial Planning

Clason, George C – The Richest Man in Babylon

Hansen & Allen, Mark Victor and Robert – The One Minute Millionaire

Kay, Herb – How to Get Filthy, Stinking Rich & Still Have Time for great Sex

Kiyosaki & Lechter, Robert & Sharon -Rich Dad Poor Dad

Kiyosaki & Lechter, Robert & Sharon – The Cashflow Quadrant

Kiyosaki & Lechter, Robert & Sharon -Retire Young Retire Rich

Kiyosaki & Lechter, Robert & Sharon – Rich Dad's Guide to Investing

Stanley & Danko, Thomas & William – The Millionaire Next Door

Whittaker, Noel – Making Money Made Simple

Yager, Dexter – A Millionaire's Common Sense Approach to Wealth

Influential Training

Training & Assessment Cert IV Part 1 – (Inspire Education Perth 2013)

Wow Marketing Accelerator – John Dwyer (Universal Stars Perth 2013)

8 Week Author – Emily Gowor (GIP Online 2013)

Yoga for Beginners – Chioni Hicks (Chi Yoga Perth 2013)

How to Win More Deals More Often – John Denton Perth 2013)

The Breakthrough Experience – Dr John F Demartini (Global 1 Events Perth 2013)

Creating Powerful Action-Based Sales Meetings & Presentations – Phil Cronin (Cronin Communications Perth 2012)

Acting Weekend workshop – Loren Johnson (Acting Classes in Perth 2012)

Ancient Hawaiian Huna Intensive – Dr Serge Kahili King (QC Seminars Byron Bay 2012)

Renovating for Profit – Cherie Barber (RFP Perth 2012)

Business Networking – David Bearsley (SBN Perth 2012 to present)

Industry Rockstar Intensive (Business & Personal Strategic Planning) – Jeff & Kane (Universal Events Perth 2012)

Introduction to Acting – Loren Johnson (Acting Classes in Perth 2012)

Internet Rockstar – (Universal Events Sydney 2012)

Preparing a Business Ready for Sale – John Denton (Stirling SBC 2012)

Coach's Master Class (Certified Coach) – Jeff Slayter, Kane Minkus & Dr Carl Buchheit – (Industry Rockstars & UpCoach Sydney & Melbourne 2011-2012)

Master Practitioner of NLP (2nd time) – Jeff Slayter, Kane Minkus & Carl Buchheit – (Industry Rockstars & Universal Events Sydney & Melbourne 2011-2012)

Business Mastery – Jennifer Castle (Streetsmart Business School Perth 2011-2012)

Rockstar Trainer (Platform Selling Speaker Training) – Jeff & Kane (Industry Rockstars & Universal Events Sydney 2011)

Certified Trainer of Neuro Linguistic Programming (NLP) – George Faddoul & Nic LeForce – (QC Seminars Sydney 2011)

Million Dollar Speaker (Speaker Training) – George Faddoul & Nic LeForce – (QC Seminars Sydney 2011)

Master Practitioner of NLP (1st Time) – George Faddoul & Nic LeForce – (QC Seminars Sydney 2011)

Publicity for Profit – Sue Papadoulis (Bliss Communications Perth 2011)

Coaching Boot camp – Dan Kennedy (DK CD Series 2011-2012)

Social Media Marketing – John Denton & Peter B Butler (Smarter Workshops 2011)

Publish Your Passion for Profit – Mike & Jane Pelusey (Stirling BEC 2011)

Secrets of Industry Rockstars – Jeff & Kane (Industry Rockstars & Universal Events Perth 2011)

Practitioner of NLP – George Faddoul & Dr Matt James – (QC Seminars Perth 2011)

Advanced Business Mentoring – John Denton (Stirling BEC Perth 2010 to present)

Business Mentoring Basecamp – John Denton (Stirling BEC 2009 to 2010)

Learn to Sail – (Royal Perth Yacht Club 2009)

Rescue Diver – P.A.D.I. (Malibu Dive Perth 2007)

Emergency Response First Aid Course – (Malibu Dive Perth 2007)

Advanced Open Water Scuba Diver – P.A.D.I. (Malibu Dive Perth 2006)

Open Water Scuba Diver -–P.A.D.I. (Malibu Dive Perth 2006)

Emotional Intelligence (EQ) – (BSA Perth 2004)

Speed Reading – (BSA Perth 2004)

Time Management – (BSA Perth 2004)

Marketing through the Internet – (BSA Perth 2004)

The Breakthrough Experience – Dr Pamela Evans (Demartini Trainer Perth 2003)

Get the Edge Program – Tony Robbins (R.R.I. 2002 ongoing)

Personal Power Programme – Tony Robbins (R.R.I. 2002 ongoing)

Business Improvement Programme – (Curtin Uni Centre for Entrepreneurship Perth 2002)

Certificate in Transport Management – (University of Sydney 2000)

Motor Vehicle Dealers Licence – (MTAWA Perth 2000)

Yard Manager Certificate – (MTAWA Perth 2000)

Sales Manager Certificate – (MTAWA Perth 2000)

Open Tours & Charters Licence – (WA Transport Dept Perth 2000)

HR (Bus/Truck) & F (Tour Bus) Driving Licence – (WA Transport Dept Perth 2000)

Website Design – (Curtin Uni 2000)

Quicken Bookkeeper Training – (Perth 2000)

Special Facility Liquor Licence – (ORGL Perth 1999)

Approved Manager for Liquor Licence – (Aragon Training Perth 1999)

The Internet – (Prime Learning Perth 1997)

Management Development Program – (Big W 1991)

Influential Training

Agency Management Development Course – (A.M.P. 1989)

Tom Hopkins Sales and Management Training A-Z – (Video series Perth 1989)

Agency Management Course – (Nat Mutual Perth 1989)

Bachelor of Business – (Commenced but not completed WACAE 1989)

Business Maths – (Curtin Uni 1988)

ATAA – (TISC Perth 1988)

Management Trainee Programme – (Target Perth 1986-1987)

Finance for the Non-Financial Manager – (Highlands College Jersey 1984)

Profit through Merchandising – (CICS Training Jersey 1983)

The Skills of Management – Dr Andrew Jones (Highlands College Jersey 1983)

Small Business Management – (Highlands College Jersey 1983)

Certificate in Distributive Management Studies – (I.G.D. UK 1982-84)

Private Pilot's Licence – (FAA of USA C.I. Aero Club Jersey 1983)

Flying at Night Rating – (CAA UK C.I. Aero Club Jersey 1981)

Radio-Telephony Operator's Licence – (CAA UK C.I. Aero Club Jersey 1980)

Private Pilot's Licence – (CAA UK C.I. Aero Club Jersey 1980)

Job Instruction – (CWSTS Jersey 1980)

Management Trainee Programme – (CICS Perth 1979-1980)

Victoria College Jersey – (High School education 1972-1979)

Acknowledgments

I am delighted to present this as the first non-fiction book that I have completed on my own, yet even as I say that I am reminded that in truth we never achieve anything completely without help from someone, and in this case, there are many who have inspired me. Please forgive the possibility of this sounding like one of those Hollywood Oscar speeches, but it's an opportunity to thank so many wonderful people.

I have dedicated this book to my parents, Bill and Vera Inman, though in particular to my father, who sadly passed away in 2011 at the grand age of ninety. It is often only with hindsight that we realise just how profound an impact people have had on your life, and I am truly grateful to my parents for instilling fine values in all of their children and for providing me with both a great education at Victoria College in Jersey and a great example as conscientious and ethical business people who truly cared about their customers. There are way too many people to thank here, so if I miss you please forgive me.

My wonderful partner, Joanne has encouraged and supported my efforts in producing this book and throughout my many challenges and adventures over the last seven years. My grown-up children, Craig and Kim, along with Kim's partner, Marty, and my grandson, Hayden, plus step-son, Troy, have all played their part in keeping me grounded and in reminding me of what's important in life. My siblings, Cheryl, Geoff, and Peter, and their respective families are a terrific bunch of people, as are my extended family of Ann and the Tassie crew.

I am blessed to have an amazing global family of friends, in no small part due to having run a backpacker tourism venture for fourteen glorious years, along with my many and varied business activities. I have indeed led a wonderful life thus far, and though I am proud of my accomplishments to date, my 'bucket list' of things still to do seems only to get longer, despite how many items I cross off the list! When I reflect on all of the folk who inspired me along my journey, you'll see in the book that this would run into thousands if I included all of the actors,

Acknowledgments

musicians, authors, world leaders and coaches. If I have cited them, you can take that as confirmation of their influence.

In terms of personal growth, I have had many teachers, from my early schooling in Jersey, the bosses in my various jobs, through to mentors in business and in my studies as a coach and consultant. Plus there have been flying instructors, diving instructors and sports coaches. There are a few people I feel I need to pick out of that massive supporting cast, however.

In terms of influence, of course, my two ex-wives, Joyce and Lesley, played quintessential roles in my development, and I will always be grateful to them. Notable girlfriends, who impacted in a bigger way than most included Vanessa, Jane, Tracey, Viktoria, Tricia and Sarah. Plus of course the two who were in some way meant to break my heart, Dawn and Kate.

From school, I thank my best friends Tony Pitcher and Dave Omissi as well as my teachers of course. I loved all of my friends at the Jersey Aero Club, but I have to mention the irrepressible Percy Thorne, who was my best man and flying buddy. At work in Jersey, my biggest mentor was my good friend, David Palmer, and I'd also like to thank my friends Sue and Angela, who also helped me deal with difficult situations.

My many staff played their parts over the years and were friends too, in particular, the two Dans, Deonne, Annika, Keef and Sharon, Haley, Glen, Greg and my nephew, Mick. Other long-term ex-staff who have remained in regular contact have included Paul, George, Rhys and, of course, Nicole, Alan and Glenn, my musical pal. There are many others who keep in touch via social media. You know who you are, and I thank you. There will have to be a book about those crazy days at some stage before we all become too addled to remember all the stories. Friends who helped me through my post-marital crisis included the musketeers, Brett, Glen, Ian and the so-called 'Blind Crew'.

Other influential business people who have helped me along the way have included sounding boards Rell, now in Bali; Paul Brinsley, Bernie Kroczek, John Denton and Peter B. Butler. I also really appreciate my friends at the Stirling Enterprise Centre and David's crew at Superior Business Networks plus the huge list of fellow seminar participants, especially at Jeff and Kane's coaching master classes and George and Nic's NLP training. Thank you to Phil at Curtin University for inviting me to become a mentor at the Centre for Entrepreneurship at a time that really boosted my confidence.

My other support team members include my accountant, Auntie Diane; long-supporting mechanic, Mick; insurance boffin, Alison; finance guru, Colin; current right-hand man, Rajeev; writing inspiration source, writing coach and publisher, Emily Gowor, and my fantastic life coach, Vanessa Dichiera.

I would also like to acknowledge my diving buddies, my soccer club mates at Victoria Park Masters, the volleyball and beach volleyball crews and, of course, Andy, Emma and Guy who played their parts in unconsciously helping with my first novel, *The Parrot and the Lady*.

Thank you to the over thirty-five thousand people who stayed at my tourist accommodation business in Perth, the thousands more who rented our hire cars, and to my many coaching and consulting clients as well as the customers and property managers with whom I deal in my strata cleaning and property maintenance business.

About the Author

Tony Inman is 'The Reinvention Specialist' in that his life and career has been a fascinating journey. Born on the holiday isle of Jersey, Channel Islands, to parents from the North of England, Tony grew up helping in family hotels. That's where his work ethic evolved.

Initially pursuing a successful retail management career, Tony moved to Perth in 1985 in search of more opportunity and the 'Great Australian Dream' of an affordable family home. He soon moved up the executive ranks of some of Australia's retail giants while exploring a number of part-time business ventures, including insurance and network marketing, before he set up in business full-time in 1996.

Tony went on to start up and grow over twenty-one small businesses, including a backpackers' tourist accommodation and hospitality, holiday apartments, adventure tourism, a car dealership, vehicle servicing workshop, car rentals fleet, vehicle towing and transportation, domestic and commercial cleaning, office furniture removals, musical events, property investments and specialized cleaning services.

Almost losing everything in the Global Financial Crisis, Tony reinvented himself again as a certified business and life coach, consultant and mentor, helping owners of small businesses to increase profits while balancing their lifestyles. He has mentored in Entrepreneurship at Curtin University and has been published in business newspapers.

Tony has two grown-up children and a grandson, and he now lives with his girlfriend and step-son. Tony enjoys scuba diving, flying, soccer, and beach volleyball with a commitment to self-expression through playing guitar and writing. He is inspired by travelling the world and helping people on their journeys.

Also by Tony Inman

The Parrot and the Lady – Introducing Randy Short 008

The South Pacific island of Espiritu Santo is the backdrop for this tongue-in-cheek spy thriller. The action centres on a quest for treasure aboard a WW2 shipwreck whose mysteries link government secrets of the past with a modern world confused by political correctness. Randy Short juggles a stable family life with his role of Australian Secret Service Agent. His family vacation is interrupted by a call to duty that will pit him against dangerous foreign operatives in a race to solve the enigma. From an eclectic cast, the Aussie befriends CIA mercenary Gus McThompkins in their personal 'War against Terror'.

Available from: www.tonyinman.net/shop

Recommended Retail Price:

$29.99 Paperback

$49.99 Hardback

$9.99 E-Book

Link to Sample Chapter: www.tonyinman.net/pdf/Sample-Chapter-13.pdf

Special Offer for You, the Reader

There will be special offers for readers of this book, which may change from time to time, as my journey continues and, I hope, as my wisdom grows.

So, I thought the best way to proceed was to suggest that you go the following webpage:

www.tonyinman.net/vip-reader-specials
and enter the promotional code 'vipreader' to claim your special offer.

Firstly, let me thank you for reading my book and coming along with me on this journey. I really hope that you have found it worthwhile. If you did find it useful and you either learned something new or found yourself inspired to do something different to improve your life or the lives of others around you, then please tell all your friends. Please also tell me! I love to hear stories of peoples' journeys and their successes.

The good news is that there are several ways to continue your journey with me if wish to do so. I have two consulting websites at www.clubred.com.au and www.tonyinman.net – both of which have blogs and the opportunity to subscribe to newsletters and updates.

I also conduct seminars, mentoring workshops and events; the details of which are on my websites and social media pages. There will also be further books and other products in the pipeline, so watch the sites for details.

Last, but not least, I offer consulting, coaching and mentoring services in both business and lifestyle areas. If you wish to chat, please drop me an email at info@clubred.com.au.

Also, don't forget to check out my recommended reading list on my website.

www.clubred.com.au/resources/a-recommended-book-list-for-success

Plus, if you want some ideas on what you can do to spice up your life, check out these ideas for your own 'bucket list': www.tonyinman.net/resources/bucket-list-ideas

www.ingramcontent.com/pod-product-compliance
Ingram Content Group UK Ltd.
Pitfield, Milton Keynes, MK11 3LW, UK
UKHW021314180426
11947UKWH00015B/1231